explo

TUNISIA

Sylvie Franquet and Anthony Sattin

AA Publishing

Written by Sylvie Franquet and Anthony Sattin
Original photography by Steve Day
Edited, designed and produced by AA Publishing
Maps © The Automobile Association 1998

A CIP catalogue record for this book is available from the British Library.

ISBN 0 7495 1717 4
Published by AA Publishing (a trading name of Automobile Association Developments Limited, whose registered office is Norfolk House, Priestley Road, Basingstoke, Hampshire RG24 9NY. Registered number 1878835).

Colour separation by Fotographics Ltd
Printed and bound in Italy by Printer Trento srl

Titles in the Explorer series:
Australia • Boston & New England • Britain
Brittany • California • Caribbean • China • Costa Rica
Crete • Cuba • Cyprus • Egypt • Florence & Tuscany
Florida • France • Germany • Greek Islands • Hawaii
India • Indonesia • Ireland • Israel • Italy • Japan • London
Mexico • Moscow & St Petersburg • New York
New Zealand • Paris • Portugal • Prague • Provence
Rome • San Francisco • Scotland • Singapore & Malaysia
South Africa • Spain • Tenerife • Thailand • Turkey
Venice • Vietnam

AA World Travel Guides publish nearly 300 guidebooks to a full range of cities, countries and regions across the world. Find out more about AA Publishing and the wide range of services the AA provides by visiting our Web site at www.theaa.co.uk.

Cover (front): restored *ghorfas* at Ksar Ouled Soltane
Page 2: Arab horseman, National Sahara Festival, Douz
Page 3: Zaouia of Sidi Sahab, Kairouan
Page 4(a): landscape near Chenini
Pages 4–5: mosaic of two severed heads, Kasbah Sousse Museum
Page 5(a): Arabic script, Zaouia of Sidi Sahab, Kairouan
Page 5(b): 'Hand of Fatima', troglodyte house, Matmata
Pages 6–7: fisherman, Houmt Souk
Page 6(b): seafront villas, Hammamet
Page 8(a): Temple of Caelestis, Dougga
Page 9(a): monument in honour of President Ben Ali, Tunis
Page 27(a): symbol of Tanit, the Phoenician moon goddess

How to use this book

This book is divided into five main sections:

❑ Section 1: *Tunisia Is*
discusses aspects of life and living today, from geography to arts and culture

❑ Section 2: *Tunisia Was*
places the country in its historical context and explores past events whose influences are still felt

❑ Section 3: *A to Z Section*
covers places to visit, arranged by region, with suggested walks and drives. Within this section fall the Focus On articles, which consider a variety of topics in greater detail

❑ Section 4: *Travel Facts*
contains the strictly practical information that is vital for a successful trip

❑ Section 5: *Hotels and Restaurants*
lists recommended establishments in Tunisia, giving a brief résumé of what they offer

How to use the star rating
Most places described in this book have been given a separate rating:

▶▶▶ **Do not miss**

▶▶ **Highly recommended**

▶ **Worth seeing**

Not essential viewing

Map references
To make the location of a particular place easier to find, every main entry in the A to Z section of this book is given a map reference, such as 48A2. The first number (48) indicates the page on which the map can be found; the letter (A) and the second number (2) pinpoint the square in which the main entry is located. The map on the inside front cover is referred to as IFC.

Contents

5

Quick reference

This quick-reference guide highlights the elements of the book you will use most often: the maps; the introductory features; the Focus On articles; the walks and the drives.

Our Tunisia

by Sylvie Franquet and Anthony Sattin

For several years in the 1980s, Sylvie spent her summers studying Arabic in Tunis. A few years ago we both went back with our newborn son and rented an apartment on the beach. We swam in the Mediterranean, shopped in the market, visited museums, sites and souqs, drove to a friend's villa in Hammamet and to remote beaches in the north. It was a summer coloured by bougainvillaea, flavoured with jasmine and spices, and refreshed by syrupy mint tea and chilled wine.

Tunisia has a reputation for mass-market resorts, some of which have aged badly. Tourism and industry have also changed the character of many coastal towns and of their inhabitants who, until earlier this century, were still living within Arab fortifications, supported by agriculture and fishing. Although the beaches are some of the best on the Mediterranean, we learned to choose hotels and resorts with care.

Happily, Tunisia still has much to offer independent travellers such as us. The interior is particularly worth while. It has important ruins and picturesque towns, fertile hills and the awesome desert. Furthermore, in spite of the dominance of Tunis, the interior remains Tunisia's heartland where the national identity – that curious blend of Berber, Phoenician and Arab, privacy and hospitality, Mediterranean and Saharan, traditional and liberal – can best be understood, and where conversations are less likely to come round to your buying souvenirs.

In the southern oases, we ate succulent dates and talked about trans-Saharan travel. In the hilly Tell, we bathed in the warm waters of a natural spring that has been used for more than two thousand years and saw plays performed on a Roman stage. Even though much of the coast has been transformed, when we returned to old haunts around Tunis we found the welcome as warm, the sea as clear, the jasmine as sweet and the food as delicious as before. In Tunisia, some things never change.

Belgian-born Sylvie Franquet studied Arabic while travelling in Tunisia as a teenager. After living in Cairo for six years and spending summers in Tunis, she now divides her time between London and the Middle East, bringing up her sons, writing and travelling.

Anthony Sattin is the author of several books, including a novel, and is a regular contributor to the *Sunday Times* travel and books pages.

Together they have written AA *Explorer* guides to Egypt and the Greek Islands, AA *Citypack* guides to Bangkok and to Brussels and Bruges as well as the AA *Essential* guide to Morocco.

TUNISIA IS

■ Tunisia is bordered by the Mediterranean to the north and east, by the last flourishes of the Atlas Mountains to the west and by the great Sahara Desert to the south. Within the country there are extremes of climate and great variety of landscape, from lush coastal plains and olive groves to oases and sand-dunes. ■

The coast The Tunisian coast runs along the north and east of the country. Pliny, the Roman historian, thought it one of the finest coasts in the world, and many have agreed with him since. The northern coast is more rugged, while the east has some of the Mediterranean's finest beaches. The Cap Bon peninsula, located in the north-east, stands out in particular, its limestone hills rising immediately inland from the coast.

❏ Tunisia, the northernmost country in Africa, covers 164,150sq km (63,378sq miles), an area about the size of England and Wales, or half the size of Italy. Almost half the country is desert, and it has some 1,300km of coastline and 600km of beaches. The highest mountains are Jebel Chambi (1,544m) and Jebel Mrhila (1,378m). ❏

The Chott el Jerid, one of Tunisia's great salt lakes

The Kerkennah Islands and Jerba, meanwhile, share the same features as the mainland, to which they were once joined. The main tourist resorts are built around the finest beaches, as at Hammamet, but there are also beaches that have escaped large-scale development, as at Raf Raf, north of Tunis.

The Tell The main geographical feature of the north is the range of rolling hills called the Tell, the easternmost extensions of the Atlas Mountains which run across North Africa from Morocco. The Northern Tell and the Dorsal are divided by the Mejerda, Tunisia's most important river. The Mejerda Valley is the country's prime fertile region and an important grower of cereals; even in antiquity it was the country's main farming area. The hills of the Northern Tell, rising over 1,000m, are covered with oak and pine forests. The Dorsal is more rugged and less fertile, cuts across the country south of the Mejerda and contains major phosphate reserves.

Rocks quarried at El Haouaria were used in the building of Carthage

The Sahel South-east of the Tell is the Sahel (meaning the 'Shore'), a region of immense olive plantations that contains some two-thirds of Tunisia's olive trees: 15 million according to some estimates. The Sahel's olives are highly regarded and the oil they yield is of export quality.

The salt lakes Beyond the arid hills around Gafsa, the landscape becomes increasingly Saharan. To the south-west lie the country's two great *chotts* (salt lakes), Chott el Jerid and Chott el Gharsa, which sit below sea-level and are surrounded by some exceptionally beautiful oases. Around the *chotts* and running back towards the eastern

The forested region around Makthar offers beautiful scenery

coast are bare brown hills, some eroded by water into beautiful shapes and exposing brightly coloured rock strata. Near the coast, the rugged mountains around Jebel Demer are still home to Berbers, who have built remarkable fortresses and landscape-hugging houses.

The Sahara Further south and west the true Sahara begins, the edge of the sand-dunes being known as the Grand Erg Oriental. Before the Grand Erg there is little cultivation beyond date palms, these fed by spring water. The erg itself is a classic desert of rolling sand hills, suitable only for camels and four-wheel drives.

Climate The north and most of the east of the country enjoy a Mediterranean climate. Summers are usually hot and dry, winters wet and mild. More rain falls on the Tell, especially on higher ground, where there is also occasional snow. Average rainfall each winter in the north is 406mm; in the south it is less than 152mm. Rainfall is irregular throughout the country, and central and southern regions are also prone to periodic droughts. The southern interior experiences great extremes of temperature: in Tozeur in July, for example, the temperatures can rise to 40°C during the day and drop to 0°C at night. The arid dunes of the Sahara often go several years without receiving any rain.

■ Unlike its neighbours, Libya and Algeria, Tunisia under President Ben Ali is generally politically stable, thanks partly to successful economic reforms. But there are social and religious pressures, and the voice of a democratic opposition is still clamouring to be heard. ■

The government Tunisia gained independence from France in 1956. Under the 1959 constitution, its parliament, the National Assembly, is elected every five years by universal suffrage by all citizens over the age of 20. The government and prime minister are answerable to the president, who is also elected. The president, who is chief executive of the government and commander-in-chief of the armed forces, is limited to three five-year terms of office. The country is divided into 23 *wilayas* (governorates), whose governors report directly to the president. The judiciary has its independence guaranteed by the constitution.

President Ben Ali American-educated Ben Ali took power in 1987, promising government reforms. Treading a delicate line between powerful right-wing army factions and popular Islamist groups, he brought in immediate changes, relaxing press censorship. Ben Ali was unopposed in the presidential

One of Ben Ali's pet projects is environmental conservation

elections of 1989 and 1994. According to the constitution, 1999 will be the last time he is eligible to stand for office.

Political parties The Rassemblement Constitutionnel Démocratique (Democratic Constitutional Assembly, or RCD,

The date Ben Ali came to power

To avoid a domestic crisis, Ben Ali banned Islamist movements

formerly known as the Destour Socialist Party) is the party of government and until 1981 was Tunisia's only legitimate political party. Since then, opposition parties have been legalised and fielded candidates in the 1994 legislative elections. However, with a system of 'first past the post' rather than proportional representation, the RCD won an overwhelming majority.

Islamic fundamentalism Islamist groups are banned from the political process under a law which forbids political parties with religious, regional or ethnic programmes. This is understandable, given events in neighbouring Algeria. Although the government has taken a tough stand on Islamic fundamentalism since 1991, the outlawed Islamist party El Nadha (the Renaissance) still has support in Tunisia. As a result of the perceived fundamentalist threat, Ben Ali has reneged on many of his liberalising views, especially with regard to press censorship.

Arab Maghreb Union President Ben Ali was central to creating this economic alliance of north-west African states. In 1987 he restored ties with Libya, which had expelled

30,000 Tunisian workers two years earlier. He then paved the way for a reconciliation between Morocco and Algeria over the disputed Western Sahara. In 1988 Tunisia, Morocco, Algeria, Mauritania and Libya created the Union du Grand Maghreb (Arab Maghreb Union) to help counter the effects of the European Community. They intended to follow the European model by ending customs regulations, but the situation in Algeria has hindered progress.

Foreign policy Tunisia pursued a pro-Western policy in the 1980s, but the 1990–1 Gulf crisis brought new difficulties. Although Ben Ali spoke out against the Iraqi invasion of Kuwait, unlike Morocco he did not send troops to join the US-led coalition of Desert Shield, much to the surprise of the US and Gulf States, which had until then been the largest providers of aid to Tunisia. Since the end of the war, however, Tunisia has not only made efforts to improve relations with the US and Gulf States, but has also sought to strengthen ties with the European Union through its former colonial power, France, and its nearest EU neighbour, Italy. This policy paid off in 1995 when Tunisia became the first southern Mediterranean country to sign an association agreement with the European Union.

Islamic

■ **Tunisia is not an Islamic republic like Iran or Saudi Arabia, but Islam is the state religion. Tunisian laws, attitudes and behaviour are shaped by it, and the majority of Tunisians are guided by Islam in all aspects of their lives.** ■

14

In the beginning The Prophet Muhammad was born around AD 570 in Mecca and, after he was orphaned, was raised by his uncle, a merchant. According to Islam, in his 40th year Muhammad had a vision in which he received the word of God through the Archangel Gabriel. As he was illiterate, Muhammad was made to learn the message so that he could recite it, hence the Koran (meaning 'the Recital'). Between 610 and 612, Muhammad passed on the message to his followers, but some members of the tribe grew nervous of Muhammad's power and he was forced to flee to Medina in 622. This journey, known as el-Hijrah, is the starting point for the Islamic calendar. Muhammad's message was popular, but from the very beginning his followers had to fight for the right to worship and to fulfil Muhammad's vision that Islam was meant for all people, not just the Arabs. While preparing for a campaign in the north of the Arabian Peninsula, Muhammad fell ill and died in 632.

The Koran It was only 18 years after Muhammad's death that the divine message he had received was written down, its accuracy confirmed by those closest to the Prophet, its sanctity affirmed by the beauty of the message and of the language in which it was given. Islam rests on the Koran, the word of God delivered directly to and in the language of the people, and on the Sunna, the sayings and actions of Muhammad,

Devoted pilgrims flock to the Zaouia of Sidi Sahab in Kairouan

Megaphones and tape recorders now summon the faithful to prayer

on which many Islamic laws are based.

Sunni or Shiite Muhammad died without naming a successor, and soon after his death Muslims were divided over who should lead them. The prophet's companion, Abu Bakr, was accepted as the Caliph Rasul-Allah, or Successor to the Prophet of God, but Ali, Muhammad's son-in-law, claimed that he was the natural successor. Ali and his son Husayn were both killed in the ensuing struggle, but their followers, members of the Shiah sect, believed that only Ali's descendants had the right to lead Muslims. The divide continues to this day. The majority of Tunisians are Sunnis.

The final word The Koran regards Jews and Christians as 'people of the Book', who received the message of the one true God but, through weakness and corruption, failed to be true to it. Muhammad is regarded

as the last prophet, the successor in a line of prophets stretching from Abraham and Moses to Jesus.

❏ Tunisia is also home to Christian and Jewish communities. Jews claim to have founded their first Tunisian synagogue, on the island of Jerba, in 590 BC. Tunisia was a haven for Jews fleeing the fall of Jerusalem in AD 70, and again in the 16th century, after they were expelled from Catholic Spain. Both Arabs and Turks were tolerant to Jews in Tunisia, although there were some prohibitions (later abolished in 1881 under the French). When the Germans took Tunisia during World War II, Jews were obliged to buy their survival with gold. There were more than 100,000 Jews in Tunisia after the war, but tension generated by the Arab–Israeli conflict has since reduced that number to mere hundreds. ❏

The Five Pillars of Islam All Muslims are expected to fulfil the following five rituals on which their faith is based: to declare publicly that 'there is but one God, Allah, and Muhammad is his prophet'; to pray five times a day at specific hours, facing the direction of Mecca; to observe the daytime fast during the month of Ramadan; to make the hadj (pilgrimage) to Mecca at least once in their lifetime; and to pay a religious levy for the poor and ill and for the defence of Islam.

All visitors must remove their shoes before entering a mosque

■ In antiquity Tunisia's economy was based on agriculture, and although this remains the case today substantial natural resources are raising the prospect of an unexpected boost to the economy. In the meantime, tight fiscal control has left Tunisia with one of the region's most buoyant economies. ■

16

Agricultural base Some 31 per cent of Tunisia consists of arable land or orchards, 20 per cent is animal pastures or meadows, 4 per cent is covered by woods or forests and 45 per cent is given over to non-agricultural purposes. The Mejerda is Tunisia's main and only sizeable, perennial river. Its valley, extended through intensive irrigation channels, is the centre of the country's main cereal-growing region. The fertile peninsula of Cap Bon, jutting out into the Mediterranean south of Tunis, offers the most easily cultivated land in the country. As well as cereals, grapes, peppers (used in the production of *harissa* sauce) and spices are grown here.

In the centre of the country are the plains of the Sahel, the focus of intensive olive cultivation (see page 108). In antiquity the olive harvest generated enough profit to build an amphitheatre that rivalled the Colosseum in Rome. They don't build them like that any more, but the olive business is still profitable. However, despite the fact that

Due to poor investment, only 25 per cent of Tunisia's farm output comes from irrigated plots

Tunisia remains the world's second-largest producer of olive oil, the local product is rarely marketed under its own label in the competitive European and North American markets, although it does find other ways of arriving on our tables (it is sometimes mixed with Italian oils). In the south, the date, particularly the internationally acclaimed deglet ennour (see pages 150–1), is the most exportable agricultural product.

Rival industries Although more Tunisians work in agriculture than in any other industry, diversity has become the mainstay of the economy. The mass-market tourist industry was developed relatively early on and, after a period of decline, has recently enjoyed the beginnings of a revival. The exploitation of mineral, gas and oil deposits is also making substantial contributions to the gross national product.

❏ 'The old story has it that when a Tunisian peasant picks up an olive, he says, "This is my gold."' From *Inside Africa* by John Gunther (1955). ❏

Modern reforms In 1984, the International Monetary Fund (IMF) expressed concern at the level of Tunisia's mounting foreign debt and insisted that the government slash food subsidies. As in other North African countries forced to take similar measures (such as Egypt), food riots followed. In 1988, newly installed President Ben Ali embarked on a dramatic economic reform programme that attempted to free the economy from tight state controls and encourage the development of the private sector. In 1994 the government offered new incentives to attract foreign investment. The following year it became the first southern Mediterranean state to reach an agreement of association with the European Union, this giving it trading privileges.

❏ Tunisia's main exports include textiles, clothes and animal skins (35 per cent); oil and petroleum products (18 per cent); and phosphates (13 per cent). Tunisia's main imports include textiles (22 per cent); machinery (22 per cent); petroleum (9 per cent); and vehicles (3 per cent). ❏

The power station at Sousse

17

Prospects Economists praise Tunisia for its successful economic reforms, which have in turn contributed to the country's relative political stability. The major obstacles to continuing development are cited as the youth of the population, the number of smallholdings (the majority of farmed land is held in plots of less than 10 hectares), and a lack of investment in agriculture and tourism. Since the majority of farmers rent their land

and absentee landlords lack incentives to invest in improvements, the situation in agriculture is unlikely to change. The largest question mark hangs over Tunisia's natural resources: deposits of petroleum and natural gas have been found, but their extent is unknown.

Tourism is another area of potential growth. Tunisia has considerable natural attractions, from excellent beaches to extensive deserts. If sufficient investment is made in developing facilities, then tourism revenue will certainly increase.

The majority of farms are too small to be economically viable

■ **Tunisia is squeezed between the Mediterranean and the Sahara and, as a bridge between the two, has had to adapt to both extremes. Tunisians have emerged from this, and from foreign invasions and occupation, as a people known for their tolerance and sense of compromise.** ■

A melting-pot Tunisia has seen more than its share of invaders, from Sicilian Greeks in 311 BC to Nazi Germans in 1941. The indigenous Berbers, colonised by the Phoenicians and overwhelmed by the Arabs, were also deeply marked by Romans, Vandals, Byzantines, Spaniards, Turks and French. Out of this melting-pot has been created the most liberal and one of the most stable nations in North Africa, inhabited by people who are eager both to welcome global influences and to preserve their unique identity. An often-heard comment is: 'I'm not Arab, I'm a Tunisian.'

Countryside versus town Whereas Berbers in the rest of North Africa still speak their own language and get angry at being mistaken for Arabs, Tunisian Berbers have always assimilated with the newcomers, intermarried and adopted both the Arabs' languages and religions (see

Modesty forbids most Tunisian women from donning a swimsuit

also pages 20–1). In Tunisia the divide lies not between Berbers and Arabs, but between cosmopolitan citizens of affluent coastal towns and the poorer rural population with its traditional values. Although the government is committed to raising health and education standards in the country, the huge discrepancies in wealth continue to grow.

❑ **Population** 8.9 million, with 54 inhabitants per sq km (800 per sq km in Tunis). Some 55 per cent of the population is younger than 20 and 33 per cent is younger than 14. A total of 99 per cent are Sunni Muslims. Less than 7 per cent of the population is ethnically Berber and only some 3 per cent still speak the Berber dialect.
Birth rate 25 per 1,000.
Death rate 6 per 1,000.
Infant mortality 30 per 1,000.
Life expectancy 69 years.
Literacy rate 67 per cent.
GNP per capita US$1,790. ❑

Invasion of tourists After independence, Tunisia realised – before many other countries in the same situation – that beach tourism could become a much-needed source of foreign currency. But although Tunisians are friendly and welcoming by nature, they were eager to preserve their Muslim traditions and integrity. The solution was to create *zones touristiques*, areas outside the towns where tourists could do more or less what they wanted – even sunbathe topless. At the same time, this has to a great extent allowed Tunisians to maintain their own traditions, although obviously there

In every village and town Tunisians enjoy the evening promenade

are exceptions, as in Sousse (see pages 121–3).

Tunisia's pro-Western policies have also had social side-effects. Close relations with Europe and the United States have helped to encourage more liberal behaviour than one finds in other North African countries, particularly neighbouring Algeria and Libya. This is something you will feel as you walk down a street, whether you are in a city or a resort.

Women's rights 'Women's rights within family law are unique in the Arab world' (*New Internationalist* August 1997). Although Tunisian women are rarely seen on café terraces, they do have a full role in the community outside the home, working in offices, banks, shops and markets, and in government agencies and the civil services. In the evening, they are also seen out for the promenade.

Tunisians are proud of the position of women in their society. This, in part, is the legacy of Bourguiba's civil charter, which gave women more freedom and more rights

These days it is rare to see people dressed traditionally

than in any other Muslim country, including the right to demand a divorce. Polygamy was forbidden, abortion was accepted in 1965 and more than 60 per cent of women make use of contraceptives. Many women in Tunis and other cities lead very similar lives to those of Western women, although those in the more traditional countryside still live in a patriarchal society.

■ **The Berbers are the indigenous inhabitants of southern Tunisia, the 'original' Tunisians whose history reflects the history of the country. Over the centuries invaders have forced change on them. Now a new invasion, from tourists, threatens to overwhelm the last bastions of their culture.** ■

Ancient Berbers There are no Berber histories and very little archaeology, either because no traces remain or because it has not been a priority to study them. Greek and Roman historians grouped the early inhabitants of Tunisia together as 'barbarians', but the Greek word *barbaroi* covered anyone who wasn't Greek, while the Roman *barbari* referred to people who lived beyond the imperial borders. It was the Arabs, in the 8th century, who used the word specifically to refer to indigenous North Africans, and the name still applies to the indigenous people of the North African seaboard, from Siwa Oasis in Egypt to the Rif Mountains in Morocco.

Berber confederation The Berbers were originally semi-nomadic tribes

It is the Berber women who keep up traditions

who shifted their camps according to the need for pasture or trade. Most of Tunisia was originally divided into the territories of different tribes. Some of the most important gave their name to places, as in the case of the Numidae, on whose territory the ancient kingdom of Numidia was established, and the Khroumir, whose name lives on in a range of hills. The Khroumir were in fact just one of three tribes who lived in the area, the others being the Moghod and Nefza. It was on the excuse of retaliation against the Khroumir that French troops first crossed from Algeria into Tunisia in 1881 at the start of their occupation.

❏ The Berbers had and still have their own distinct language, with many local dialects. Although little is known of early Berber, some words have certainly survived – king or chieftain, for instance, was built around the consonants 'gld', as is *aguellid*, the modern Berber word of the same meaning. Today, Berber is spoken by only a very few people, mostly in the remains of the southern communities, and is most noticeable in place-names. ❏

Berber monuments The lack of research means that information is still scarce, but ancient Berber ruins certainly do exist in North Africa, with some in Tunisia. As elsewhere in the ancient world, many are tombs, cut into hills or rocks, or built out of stones. One of the most interesting in Tunisia is the Mausoleum of Ateban at Dougga (see page 132), dating from the period of the

Numidian (Berber) Kingdom, *c.* 200 BC. In the south there are also remains of Berber citadels, which were later converted into *ksour*, or fortified settlements. Around these *ksour* villages sometimes developed, as in the case of modern-day Guermessa (see page 165).

Berber religion Nothing is known of the pre-Punic Berber religion in Tunisia. After the rise of Carthage, the Berbers practised the religion of the latest invader, adopting – or, rather, often being forced to adopt – the gods of the Phoenicians and Romans, being converted to Christianity by the Byzantines, and then changing over to Islam. When the Arabs invaded Berber territory in the 7th century, their general, Oqba ibn Nafi, won over many Berbers to Islam by pretending he was something of a prophet and miracle-worker; many who refused to convert were either forced into slavery or killed.

Berbers today The increase in the amount of land that is being farmed in Tunisia, the discovery of minerals in the desert and the extended power of modern central government have all conspired to reduce the Berber population. They sought refuge in the southern hills, isolated and inhospitable places where they

Colour, an antidote to the desert

Berbers in Guermessa still work their small plots of land

21

must have thought they would be safe to continue to live undisturbed, but they didn't count on the late 20th-century phenomenon of tourism. Being the most distinctive and picturesque cultural group in the country is enough of a reason for thousands of foreigners armed with cameras to seek them out each year. Perversely, the survival of Berber culture now depends on these regular intrusions from foreigners and the money they bring with them.

■ Tunisia's cultural life can seem very quiet for most of the year, but in the summer months, with the return of migrant workers, the entire country comes to life and embarks on a chain of festivals and weddings. A few festivals also coincide with the harvest or celebrate traditional sports. ■

Islamic holidays As a Muslim country, Tunisia celebrates Islamic feast days. The two major annual feasts, when everything shuts down, are the Eid el-Kebir or Aid el-Adha, commemorating Abraham's sacrifice of a lamb instead of his son Isaac, and the Eid es-Seghir or Eid el-Fitr, celebrating the end of Ramadan, the month of fasting (see also pages 14–15). As these feasts are dictated by the lunar Muslim calendar, dates move backwards by 11 days every year relative to the Gregorian calendar.

Festivals Tunisia's festivals used to be deeply rooted in a local tradition or event, but these days most of them are geared towards the tourist market. Local tourist offices should be able to supply a calendar of events (see page 192).

Douz's spectacular National Sahara Festival takes place in December

22

❏ Most weddings take place in summer. Traditional celebrations are impressive and can last up to 15 days, with separate male and female pre-wedding parties starting things off. The days before the big day see the bride being pampered by friends and family; at this time her hands and feet are decorated with henna, all her body hair is removed and she is instructed in conjugal duties. On the wedding day many brides will wear a heavy silver dress which can make movement difficult, but this is not usually a problem as the couple is expected to stay sitting on a throne while their family and friends eat and drink. Arranged weddings are still a common practice in Tunisia, especially in rural areas. ❏

The emblem of El Haouaria's Falconry Festival in the main square

April
Nabeul Festival of Orange Blossoms: cultural events.
Tataouine Cultural Festival.

May
Sfax Music Festival.

June
El Jem Classical Music Festival.
El Haouaria Falconry Festival: falcons hunt partridge and quail in the wonderful scenery of Cap Bon (see also page 104).
Testour Festival: *maalouf* music or Andalusian-based folk music (see panel on page 154) in the café below the Great Mosque.
Kelibia Festival of Amateur Cinema.

July
La Goulette Festival de la Karaka.
Tabarka Coral Festival.

July/August
Sousse Festival of Theatre: cultural events, with folk music and dancing.
Dougga Festival of Classical Theatre.
Kerkennah Folklore Festival.
Hammamet International Culture Festival: good music and theatre in Arabic and French at the Cultural Centre (see also page 107).
Carthage International Cultural Festival: the biggest festival of all. Staged in the restored Roman theatre at Carthage, and including

Greyhound racing is just one event held at the National Sahara Festival

dance, cinema, theatre and music. Most events are widely advertised. Tickets can be bought in advance from the ticket office at the theatre.
Jerba Folklore Festival (biennial).
Tabarka l'Université de l'Été (Summer University): attended by hundreds of students, with evening entertainment such as musical performances, debates and art shows.
Gabès Festival of Sidi Boulbaba: named after the local saint who was the Prophet Muhammad's barber; cultural and folklore events.

August
Monastir Theatre and Poetry Festival: performances are mainly in French.
Sidi Bou Said Kharja celebrations.

November
Kebili Date Harvest Festival.
Biennial Carthage International Film Festival: good Arab and African films. Listings in the local press.

December/January
Tozeur Folklore Festival: camel races and Bedouin spectacles.
Douz National Sahara Festival: attracts more than 50,000 Bedouins, nomads and tourists. Camel races, sand hockey, greyhound races, music, poetry, singing and fantasias.

■ **For centuries Tunisian artists had been influenced by the styles that prevailed in the Middle East, but with the arrival of the French at the end of the 19th century, they looked to the West for new ways of expressing their often confused identity. Since then, artists in all fields have struggled to blend their Islamic heritage and values with European aesthetics.** ■

Modern art Islam prohibits the representation of humans and animals, so the only figurative painting that existed in Tunisia before the French invasion was the painting on glass of scenes of Arab epics (you can still find these in the *souqs*) and formal court portraits commissioned by the Ottoman beys. Although at the end of the 19th century a few native painters (such as Ahmed ben Osman) entered this court scene, it was only with the arrival of the French that a tradition of painting on canvas and of figurative art was born.

❑ Paul Klee claimed that a visit to Kairouan changed his life. He wrote in his diary: 'Colour has taken hold of me … colour and I are one.' ❑

Foundation schools With the likes of Paul Klee discovering Tunisia's special light and vibrant colours, and being hugely influenced by them, a Tunisian salon was opened in 1894. Initially, this annual exhibition only admitted French painters and orientalists, but early in the 20th century the first few Tunisian painters were accepted. Among them were Yahia Turki, whose naïve paintings evoke wonderfully Tunisian scenes of street life, and Abdelaziz ben Rais, who used the techniques of glass painting and Persian miniatures to express the Tunisian landscape. Both were early members of the influential Tunis School, founded in the 1920s, and are now considered the fathers of Tunisian painting.

A patchwork of colours and shapes, typical of Paul Klee's Tunisian work

Above and below: contemporary sculpture on the beach at Mahrès

Identity crisis The struggle for independence provoked a crisis of identity amongst Tunisia's artists. Two key developments then appeared: Hatem el-Mekki began to put to secular use the previously exclusively religious art of calligraphy, and Ammar Farhat began incorporating into paintings themes from Tunisian folktales. From these and other beginnings developed an art with a Tunisian character. The next generation took the search for a national artistic identity even further. Artists like Naj Mahdaoui created bold calligraphic forms, while others – including Habib Chebli and Hedi Turki – explored abstract painting.

Literature After the French occupation, Tunisian writers began using the French language and also the essentially European forms of the novella and the play. As with visual artists, there was a debate amongst writers about how to express the national identity. One writer who stood out was Abu el-Kacem el Shabbi, often acknowledged as the father of modern Arabic poetry in North Africa, and who now has a street named after him in almost every Tunisian town. Born in 1909, he received a traditional education at the Jemaa ez Zitouna in Tunis. As he never learned a foreign language, his poetry was purely traditional in form, but his ideas were very much of the moment, inspired by anger at the colonial occupation. More recently, the novella has found new favour amongst fiction writers and is being used as a challenge to the traditionalists. Laila ben Mami writes about feminist issues, while Izz al Din al Madani attacks Islamic fundamentalism. The country's best-known contemporary novelist, however, is Albert Memni, a Tunisian Jew who now lives in Paris.

❏ The most important art galleries representing young and more established native artists are in and around Tunis. Some of the best are: Espace Alif (20 bis rue de Yougoslavie, Tunis); Galerie Yahia (1 avenue de Carthage, Tunis); Galerie Ammar Farhat (3 rue Sidi el Ghimrim, Sidi Bou Said); and Galerie Sophonisbe (Carthage Dermech). A small museum of Tunisian modern art recently opened in the Parc du Belvédère in Tunis (see page 56). ❏

Egyptian films are a popular form of entertainment among Tunisians

Flora and fauna

■ Tunisia might be small, but its varied landscape and climate provide a home for a wide range of flora and fauna. Lions and elephants lost their battle against humans long ago, but there is still plenty of natural beauty to be discovered. ■

The painted lady butterfly (left) and grasshopper are common sights

Northern hills The more generous rainfall occurring in the north of the country and in the Tell supports some thick forests, mostly of pine and oak, as well as farmed cork trees, walnuts and almonds. These forests are home to animals that have survived French colonial hunters and are now enjoying a more peaceful life, including wild boars, mongooses, the feline genet and jackals. (See also the Focus on Birdlife on pages 92–3.)

Coastal plains Throughout the country your outlook will be brightened by flowering oleander and bougainvillaea bushes, and hemmed in by the prickly pear, known here as the Barbary fig and brought to North Africa from its native Caribbean by the Spanish. The plains, the lower meadows of the Tell and the valley of the Mejerda are good places to see the springtime profusion of colourful wildflowers, from chrysanthemums and marigolds to irises and daisies.

Southern deserts Beyond the olive plantations of the Sahel and the treeless grasslands, Tunisia is transformed from a sub-Saharan landscape of acacia, tamarisk and eucalyptus trees into full desert. The southern desert oases are home to a number of fruit trees, including figs, bananas and date palms, the latter producing the sought-after deglet ennour date. The most visible animals in the region are camels, none of which are wild, however far you are from habitation. If you see a gazelle or the nocturnal fennec fox, they will be running, having been threatened with the same fate as Tunisia's lions, ostriches and antelopes before them: extinction. Rocky areas in the south are home to a number of creatures you may prefer not to meet, such as the horned viper and deadly scorpions, as well as some you won't mind, such as the desert varan, a lizard whose taste for meat luckily doesn't include human flesh.

Prickly pears, or Barbary figs

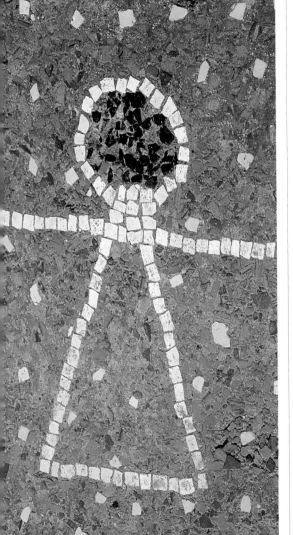

TUNISIA WAS

■ **Although the Phoenicians were not Tunisian in origin, their legacy has become a central part of the country's inheritance and their achievements are pointed to as one of the high points in ancient Tunisian culture. They also gave the ancient world two of its most exciting characters.** ■

28

Mediterranean traders The Phoenicians came from the eastern Mediterranean coast (modern-day Lebanon) and, like many contemporary Lebanese, were renowned traders. Around 1000 BC they first appeared in the western part of the sea *en route* for the copper, tin and silver mines of southern Spain. Early navigation required sailors to keep within sight of land, and the Phoenician galleys were able to cover about 30km per day. Permanent settlements developed where they made their regular overnight stops, these forming the foundations of most contemporary Tunisian coastal towns.

The Carthaginian Empire In 814 BC, Elissa, a daughter of the Phoenician king of Tyre, founded Kart Hadasht (Carthage), a city with a great destiny, on the Hill of Byrsa outside present-day Tunis. (For more on Elissa, also called Dido, see page 61.) In 550 BC, an alliance of Phoenician colonists in the western Mediterranean laid the foundation for a Carthaginian empire which included Sicily, Sardinia, Corsica, the Balearic Islands and parts of southern Spain. Defeat by Greeks from Sicily in 480 BC pushed Carthaginian traders beyond the Pillars of Hercules to Mogador (modern Essaouira in Morocco) and also into the Tunisian interior.

Daily life Despite the fact that the Cathaginians left no

The now peaceful sacrificial site of Tophet, in Carthage

written accounts of life in the city, hints can be gained from Greek and Roman records – although as they were Carthage's bitter rivals these cannot always be trusted. Like the ancient Egyptians, Carthaginians were buried in elaborate tombs with goods that would help them in the afterlife. From these and other clues we know that city life was sophisticated. Wealthy Carthaginians enjoyed a standard of living similar to that of wealthy Greeks or Romans. They prayed to a pantheon of gods, were educated to world-class standards of their time, followed local fashion and discussed philosophy and politics. Unfortunately, the city's library was burned, so works

Stela from Tophet (4th–5th century BC)

such as the famous encyclopaedia of agriculture are lost to us.

The Sicilian Wars

In 410 BC, Carthage sent a 50,000-strong mercenary army to Sicily, restarting a war which continued for another 200 years. In 311 BC the Greeks invaded Cap Bon and destroyed a string of towns. Fifty years later the Romans also staked a claim to Sicily and started the First Punic War (265–242 BC), invading Cap Bon and besieging Carthage. The matter was only settled in 242 BC when the Romans defeated the Carthaginian navy. This reveals the true cause of the war: the struggle for control of maritime trade routes.

Hamilcar and son After the defeat by Rome, the mercenary army mutinied and threatened Carthage itself. In 238 BC, the mutineers were trapped somewhere in the hills between Béja and Mejez el Bab, where the Carthaginian general, Hamilcar Barca, crucified the ten leaders and let his elephants trample the rest to death. Hamilcar subsequently became ruler of Carthage and added new territories in Spain.

Punic mask to ward off the evil eye

In 221 BC he was succeeded by his son Hannibal (see also page 64), but in spite of his heroic efforts Carthage was unable to contend with growing Roman power in the Mediterranean. After defeat in the Third Punic War (149–146 BC), Carthage was burned and flattened, and its citizens made slaves. The site was then scattered with salt so that nothing would ever grow there.

❏ The Phoenicians were one of the most advanced of the early civilisations, developing new and more efficient ways of working metals and fabrics and growing crops. They also created an alphabet on which our cursive script is based. For all their achievements, however, few records of them survived the 5th-century BC advance of the Greeks and Babylonians into Lebanon. ❏

Kerkouane gives a clear idea of a purely Punic settlement

■ **After the fall of Carthage at the end of the Third Punic War, Rome decreed that its name be wiped from memory for ever. But under subsequent Roman rule it rose again to become the centre of one of the empire's most valuable yet troubled provinces.** ■

30

The continuing conquest After the Romans defeated Hannibal at the Battle of Zama in 202 BC, Massinissa, a Numidian chief who had helped the Romans, was made king of Numidia, creating a buffer zone between Rome's newly conquered farmlands and the nomadic Berber tribes' grazing pastures. When Massinissa died during the Third Punic War, his kingdom was divided between his three sons, weakening it further. In 112 BC Jugurtha, Massinissa's grandson, reunited Numidia, provoking a forceful Roman response, though it still took them seven years to defeat him and occupy the kingdom.

Carthage's renaissance Julius Caesar arrived in Tunisia in 44 BC in pursuit of his rivals Pompey and Cato the Younger. He is credited with the inspired idea of rebuilding Carthage, although it wasn't until the reign of his successor, the great imperialist Augustus, that reconstruction began. Augustus created a city of magnificent buildings, fed by an aqueduct which brought sweet water from the hills around Zaghouan, 145km away. Along with the rest of Roman Africa, it saw funds increase dramatically after 'local boy' Septimius Severus

Depiction of Carthage's acropolis as it would have appeared in 600 BC

became Roman emperor in the late 2nd century AD. By then, Roman arms had subdued the local tribes and the empire's borders had been pushed further south.

❏ It is tempting to believe that the Romans were trying to emulate the Phoenicians when they rebuilt Carthage, literally over the ashes of the older city. But the Romans were a practical people who knew that the region was capable of producing large quantities of corn to feed the empire's soldiers. ❏

The Romans' mosaics are their most impressive legacy

Pax Romana For 200 years, until the overthrow of the Severan Dynasty, North Africa – and Tunisia in particular – enjoyed an unprecedented period of peace and stability. Amongst the benefits of this period of 'Roman peace' were that proper attention was paid to agriculture, roads were improved and trade links flourished across the Mediterranean. Increased trade brought new wealth to the North African province and the period saw an extraordinary building boom. The great amphitheatre at

Above: aqueduct near Carthage
Below: Roman villas, Carthage
Right: Roman quarter, Carthage

El Jem, the theatre at Dougga and similarly grand constructions of temples, law courts, public baths and villas sprang up across the country.

❏ The magnificent mosaic legacy from this period (see pages 88–9), much of which is on display in the Musée du Bardo in Tunis (see pages 54–6), gives a picture of the wealth and stability the peace made possible. Scenes of hunting and fishing, of Bacchus, of seductions and of the Muses all suggest that North Africa's villa-owning classes were having fun. ❏

End of an empire The fate of North Africa was tied to the fate of the imperial capital Rome, and after the fall of the Severan Dynasty in Rome (AD 235), Tunisia experienced periods of lawlessness and intervals of restored peace. A conspiracy by some wealthy landowners against the new Emperor Maximinus was put down by the frontier Third Augustan Legion, which sacked El Jem and Sousse. Diocletian managed to restore central authority towards the end of the century, but after his abdication in 305 rival Roman forces were fighting in Tunisia, and Carthage itself was sacked in 311. In 429 a Germanic tribe, the Vandals, who had blazed a trail through France and Italy, crossed to North Africa and replaced the Roman administration with their own. Some 26 years later they even launched a successful attack on Rome itself, which they looted, bringing treasure back to Tunisia.

■ **The Christian and Byzantine legacy is often overlooked in Tunisia. Although the Byzantine reign didn't last as long as the Roman, it was a glorious period and has left some magnificent works of art and buildings, the ruins of the latter even today instilling an impression of grandeur and remarkable elegance.** ■

The First Christian Empire In 312, the Roman Emperor Constantine was riding into battle against his rival Maxentius when he saw a vision of a burning cross inscribed with the words 'In This We Conquer'. After his victory, he converted to Christianity and in 313 granted civil rights and tolerance to Christians who, until then, had suffered terrible persecution throughout the Roman Empire. By 330, Constantine had moved from Rome and established a new imperial capital on the site of a Greek city called Byzantium. He called his new Christian capital Constantinople.

Christian Tunisia Constantine's reforms gave a boost to a church that had suffered badly under earlier Roman emperors. That said, pagan rituals continued into the 5th century, when the destruction of a pagan temple in Carthage sparked off riots. Tunisia's Christian community flourished and Carthage stood alongside such places as Alexandria and Antioch as one of the world's leading spiritual and intellectual centres.

❑ Born in Numidia (modern Algeria), St Augustine (354–430) trained at Carthage in public speaking in preparation for a legal or political career. He then became a teacher of rhetoric in Carthage, in Rome and finally in Milan, where he converted to Christianity in 386. After his dramatic conversion, Augustine returned to North Africa to establish a religious community dedicated to the intellectual quest for God. Visiting Hippo (modern Bone, in Algeria) in 391 he was made a priest (and later a bishop) by popular demand. Augustine's theology has since had a profound influence on Western thought and culture. ❑

Justinian's reconstruction
Throughout the 5th century, Tunisia was held by the Vandals, who themselves practised a form of

The impressive Byzantine fortress at Haïdra shelters five churches

Christianity. The Vandals had destroyed much of the fabric of Roman Africa, demolishing aqueducts and doing nothing to encourage agriculture. In 533, with the main Vandal army on its way to Sardinia, the Byzantine Emperor Justinian sent 15,000 men under his general Belisarius to recover Tunisia and hence established a new era. With the Vandals out of the way and the Berber tribes either defeated or drawn into new treaties, Byzantine administrators ushered in a new period of prosperity. They oversaw much of the Mediterranean corn trade and controlled a small empire

Typical Christian imagery on a 4th-century Byzantine sarcophagus

The Church of Hildegun at Makthar is named after a man of Vandal descent buried near its entrance

within the Byzantine Empire, which included the Balearic Islands, Corsica and Sardinia.

❑ Belisarius (505–65) was a brilliant general responsible for many of Justinian's successes. He defeated the Persians between 527 and 531, suppressed riots in the empire's capital, Constantinople, and then sailed off to North Africa, where he defeated the Vandals in Tunisia. By this time Justinian was afraid that Belisarius was becoming too successful. When Belisarius moved against the Ostrogoths in Italy, Justinian refused to supply enough troops and the Italian campaign dragged on until Belisarius was recalled to Constantinople in disgrace. ❑

The Byzantine legacy The era of peace that followed Belisarius's defeat of the Vandals created another building boom. Fortresses and villas were constructed, Carthage's port was restored and, in place of the closed pagan temples, the Byzantines built a series of remarkable churches in their own inimitable style. Traditional Roman decorations, particularly mosaics, were also used to new and startling effects. In 620, Emperor Heraclius considered adding to the grandeur of Byzantine Tunisia by moving his capital from Constantinople to Carthage, although he was wise not to, for in 647 a new force arrived on the scene.

■ **In the early 7th century a new religion came out of Arabia, and with it an army of conquering tribesmen. After overcoming Byzantine forces and subduing serious resistance put up by the Berbers, the Arabs took control of North Africa, changing its face to give it the character with which we now associate Tunisia.** ■

The Arab conquest Within ten years of the Prophet Muhammad's death in 632, his followers had overrun Persia, Syria and Egypt, and laid the foundation for one of the world's great empires; 100 years after his death, Arab armies stood on the thresholds of France and India.

In Tunisia the Arabs showed courage and intelligence against Byzantine forces. After a Byzantine army had been defeated near Sbeïtla in 647, the legendary Arab general, Oqba ibn Nafi, arrived in Tunisia in 670 with plans to stay. Instead of attacking coastal strongholds, he remained inland and founded a new Islamic city at Kairouan. Although Byzantine forces were on the run, indigenous Berber tribes were far from subdued and in 682 they forced an Arab retreat. Twelve years later another exceptional Arab general, Hassan ibn Numan, defeated the Berbers and moved into Carthage after the city had been betrayed by its governor. By 705, an Arab emir (governor) ruled over the whole north-west of Africa from Kairouan for the caliph in Baghdad.

❏ Amongst the many extraordinary figures of the Arab invasion, one of the strangest is a woman called El Kahina, a Berber queen, also reputed to have been Jewish, who stood against Hassan ibn Numan at Gabès and again at El Jem. According to the legend, Ibn Numan, having failed to trap her inside the Roman amphitheatre at El Jem, chased her all the way to Tabarka on the north coast, where she was killed. ❏

Most of Tunisia's magnificent mosques do not admit tourists

Above: carving of a tiger on the Borj el Kebir, Mahdia
Left: Jemaa ez Zitouna, Tunis

that plunged North Africa into unrest for more than 20 years.

The Berber response After initial confrontations, many Berbers accepted the Arabs as new rulers and converted to their religion. Many also joined the Arab mercenary armies. But the arrogance of the Arabs was a source of bitterness which encouraged the spread of Kharijism amongst Berbers. Kharijism was a puritan Muslim creed which appealed to the desert-hardened character of the Berbers, particularly since it stressed the equality of men and that leaders should be removed if unworthy. In 739 a Berber garrison in Morocco, attempting to put the belief into practice, sparked a revolt

Strong towers and crenellated walls at Sousse's Great Mosque

The Aghlabids The size of the Arab Empire made the caliph in Baghdad reliant on governors and spies to control his provinces. But in further-flung parts of the empire, such as Tunisia (or Ifriqiya as the Arabs called it, their interpretation of its Roman name), not even the caliph's spies could keep track of the governor. When the Baghdad-appointed governor of Tunisia was unable to suppress an Arab revolt in 797, Ibrahim ibn al Aghlab stepped in, restored order and founded a dynasty, which the Baghdad caliph, Haroun el Rashid, was obliged to accept, though the situation was made sweeter by annual payments of tribute.

The golden age The rule of Ibrahim and his descendants lasted for a golden century. They built a string of *ribats* (fortified monasteries), of which those at Monastir and Sousse are some of the oldest Islamic buildings in the country, and left Tunisia with some of its greatest monuments, including the Jemaa ez Zitouna mosque in Tunis and the Grand Mosques at Kairouan and Sousse. They also provided a boost for agriculture and local trades, although the country's most valuable commodities were brought across the Sahara and through the Berber lands to be traded along the coast – namely gold and slaves. The wealth generated by these and other trades allowed the Aghlabid rulers to indulge their passions, which they did to such an extent that few were prepared to defend them against the next reformist movement.

■ After the decadence of the Aghlabids, Tunisia was ruled for more than four centuries by dynasties with international interests and ambitions. As a result, the country became a pawn in an Arab power struggle from which it suffered badly – farming was neglected, towns declined and local government collapsed. ■

Skifa el Kahla gateway, Mahdia, only entrance to the Fatimid palace

Descendants of Muhammad The crisis of loyalty that Muslims faced after the death of Prophet Muhammad – namely, who should succeed – re-emerged in Tunisia when the Ismailis, a severe Shiah sect, claimed the caliphate in the name of Ali (Muhammad's son-in-law) and Fatima. Their leader, Ubaydallah, deposed the last Aghlabid ruler in 909, proclaimed the Fatimid Dynasty and built a well-defended city at Mahdia in anticipation of objections. In spite of heavy taxation and the persecution of Sunni Muslims, particularly at Kairouan, there were few.

Fatimid ambitions Mahdia, perched over the Mediterranean, was to be a springboard for the Fatimid assault on

❑ Fatimid leaders were extremely superstitious and kept astrologers at court to advise on whether moments were propitious or not. When the Fatimids invaded Tunisia, the planet Jupiter was aligned with Saturn in the sign of Aries. Before their final assault on Egypt, a Muslim convert, Yacoub Ibn Killis, arrived with secrets of the Egyptian defences. As the planets were in the same alignment as during the Tunisian conquest, Ibn Killis was believed. The victory was complete. ❑

36

the rival caliphate ('successor' to Muhammad) in Egypt. The Fatimid army conquered Sicily in 912, Alexandria and the oasis of Fayoum in 914 and, with a 100,000-strong army led by a Greek general called Gohar, the rest of Egypt in 969. In 973 the new Fatimid caliph, al-Mu'izz, left Tunis with the bones of his ancestors for Cairo, the palace-city that had been built for him.

After the Fatimids The Caliph al-Mu'izz had left a general, Buluggin, in charge of his North African territory. As was often the way, Buluggin created a new ruling dynasty, the Zirids, who assured their independence but soon began to see their authority undermined at home. The crisis culminated, in 1016, in the massacre of some 20,000 Shiites by the majority Sunni Muslims. When the Zirids bowed to popular pressure and backed the Fatimids' rivals, the caliph in Cairo retaliated by encouraging the westward migration of an Arab tribe, the Beni Hilal. Whether coincidence or as a direct result of these semi-nomadic herders, the balance of Tunisia's countryside shifted, settled farming was neglected, towns and cities which had relied on agricultural trade went into decline and local government broke down. It was a disaster for Tunisia and didn't help the Fatimids either because the link between the

Mahdia's rock-cut Fatimid port

east and west of their empire had been severed.

Moroccan rulers For two decades in the 12th century, the strong Norman king of Sicily, Roger II, capitalised on Tunisia's weaknesses and occupied several coastal towns, including the old Fatimid capital of Mahdia. But the Normans were unable to resist the Almohad army, which marched east from Morocco and brought the whole Maghreb under a single Maghrebi ruler for the first time. The Almohads were religious revivalists with a vision of a new Muslim community. Coming out of the Atlas Mountains, they also had strong links with the Berber tribes. In 1230, Abu Zakariyya, the Almohad governor of Tunisia, had sufficient strength to proclaim independence from the rulers across the mountains in Marrakech. In the process, he created a dynasty which ruled Tunisia for 300 years.

Modern copy of Mahdia's 10th-century Great Mosque

❑ The migration of the Beni Hilal is the subject of one of the great epic poems of the Arabic language, the *Hilalia*. There are many similarities between the *Hilalia* and ancient Greek epics such as the *Iliad* and *Odyssey*, not least the fact that they were part of an oral tradition. The *Hilalia* has never been fully transcribed, but there are some story-tellers who claim to be able to remember the entire, million-line epic. ❑

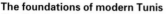

■ **Tunisia as we know it came into its own under the Hafsids, successors to the Almohad rulers. This was a period of increased international involvement as the Hafsids developed wider trade links and were dragged into complicated wars that saw all the powers in the region fighting for supremacy.** ■

The foundations of modern Tunis

Abu Zakariyya, direct descendant of the influential chief of the High Atlas tribes Abu Hafs Umar, was an Almohad governor of Tunisia. In 1230, he saw an opportunity to declare independence from his Moroccan rulers and took it. Over the next couple of years he showed the extent of his ambitions by taking control of Algeria, declaring himself caliph and sending military help to the hard-pressed Spanish Muslims.

Abu Zakariyya's son, Al Mustansir, became the pre-eminent ruler in the Muslim world and during his reign the trans-Saharan trade in gold, slaves, ebony, ivory and all the other exotica of central Africa was increasingly channelled through Tunisia. With the revenue this generated, his capital, Tunis, began to reflect his new status and witnessed a period of great expansion.

❏ The 300 years of Hafsid rule saw a transformation in international trade and travel. The opening up of Europe that accompanied the Renaissance, as well as a period of stronger government in the Levant, helped traders develop the Silk Route from China, across Central Asia to the Mediterranean. This was the period when the Italian Marco Polo embarked on his travels (1271–95), followed by many others. Some of the greatest Arab travellers were also on the move, including Ibn Battuta, who visited China (1325–54), and the Tunisian-born Ibn Khaldoun (see page 69). ❏

Despite continuous threats, the Hafsids held Tunisia for 300 years

Most of Kairouan's Zaouia of Sidi Sahab is Hafsid

Their glorious rule The timing of the rise in the Hafsids' power was fortunate. There was a rare stability in the Mediterranean and Eastern world, in spite of the occasional crusade. Their military strength and, when that failed them, their political skills, created the conditions under which not only international trade but also local agriculture thrived. Hafsid rulers were also fortunate in having a new source of skilled labour to draw upon: refugees arriving in North Africa from Muslim Spain, who were drafted into the army or given positions in the administration.

The French Crusade In 1270, the French King Louis IX, beatified as St Louis in 1297, arrived at Carthage as part of the Eighth Crusade. The reasons behind the landing are unclear, although the most likely explanation is that it was connected to the territorial ambitions of Louis's brother Charles, king of nearby Sicily. The invasion was ill-advised. After two battles, fought in the heat of summer, the Hafsids were saved from near-certain defeat by the sudden death of Louis, after which Charles negotiated for peace.

Hafsid decline Al Mustansir's successors struggled to hold the country together, losing out to both the Berber tribes and to Spanish Christians, who took Jerba and the Kerkenneh Islands. Under Abu Abbas (1370–94), the Hafsids clawed back some of their lost territory in the south, as well as Algeria and Morocco, while the Hafsid fleet had become sufficiently strong to provoke a joint French, Genoese and Spanish blockade of their naval base at Mahdia. The Hafsid fleet survived the encounter and Abu Abbas split the alliance against him by concluding treaties with both Genoa and Venice. It was the power struggle across the Mediterranean between the French, Spanish, Genoese, Venetians and Ottomans that eventually overwhelmed Hafsid Tunisia.

> ❏ Under the Hafsids, the city of Tunis grew both to the north and south. The first palace building was erected on the site of what is now the Musée du Bardo, and quarters were devoted to Muslim refugees from Spain and to European envoys and merchants. At the Jemaa ez Zitouna mosque a minaret and *medersa* (Koranic school) were built, while the Great Mosque at Kairouan was also restored. ❏

The Hafsids restored the Great Mosque in Kairouan

■ **In the 16th century Tunisia was a battle ground for a war of religion, ideology and power between Ottoman Turks and Hapsburg Spanish, and between Christians and Muslims. With the help of two extraordinary brothers, the notorious Barbary pirates El Uruj and Kheireddin (Barbarossa), Tunisia came under Ottoman control to enjoy once again a period of stability.** ■

Hapsburgs and Ottomans After the fall of Granada, the Catholic monarchs of Spain capitalised on their victory by sending ships against a string of North African ports. The most effective resistance was provided by two brothers, El Uruj and Kheireddin (Barbarossa – see box), who built up a force of swift galleys manned by Christian slaves, operating out of La Goulette and Jerba and, after 1516, out of Algiers. In this period of fast-shifting alliances, Barbarossa was attacked by Hafsids, Spanish and Berbers. In the early 1530s, after the death of El Uruj and faced with increased Hapsburg pressure, Barbarossa appealed to the great Ottoman sultan, Suleyman I ('the Magnificent'), for help. In 1534 he took Tunisia, which provoked Charles V to retaliate the following year, landing with a force of 30,000 soldiers and retaking Tunis.

Barbary pirates After Barbarossa's departure, his successor, Dragut, re-established Ottoman control over

Charles V captured Tunis in 1535 from the famous pirate Barbarossa

Piracy thrived along the North African coast

southern Tunisia. For more than 300 years Barbary pirates – or corsairs as they came to be known – continued to attack ships along the North African coast. Even American efforts in 1801 and 1815 failed to end piracy, which continued until France invaded Algeria in 1830.

❑ El Uruj and Kheireddin (Barbarossa), brothers from the Greek island of Lesbos, made a name for themselves helping Muslims escape from Spain, and subsequently emerged as the most powerful pirates in North Africa. After offering his services to the Ottoman sultan, Kheireddin was made admiral of the Ottoman navy in 1533 and gained a reputation for himself by attacking Spanish and Italian fleets throughout the Mediterranean. In 1544 he retired to Constantinople, where he died two years later. ❑

Ottoman pashas In 1574 the
Ottoman commander Eulj Ali
recaptured Tunis for the sultan in
Constantinople. Apart from resuming
control of the previously Spanish-
held fortifications along the coast,
the sultan's governor, or pasha, ruled
the country with the help of *deys*
(commanders) and their janissaries
(Turkish soldiers), 4,000 of whom
were stationed in Tunis. History
repeated itself again: the distance
between governor and sovereign
was too great and, just as the
Aghlabids broke with the caliph in
Baghdad, so the *deys* declared
practical independence from

The Dar Ben Abdallah, Tunis

*The Borj el Kebir in Houmt Souk,
stormed by Dragut in 1560*

Constantinople and appointed their
own pasha, though they still
acknowledged the sultan's
sovereignty. Under its new rulers,
Tunisia thrived, attention was paid to
agriculture at home and to trade
abroad, and some of the damage
inflicted during the Hapsburg–
Ottoman struggle was repaired.

The Husseinites Hussein ibn Ali
Turki took power in 1705 and, break-
ing with the tradition of an elected
ruler, established a dynasty which
lasted until 1881. Constant hostility
from Algeria was of little concern
compared to the growing presence of
the European powers. Under strong
rulers, like Hammouda Pacha II
(1781–1813), the Algerians stayed
their side of the border and the
Europeans generally kept their attention on business. Under the weaker
rulers who succeeded Hammouda,
however, the Europeans encroached.
In 1819 they forced the bey to end
piracy, which immediately deprived
the treasury of much-needed
income, and at a time when less than
10 per cent of fertile land was being
farmed and therefore agricultural
revenues were at an all-time low.
Tunisia's weak and extravagant beys
ran up debts in Europe which they
were unable to repay, thereby bringing an end to the Husseinite Dynasty
and to Tunisian independence.

■ France had long held ambitions to control the Maghreb. In 1830 it invaded Algeria and in 1881 it took control of Tunisia. Morocco, however, didn't 'fall' until 1912. After the incompetence of previous Tunisian governments, the advantages of the colonial administration and the period of growth that accompanied it were almost welcome, for a while at least. ■

INVESTITURE DU NOUVEAU BEY DE TUNIS

The French administration operated alongside the traditional beylical structure

didn't renounce their claim to Tunisia until 1923.

The 'blessings' of colonisation The French installed their own administration alongside the traditional Tunisian government, much as the British did in Egypt. Although the bey remained the nominal head of state, the French resident minister ruled the country with the help of French civil servants. While Tunisians were subject to Islamic law, Europeans were answerable only to French courts, a cause of much tension.

❑ Under the French administration, Tunisia experienced a period of what would now be called 'sustained growth'. Nearly 13,000km of new road and 2,000km of railway were laid, borders were secured and the southern tribes pacified (or suppressed). There were new schools, hospitals and entertainments, although mostly for an élite. The area of cultivated land trebled, and in spite of French oppression the native population quadrupled from 1 to 4 million during the protectorate. ❑

The pretext France had wanted to extend its rule over North Africa for many years, but Husseinite beys resisted. In 1871, the bey of Tunis even approached London with the idea of Tunisia becoming a British protectorate. Under the terms of the 1878 Congress of Berlin, Britain and France came to an agreement over their interests around the world: Britain would 'have' Cyprus, and France Tunisia. Three years later a French force crossed the Algerian–Tunisian border on the pretext of chasing a group of Kroumiri tribesmen and carried straight on to Tunis. Tunisia became a French protectorate under the Treaty of the Bardo (1881), but after Mohammed VI's death a new agreement was reached with his successor, Ali IV, at the La Marsa Convention (1883). In spite of these treaties, the Ottomans

Holding the land Tunisia attracted the French for one of the reasons that it had attracted the ancient Romans: its fertility. There were already French landholders here before the protectorate was established, and after 1892 new colonial

settlers were further encouraged with cheap land, easy credit and improved roads. By 1915, French settlers owned 20 per cent of Tunisia's cultivated land. The poverty this created amongst dispossessed Tunisian farmers was one of many reasons for the support of the independence movement.

The new look The Ville Nouvelle of Tunis was laid out long before the protectorate, but it developed rapidly in the late 19th century. This was where the French 'shadow' adminis-trators were based. As it developed,

The Cathedral of St Vincent de Paul in Tunis, a cocktail of styles

The theatre was reserved almost exclusively for the French

so it drew some of the life and func-tions from the old city. The creeping influence of the colonisers, from the European-style uniforms of the army to the spread of the French language, also added to the bitterness.

Tunisia at war During 1914–18, more than 60,000 Tunisians went to Europe to support the French war effort, 10,000 of whom were either killed or went missing. During World War II, Tunisia once again became a battlefield. After France fell to Germany, the French administration in Tunisia blocked the ports of Tunis and Bizerte to both Allied and Nazi shipping. In 1941, German forces landed in Bizerte, Tunis, Sousse and Sfax. The Allies landed troops in Algeria, while Montgomery's British Eighth Army moved east from Egypt against Rommel's Afrika Korps and Italian forces. Resistance was stiff, as the rolling landscape favoured the defenders: it took particularly bitter fighting to shift the German panzer units defending the Gabès and Kasserine gaps. Fighting continued throughout the winter, switching from the Libyan border to the slopes of the Tell, with the area around Mejez el Bab seeing some of the bloodiest fighting. In April 1943 the east and west Allied armies met up, and on 13 May the Germans and Italians surrendered.

■ **The French held their North African colonies through both World Wars I and II. But pressure to withdraw was increasing at home, in the colonies and amongst world politicians. Meanwhile, a new Tunisian leader had been trained in France, one who would spearhead the country's struggle for independence.** ■

The beginning of the struggle The French met with resistance from the moment they occupied Tunisia in 1881, but it wasn't until the 20th century that the independence movement began to make itself heard. In 1911, rumours that French authorities had plans to redevelop the southern Muslim cemetery in Tunis led to riots.

After World War I an independence group calling itself the Young Tunisians, modelled on the Young Turks, emerged. In 1920 it founded the Destour (Constitution) Party. Within a decade, the Destour was divided between moderates and extremists. A split was inevitable.

The Neo-Destour In 1934, the radical Habib Bourguiba (see box opposite) and his sympathisers came into

Habib Bourguiba was eventually declared mentally ill in 1988

conflict with the Destour committee. Bourguiba promptly left the party and formed the Neo-Destour (later the Socialist Destourian Party). It was immediately banned and its leaders imprisoned, which resulted in a huge surge of support for Bourguiba. The Destour and Neo-Destour continued to agitate for independence, but their agendas differed widely, the Destour taking the more conservative line.

To independence The post-War French government of Charles de Gaulle attempted to suppress North African independence movements. Farhed Hached's trades union-based UGTT, for example, was severely restricted. As activists became more radical, Bourguiba seemed an attractive option and subsequently became involved in the formation of the 1950 pro-nationalist cabinet, still presided over by a French resident general. In 1952 confrontation escalated across the Maghreb. In Tunisia, Bourguiba was rearrested, a state of emergency declared and Farhat Hached assassinated. The following year the conflict developed into a civil war.

Celebrating the founding of the Tunisian Republic

Above: Zini El-Abidine Ben Ali
Left: Bourguiba's statue still stands in the centre of Tunis

In 1955 Bourguiba returned from France, having agreed to an autonomous Tunisia (his arrival at La Goulette on 1 June is still celebrated as the annual Victory Day holiday). On 20 March 1956 Tunisia declared independence, and a year later the last of the beys was deposed and a republic proclaimed. Morocco also achieved independence in 1956, Algeria following suit in 1962.

Bourguiba's legacy Bourguiba has been called both the father of the nation and another Third World despot. His Neo-Destour party ruled with a 100 per cent majority in the National Assembly; his security services were said to be as repressive as the occupying French; he was ruthless with his opponents; and neither the socialist economy of the 1960s nor the mixed economy of the 1970s created the social opportunities he promised. Bourguiba insisted that Tunisia should be secular. He brought the religious establishment under government control, gave women equal rights and provided for universal education. Whatever his faults, however, he does seem to have spared Tunisia the civil turmoil that has overwhelmed Algeria.

❏ Habib Bourguiba was born in Monastir in 1903 and educated at the respected Sadiki College in Tunis and in Paris, where he studied law. In 1928 he returned with his French wife (his second wife was from Le Kef) and immediately became embroiled in protest politics. In 1929 he defended the right of women to wear a veil and in 1930 called for the removal of French statues. In 1934 he formed the Neo-Destour Party, and was frequently imprisoned in France and Tunisia between 1938 and 1955, the year he accepted a French plan for an autonomous Tunisia. In 1956 he became leader of independent Tunisia and in 1956 president of the new republic, a post which he held until November 1988, when he was declared senile. ❏

Ben Ali brought in a multi-party system and legislative elections

TUNIS A to Z

47

TUNIS

The scent of summer
If you visit Tunis in the summer you will undoubtedly see – and smell – the jasmine blossoms here. This distinctive flower has become one of the emblems of the season, a tradition imported by refugees from Andalusia in the 13th and 16th centuries. For some people, jasmine has become part of the vocabulary of love: if a man wears one of the tight bouquets wrapped around a stick behind his left ear, he's announcing that he is available; behind his right ear, that he is already attached. If a girl accepts a necklace of jasmine from a man, she is also accepting his attentions. For other people, jasmine is just a pleasant scent carried on the evening air.

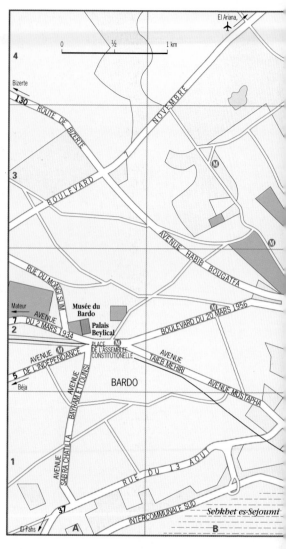

Tunis This is a city of several faces whose character has been shaped by some 3,500 years of history. It's also a city of two different paces: the modern, sometimes brash Mediterranean port and the slower, traditional, old Arab heart.

Modern Tunis As you fly, drive or sail in, Tunis looks modern: dual carriageways, a few high-rise buildings (particularly the landmark Africa Hotel) and one of North Africa's busiest ports. Over the past few decades, modern Tunis has sprouted a couple of large tower hotels, office blocks and an industrial quarter. For several years it was home to the Arab League, in protest at Egypt's peace deal with Israel, although the League has since moved back to its original headquarters in Cairo. Modern Tunis also makes itself felt in beach suburbs such

Previous pages (main photo): view over the Jemaa ez Zitouna mosque

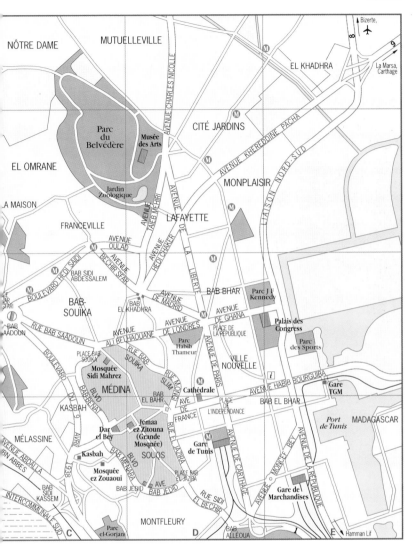

as Gammarth and La Marsa, spacious, leafy and crowded in summer, where the bikini rather than the veil is the essential fashion item and there are queues at night for pizza and ice-cream.

The colonial legacy Closer to the centre is colonial Tunis. Its streets of whitewashed Franco-Arab buildings borrowed their inspiration from around the Mediterranean, and the resulting mix is somehow uniquely Tunisian. The French occupied Tunis for more than 70 years and embellished their colonial capital. The Ville Nouvelle, the new quarters around the old city, was laid out along lines that will be familiar to anyone

Tunis' main artery is the shady tree-lined avenue Habib Bourguiba, officially called avenue du 7 Novembre

TUNIS

Right: cafés in the Médina are lively and atmospheric

Opposite: picturesque Tunisian doorway

Italian craftsmen decorated much of the elegant Mosquée de Hammouda Pacha

Two-day itinerary
Day one
Morning: Carthage.
Afternoon: Musée du Bardo.
Sunset: Sidi Bou Said
(by TGM).
Dinner: La Goulette
(by TGM).

Day two
Morning: *medina* and
souqs in Tunis.
Afternoon: Musée des Arts
Populaires et Traditions
(Dar Ben Abdallah).
Sunset: La Marsa
(by TGM).

who has been to France: broad, tree-lined avenues, colonnaded buildings, a large central market, and parks on the high places where you can catch the Mediterranean breeze. The colonists were sufficiently numerous (250,000 throughout the country) to have left their mark on more than the architecture and town planning. There are cafés where you can drink good coffee and read French-language newspapers, restaurants with excellent-value set menus, patisseries with French specialities and, twice a day in shops and restaurants, fresh deliveries of baguettes.

The Médina The visible heart of Tunis, the building that stands out at its centre, is the Jemaa ez Zitouna (Mosque of the Olive Tree), founded in AD 732 by Umayyad rulers. The physical and spiritual centre of the city is also the original commercial centre. Around the mosque there were many *souqs*, each one specialising in a single trade; today some continue to maintain the old traditions. Mainly pedestrian and still the most densely populated place in the city is the old *medina*, with the elements of the traditional Muslim community still intact – mosque, school, bakery, bath, square and *souq*. The pace of life is slower here, as though the weight of time is holding it back.

The ancient city Long before the Prophet Muhammad was born, the ancient city of Carthage had already earned its place in history. One of the great cities of antiquity, it had been a rival to Rome and later, under Roman protection, became one of the vital centres of the early Christian world. The ruins of Carthage, now surrounded by beautiful villas and well-tended gardens, lack the grandeur of Rome or Athens, but as in Alexandria there are just enough of them left on the ground to give a sense of what is missing. It is in the city's museums that the past really comes alive, particularly in the wealth of vivid mosaics.

The Mediterranean city If you are sailing in from Palermo or some other northern port you will need no reminder that Tunis lies on the sea. Apart from the spring that the Mediterranean air seems to put in everyone's step and the lilt in their voice, as happens from Barcelona to Beirut, the main reminder of the sea in the city itself is found in the freshness of the seafood. But leave the city centre for La Goulette, the old pirate base, or for the beaches of the northern suburbs, and you will be treated to yet another face of this intriguing city.

TUNIS

Get lost
You can stick to the main arteries of the *medina*, but one of the most pleasant things to do is to wander off and stumble into a lovely *medersa*, peep through a monumental doorway or stop for a cup of tea in a corner café. The thing to remember is that the *medina* is not as big as it seems, and that if you ask anyone to be directed towards the Zitouna mosque or the Bab el Bahr (the two main landmarks), they will show you the way with a smile. Remember that the *medina* in Tunis is a real place where people sleep, pray, work, study, shop and have fun.

The minaret of the Jemaa ez Zitouna, as seen from a roof terrace in one of the surrounding souqs

▶▶ **Jemaa ez Zitouna (Great Mosque)**   49D1

rue Jemaa ez Zitouna, Médina
Open: Sat–Thu 8–12. Closed Fri and Muslim holidays.
Admission charge: moderate
The Jemaa ez Zitouna, meaning 'Mosque of the Olive Tree', is the city's Great Mosque and is the largest (5,000sq m) and oldest in Tunis, and second in Tunisia only to that at Kairouan. Work was started by the Umayyad rulers in 732 and completed by the Aghlabids in 864. The Zirites enlarged it in the 10th century, as did the Turks in 1637. The minaret was constructed in 1894 and the whole structure was restored between 1962 and 1975. Non-Muslims enter from the imposing eastern gallery, but can only view the courtyard and patio. The sombre prayer hall is supported by 184 columns, most of which were brought here from ancient Carthage.

▶▶▶ **Médina**   49C2

The once high-walled *medina* of Tunis is the largest and best maintained in the country, and has been placed on Unesco's World Heritage List. Around the perimeter of the *medina*, a ring road follows the line where the walls once stood. At its heart is its oldest surviving building, the 9th-century Jemaa ez Zitouna (see above). The *souqs* surround the mosque and occupy much of the *medina* (see pages 58–9), but there is a lot more to see if you can take your eyes off the shops. To the right of the Zitouna, at 9 Impasse ech-Chammaia, stands the **Tourbet Aziza Othmana▶**, a 17th-century mausoleum for the family of Princess Aziza, who was renowned for her generosity. Further to the right at the end of rue Sidi ben Arous is the

JEMAA EZ ZITOUNA (GREAT MOSQUE)–MÉDINA

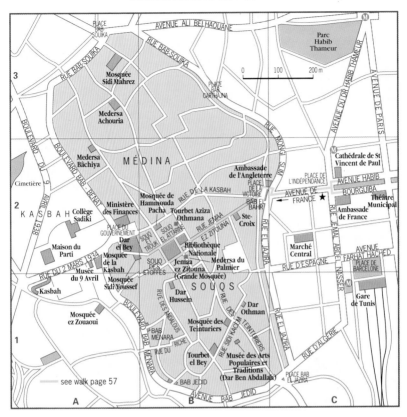

Mosquée de Hammouda Pacha►►, with an elegant minaret and rich decoration, the latter inspiring the architects of the mausoleum of Bourguiba in Monastir. Walk through the old Souq des Chechias to the 17th-century Mosquée Sidi Youssef►► and admire its unusual octagonal minaret, then continue to the Dar el Bey, offices of the prime minister.

Back at the Zitouna, take a left turn into rue des Libraires. This is home to three 18th-century *medresa* (Koranic schools): the Medersa du Palmier►, named after the palm tree in its courtyard; the Medersa Bâchiya►, now a school for crafts; and the Medersa Slimania►►, with a lovely tiled porch. Opposite the latter is one of the most authentic hammams in the *medina*, the Hammam Kachachine►►► (men only. Open 5am–5pm), entered through a barber's shop. Turn left into rue Tourbet el Bey to reach Tourbet el Bey►►► (Open Mon–Sat 9.30–4.30. Admission charge moderate), the splendid mausoleum of the Husseinite princes. From there follow rue Sidi Kacem to the Dar Ben Abdallah►►► (see page 54), then cross rue des Teinturiers into rue el-M'Bazz to visit the early 17th-century palace of Dar Othman►► (Open Mon–Sat 9.30–4.30. Admission free). Return to rue des Teinturiers to see the Mosqueé des Teinturiers►, then explore the side-streets where dyers still employ age-old techniques. Head back to rue Tourbet el Bey and stroll through elegant rue des Andalous and rue du Riche.

The courtyard of the Jemaa ez Zitouna

TUNIS

Conservation of the medina

Covering 270 hectares and with more than 100,000 inhabitants, the Tunis *medina* is not an area to be neglected, and since it was added in 1981 to the World Heritage List sponsored by Unesco, much progress has been made towards conservation. The Association de la Sauvegarde de la Médina goes from strength to strength and their projects have won numerous prizes. There is also increasing interest from local councillors, as well as from Tunisois.

Above right and below: the Musée des Arts Populaires et Traditions

Palatial museum

The Musée du Bardo is housed in a mid-19th-century beylical palace built in a mix of styles, mainly Moorish with a touch of classicism. From the 13th century onwards the Husseinite rulers preferred to live in outlying locations on hilltops rather than in the old *medina*. By the time this palace was built, the whole area was covered with palaces, harems and grand houses, few of which survive today.

▶▶▶ Musée des Arts Populaires et Traditions (Dar Ben Abdallah) 53B1

rue Sidi Kacem, off rue des Teinturiers (tel: 01 256 195) Open: Tue–Sun 9.30–4.30. Closed Mon. Admission charge: moderate

Walking up to the Museum of Popular Arts and Traditions is a pleasure in itself as it takes you away from the main tourist hubbub into the real *medina*. After the walk, this 18th-century palace never fails to impress. The Dar Ben Abdallah offers a rare glimpse of the grandeur hidden behind some of the walls and closed doors of the *medina*. The dark entrance corridor, lined with benches, is where callers would have waited to be summoned for an audience with the noble master of the house. Inside, the four T-shaped rooms off the peaceful and dazzling courtyard show the traditional arrangement of such grand houses whereby all the wives received the same treatment from their husband. The rooms contain exhibits of models dressed in traditional costumes, including men drinking tea together, a bride being prepared for her wedding, women chatting and an exquisite trousseau for a baby boy.

▶▶▶ Musée du Bardo (Bardo National Museum) 48A2

6km from the centre, route de Bizerte, Quartier Le Bardo (tel: 01 513 842) Open: summer Tue–Sun 8.30–5.30. Rest of year Tue–Sun 9.30–4.30. Closed Mon and public holidays. Admission charge: moderate; extra ticket for using a camera. Bus no 3 from the TGM station, avenue Habib Bourguiba and avenue de Paris; or nos 4, 16, 42 from Parc H Thameur

As Tunisia's national museum, the Bardo is the repository for the country's archaeological treasures. The mosaics are its star attraction, those from the country's various Roman sites forming one of the most important collections in the world. The museum is never fully open as rooms are constantly being rearranged, but in any case it would probably be impossible to see everything at once.

Ground floor The downstairs rooms display a large collection of sarcophagi, stelae and statues from the

MUSÉE DES ARTS POPULAIRES ET TRADITIONS–MUSÉE DU BARDO

Carthaginian and Roman periods. In **Room A** look out for the splendid 1st-century AD terracotta statue of Baal Hammon, chief god of Carthage, sitting on a throne and wearing a feathered head-dress. Note, too, the magnificent sarcophagi of the Muses opposite the door of **Room V**. The gigantic arms in **Room VIII** belonged to a cult statue of Jupiter found at Thuburbo Majus; its feet can be seen upstairs amongst the Sousse exhibits. From Bulla Regia is the remarkable 3rd-century AD mosaic of Perseus and Andromeda with a sea monster, now in **Room VI**.

First floor The main bulk of the mosaic collection is upstairs, laid out from floor to ceiling, with so many examples that some exquisite ones get lost in the crowds. The Ulysses Room is named after the famous 3rd-century AD mosaic of Ulysses, found in Dougga, which shows the hero bound to the mast of his ship to prevent him being lured by the sirens. In the corridor outside is a 4th-century AD wedding mosaic of Ariadne and Bacchus from Thuburbo Majus. Look out in the Dougga Room for the splendid 2nd-century AD mosaic of Neptune in his chariot, and opposite it the mosaic of three giants working the forge of a volcano. The Lord Julius mosaic in the spacious Sousse Room shows the life of a wealthy man and the goings-on at his estate. The two mosaics on the floor in the Carthage Gallery represent lovely hunting scenes and Bacchus surrounded by cupids. The Virgil Room, with a wonderful dome of carved plasterwork, houses the famous 3rd-century AD

The Ulysses mosaic, depicting the hero tied to his ship's mast to prevent him being lured by the sirens, is one of the Bardo's star attractions

The 'tears of Carthage'
'After any rain you may walk across the earth and find handfuls of blobs of iridescent glass, thousands of years old, relics of the ancient glass factories. They glisten and gleam on the top of the soil, and the Arabs have called them the "tears of Carthage." Their legend-loving minds have woven these bits of glass into romance. To them they are nothing less than the tears of the Carthaginians, crystallised and preserved; tears that were shed over the ruins of the wonderful city, now shining again at the feet of the prosaic men who are trying to reconstruct the glory that was Carthage.' From *Digging for Lost African Gods* by Baron Khun de Prorok (1926).

The floors in the huge Sousse Room are covered with a vast Roman mosaic depicting the Triumph of Neptune

The lake and fountain in the Parc du Belvédère provide a pleasant backdrop for the courting couples who come here for a drink on the popular café-terrace

mosaic of the poet Virgil (70–19 BC) between the Muses of History and Tragedy, found in Sousse. It is the only portrait of the poet, and is very well preserved.

From the first floor a staircase leads down into the Folk Art and Traditions Room, from where it is possible to ascend to the Arab Museum, a curious collection set in an older building. It houses some interesting calligraphy, weapons and various miscellany, but it is also worth a visit for its lovely Moorish décor and tiled courtyard.

Second floor The first gallery on the second floor contains interesting terracotta statuettes of gods and other objects found in tombs dating from the 1st to 3rd centuries AD. Walls and corridors here are filled with yet more mosaics. Note the fine 4th-century AD mosaic of Theseus killing the Minotaur and a 2nd-century AD mosaic of a thoughtful poet perched on a column shaft. Finally, the Acholla Room contains mosaics and other items found in private houses near Sfax.

▶ Parc du Belvédère 49C3

avenue Taieb Mehiri

Zoo open: Tue–Sun 10–4. Closed Mon. Admission charge: cheap. Bus No 5 from avenue Bourguiba to the nearby place Pasteur

The northern hill of Tunis was landscaped into a park by the French so that their wives and children could enjoy a breath of fresh air. It is still a good place to recover from the heat – either in the park itself or in the popular café on the island in the middle of the lake. The pleasant and well-kept little zoo contains dwarf hippos, snakes, monkeys, small mammals and birds, and is popular with courting couples. The elegant 17th-century *koubba*, or pavilion, was originally constructed for a palace and was moved to the park early in the 20th century. In summer there are often performances in the park's two theatres.

Nearer to the centre of Tunis is another park, Parc H Thameur, which is rather pleasant but suffers from its popularity, particularly with boisterous young men.

Palace of Clocks

'The palace of the Bardo is even more dilapidated and desolate than the Dar-el-Bey. The great courtyard is full of refuse, and the harem has been turned into a museum of no particular interest. The walls of the saloons are mostly covered with badly executed portraits of Victor Emmanuel, Louis Napoleon Bonaparte and recent Beys. You are perhaps chiefly struck by the unnecessary profusion of ormolu clocks. In one room I counted no less than fifteen …' From *Tunisia* by Herbert Vivian (1899).

Walk *From new to old Tunis*

See map on page 53.

Above: the Bab el Bahr (Sea Gate)

This is an easy walk from modern Tunis into the medieval maze of the *medina*. It should preferably be done in the morning, when the mosque is open and the *souqs* at their liveliest. Allow one hour for the walk, or more if you plan on browsing in the *souqs*.

Start in place de l'Indépendance at the Cathédrale de St Vincent de Paul (see page 59). Directly opposite stands the **Ambassade de France (French Embassy)►**, built as the office of the resident French governor in 1862. Follow the tree-lined avenue de France through the rather elegant arcades to the place de la Victoire, recognisable by the arched **Bab el Bahr (Sea Gate)►**. The handsome green and white stucco façade on the north side of the square marks the **Ambassade de l'Angleterre (British Embassy)►►**, home also to the British Council Library.

From the Bab el Bahr follow rue Jemaa ez Zitouna, the *medina's* main thoroughfare, taken over by souvenir shops; remember that this is no place to find a bargain. To the left is the old Catholic **Église Ste-Croix**, now serving as municipal offices, and the **old rectory**, now occupied by the beautiful pottery shop of el-Hanout. On the right after 150m is the elegant **Bibliothèque Nationale►**, built by Hammouda Pacha II as the Turkish barracks.

The street runs directly up to the **Jemaa ez Zitouna►►** (see page 52), its entrance lying up the steps. Follow the walls of the mosque to the right to enter the **Souq el Attarine (Scent-Makers' Market)►►►**. At the next junction turn left into the **Souq des Etoffes (Cloth Market)►►**, with its red- and green-painted columns, or continue 50m further to the right for refreshments at the M'Rabet café (see page 200) in the **Souq et Trouk (Market of the Turks)►►►**. Return to the Souq des Etoffes, follow the walls of the mosque and return to the start point via the rue Jemaa ez Zitouna.

A world of perfumes
Until the 20th century scent-making was the noblest trade of all, and throughout North Africa Tunis was renowned for its perfumes. Tunisians still love their perfumes and use different scents for different occasions. The guests at a wedding are sprinkled with orange blossom, while after a dinner guests are refreshed with rose water. On the eve of religious festivals Tunisians traditionally use amber, while during Ramadan, the month of fasting, no perfumes are used, which is felt as a deprivation.

Most goods sold on the rue Jemaa ez Zitouna are aimed at the tourist market, but once you are off the main drag the souqs *start to reveal secrets known only to locals*

►►► Souqs   49D1

The central complex of high-vaulted *souqs* (markets) around the Jemaa ez Zitouna (see page 52), each originally specialising in one trade, was mostly built by the 13th-century Hafsids and then rebuilt in the 18th century by the Turkish beys. To the right of the Great Mosque is the beautiful 13th-century **Souq el Attarine (Scent-Makers' Market)►►►**, whose narrow shops stock henna, various herbs and oils for perfumes, incense, amber and kitsch white baskets offered by a fiancé to his future wife. By following the mosque's walls to the left you reach the 14th-century **Souq des Etoffes (Cloth Market)►►**, which runs into the **Souq des Femmes (Souq for Women)►**.

Turn right by the tiled fountain of the Bab es-Shefa and climb the narrow **Souq el-Leffa►**, with its carpets and blankets. At No 58 is the tourist supermarket where a small tip will get you upstairs, past the vast gilt-and-mirror 'bed of the bey' to the so-called Palais d'Orient, the first of several tourist terraces that offer fine views over the *medina*'s skyline. Opposite, downhill, is the **Souq el-Kebabjia (Silk Market)**, while a short hop uphill is the lovely **Souq el-Berka►►►**. The el-Berka has a dirty past, for amongst the shopfronts in their pretty pastel mauves and pinks, reds, soft greens and golds stands the former Slave Market, one of the largest in the Mediterranean. Red and green pillars, mural tiles and jewellers are all you see now of the place where men, women and children, many of them captured Christians, were put up for auction.

From the el-Berka's far end the **Souq et Trouk (Market of the Turks)►►►** runs down to rejoin the Souq el Attarine. Yusef Dey designed the vaulted Souq et Trouk in

1630 as the city's finest thoroughfare; its reputation amongst visitors today centres on the M'Rabet café (see page 200), named after the three *marabouts* (holy men) buried at its side. At the foot of the Great Mosque's minaret to the left is the rue Sidi Ben Arous, home to the **Souq des Chechias (Chechia Market)▶▶**, where a few shops still make the traditional woollen headgear worn by men. The makers of *chechias* are mostly descended from Andalusian immigrants who left Spain in the 17th century and introduced their art to Tunisia. Beyond the Mosquée de Hammouda Pacha, turn right into the rue de la Kasbah; the **Souq el-Blaghia▶**, also known as Souq des Babouches (Slipper Market), is on the right. Follow the road further to reach the **Souq du Cuivre (Coppersmiths' Market)▶** and the constantly animated Souq el-Grana▶.

Behind closed doors
Apart from the Zitouna, none of the other mosques or *medresa* can be visited by non-Muslims. The closest you can get is a view into the Mosquée Sidi Youssef from the rooftop terrace of the Musée des Turcs, an antique shop in the Souq et Trouk. Otherwise, you'll have to keep your eyes open for a door left open into a *medersa* courtyard.

Until the 20th century perfume-making was considered a great art

▶▶　**Ville Nouvelle**　　　　　49D2

Avenue Habib Bourguiba, connecting the busy TGM station Tunis Marine to the place de l'Indépendance near the *medina*, forms the main axis of the Ville Nouvelle. The central section of the avenue is planted with trees and provides some much-needed shade in summer. Benches, flower stalls and newspaper kiosks also make it a popular place for a morning stroll or evening promenade. The tourist office and the Office de l'Artisanat are located at the intersection with avenue Mohammed V.

Downtown Tunis still has a wealth of colonial architecture. The **Théâtre Municipal▶** is built in an exuberant art nouveau style, as is the **Carlton Hotel▶** at 31 avenue Bourguiba. On the place de l'Indépendance, the statue of the philosopher–historian Ibn Khaldoun (1332–1406; see pages 68–9) forms a sightly but inconsequential link between the French Embassy (1862) and the Catholic **Cathédrale de St Vincent de Paul▶**, built in 1882 in a rather inharmonious blend of styles. More architectural treasures are found along the streets crossing the main avenue, in particular the following: along avenue de Paris, including the once-grand **Majestic Hotel▶**; on rue de Yougoslavie, especially the great art nouveau building at No 114; and avenue Habib Thameur, with the stunning **Trésorerie Générale▶**. The pedestrian rue Charles de Gaulle leads to a busy covered market, the **Marché Central▶**, surrounded by patisseries and spice shops.

Colonial architecture
The early 20th century saw a property boom in Tunis, with the construction of Italianate and French-style apartment buildings. It is interesting to see how the architects adapted the European style to the local climate by adding balconies, belvederes and roof terraces, and by using whitewashed masonry, which has become one of the capital's trademarks. At the same time, a taste for neo-Moorish architecture appeared, using traditional Tunisian decorative elements and large courtyards, still visible in many buildings today.

Excursions

Carthage practicalities
One ticket for all the sites can be bought at the Thermes d'Antonin Pius or at the Musée National de Carthage (tel: 01 730 036. *Open* summer Tue–Sun 8–7. Rest of year Tue–Sun 8.30–5.30. *Admission charge* moderate. TGM station: Carthage-Hannibal).

A troubled paradise
'Carthage had not desired to create, but only to enjoy: Therefore she left us nothing.' From *Esto Perpetua* by Hilaire Belloc (1906).

The Cathédral de St-Louis, now a cultural centre

▶▶▶ Carthage   83E2

Once the capital of an empire whose boats sailed to the ends of the known world, Carthage is now just a plush, tranquil suburb of Tunis. Here, magnificent villas set in luxuriant gardens of bougainvillaea, geraniums and jasmine spread over the hillside rolling down towards the Mediterranean. There may not be much left of ancient Carthage, whose splendour once challenged Rome, but the site is evocative and atmospheric none the less. To prevent more of the site's archaeological treasures disappearing beneath new constructions, Unesco launched a massive rescue operation in 1972.

According to the Roman poet Virgil, Carthage was founded in 814 BC by Phoenicians from Tyre led by Princess Dido (see opposite). By the 4th century BC, this 'new Tyre' was one of the most important cities in the Mediterranean world, a serious rival to both Rome and Athens. Its glory was not to last long, however, and the conflict with Rome led to the bloody Punic (Carthaginian) Wars of 264–241 BC, 218–201 BC and 149–146 BC (see page 29). Cato's famous words '*Delenda est Carthago*' ('We must destroy Carthage') were finally fulfilled in 146 BC. After a three-year siege, Carthage was defeated, pillaged and then demolished, the Romans pouring salt over its fertile lands. In 44 BC, however, Julius Caesar decided to build a new city on the site, finally constructed by his successor, Augustus. It became the capital of Roman Africa (see pages 112–13) and an important trading centre. Both Vandals and Byzantines weakened the city, which finally fell to ruin with the Arab conquest in AD 692. After that, Carthage was used as a quarry for new Islamic monuments in the *medina* at Tunis. Excavations started in 1857 and still continue today.

Continued on page 62

FOCUS ON *Dido and Aeneas*

■ **Carthage was the setting for one of history's classic tragic love stories, between the Phoenician Princess Dido and Aeneas, who washed ashore here after the fall of Troy. As told by Virgil in the *Aeneid*, it is the story of a conflict between personal emotions and public responsibilities.** ■

Mythical origins Princess Dido fled from the mighty Phoenician city of Tyre (in modern-day Lebanon) after her brother, King Pygmalion, killed her husband, Acerbas. Accompanied by a group of loyal followers, she set sail across the Mediterranean and landed on the north coast of Tunisia, where the local Numidian prince agreed to grant her as much land as could be contained within an ox hide. With typical Phoenician cunning, she cut the hide into very thin, long strips, joined them together and encircled enough land on which to build the city of Kart Hadasht, or 'New City', later to become Carthage.

Tragic love story During the time the city was being constructed, Aeneas and a band of his followers – the sole survivors of the sack of Troy – were washed ashore near by. After Dido took him in, an affair soon developed, consummated out of doors to the accompaniment of thunder, lightning and the sound of wailing nymphs. However, despite his feelings for Dido, Aeneas announced that he must complete his destiny as predicted by Apollo's oracle in Lycia, and sail to Italy to found a new Troy (Rome) for his people. Dido took his rejection badly and vowed to haunt him with 'flames of the blackest pitch'. 'Wherever you go,' she warned him, 'my spectre will be there.'

After Aeneas left, Dido had herself burnt on a funeral pyre as a royal sacrifice dedicated to the city, an act that prefigured Carthage's future destruction at the hands of imperial Rome.

Aeneas on Dido
'Nor will it ever upset me to remember Elissa so long as I remember who I am, so long as the breath of life controls these limbs.' From *Aeneid*, iv, 335, by Virgil.

61

Dido's stormy affair with Aeneas started soon after he arrived in Carthage, but by allowing it to take place Dido alienated herself from both the local Numidians and her own Phoenician followers

EXCURSIONS

Continued from page 60

Sunrise at Carthage

'... The conical roofs of the heptagonal temples, the stairs, terraces, ramparts, gradually took shape against the pale dawn; and all round the Carthaginian peninsula pulsed a girdle of white foam while the emerald-coloured sea seemed frozen in the cool of the morning. Then as the rosy sun spread wider, the tall houses tilted on the slopes of the ground grew taller and massed together like a flock of black goats coming down from the mountains. The empty streets lengthened out; palm-trees, rising out of the walls here and there, did not stir ... On the very top of the Acropolis, in the cypress wood, Eschmoun's horses, feeling the approach of day, put their hoofs on the marble parapet and whinnied towards the sun.' From *Salammbo* by Gustave Flaubert (1862); translated by AJ Krailsheimer (1977).

The **Musée National de Carthage▶▶** (for opening times see panel on page 60) sits on top of Byrsa Hill beside the 19th-century Cathédral de St-Louis, now a cultural centre. The museum houses finds from more than a century of excavations, and is clearly divided in three eras: Punic, Roman and Christian. Most objects from the Punic period came from the cemeteries in the Salammbo area, while mosaics, jewellery and sculpture found on Byrsa Hill represent the Roman period. The museum is set in a pleasant garden, and at the far end of the terrace lie the foundations of Punic houses, once several storeys high and perhaps similar to an Arab *medina*. The terrace commands sweeping views over the bay.

Byrsa Hill itself was reputedly the original settlement of Princess Dido (see page 61). Later it was used as a cemetery, a citadel and temple to the god Eschmoun. Augustus enlarged the citadel and built a Capitoline temple and forum here, which was further fortified by the Byzantines in the 6th century.

To the north of the museum, off avenue 7 Novembre, is the over-restored 2nd-century AD **Théâtre d'Hadrian▶**, where the Carthage International Cultural Festival is held during the summer (see page 23). Further up, on top of the hill, are remnants of a small **odeon▶** where gladiatorial games were held, the quite badly restored **Parc Archéologique des Villas Romaines▶**, and the ruined **basilicas of Damou and St Cyprian**. A small road leads from this site across the main road to the **Thermes d'Antonin Pius (Anthonine Baths)▶▶▶**. Once the biggest Roman baths in North Africa, this is undoubtedly the best-preserved site in Carthage. Not much was left standing after devastation by the Vandals, but the stunning location by the sea and little that is left still evoke a sense of splendid grandeur. The site is entered from the top of a peaceful garden sloping gently to the sea. On the viewing platform, a map carved into a slab of white marble gives the outlay of the vast baths, while a resurrected pillar gives an idea of the height of it all. Scattered over the garden are Punic and Roman stelae as well as the remains of a 7th-century Christian chapel.

This resurrected pillar illustrates the original height of the Anthonine Baths

Canadian students continue excavations near the museum

Follow the seashore to the **Quartier Magon►**, with Punic mosaic pavements and a model of the quarry in El Haouaria, Cap Bon, where the stones used to build Carthage were quarried. Further south along the main road towards Tunis (avenue President Bourguiba) is the **Musée Romain et Paléo-Chrétien►**. The museum houses 5th–7th-century finds from Carthage, including a beautiful statue of Ganymede with Zeus disguised as an eagle.

The commercial and military **Punic Ports►**, the basis of Carthage's power, are now little more than duck ponds; scale models give an idea of the importance they once held. Originally the ports were linked by a channel and had a common entrance from the sea. The military port, with an island in its centre and a capacity for 220 ships, was walled so that the enemy could not see the dockyards. The small, rather dull **Musée Oceanographique** is situated between the two ports.

The **Tophet►►**, or Sanctuary of Tanit and Baal Hammon, south of the Oceanographic Museum, is the oldest Punic cult site in Carthage. Now a pleasant and tranquil garden, this was where animals and probably also children (see panel) were sacrificed from the earliest days of the city until its fall to the Romans. So many children appear to have been killed, especially at times of national turmoil, that more than one layer of stelae was erected, under which the urns containing the children's ashes were buried. The stelae changed over the centuries, but always included magical and religious symbols, particularly of Tanit, the moon goddess, or the solar disc and crescent of Baal Hammon, the sun god.

Human sacrifice
Very little is known about the Carthaginians' lifestyle, but excavations at the Tophet have revealed urns containing ashes and milk teeth from 8th-century BC children, which seems to indicate that human sacrifice was practised during religious ceremonies. (Sacrifice of the first-born son was a common practice throughout the Near East.) Tens of thousands of children appear to have been sacrificed to the god Baal Hammon at the Tophet. It is believed that after the boys (aged between 2 and 12 and usually from noble families) were killed, they were cremated on a sacred fire and the urns containing their ashes buried under stelae.

63

■ The Tunisian National Institute of Heritage is reviving the image of the legendary Carthaginian general who in Western military colleges is often honoured as one of antiquity's boldest tacticians. Who else dared to cross the Alps with an army and 300 elephants? ■

A rebel with a heart
Hannibal may have been a rebellious spirit but he seems to have been a good man. Most accounts describe him as a soldierly hero with no record of gratuitous cruelty. An educated man, he spoke four languages and had two Greek tutors. As a general he led from the front. Even the Romans grudgingly admired him, the Roman historian Livy recording that Hannibal slept in his red cloak among his soldiers and guards.

The scourge of Rome Born in a tent on Carthaginian territory in Spain, Hannibal succeeded his father, Hamilcar Barca, at the age of 25 in 221 BC and became Rome's fiercest opponent during the Punic Wars. He launched his major attack on Rome in 218 BC, marching through Spain and France, then crossing the Alps with 40,000 men and 300 elephants, winning many battles as he moved southwards. Just as Rome seemed to be at his mercy, his support from Carthage dried up and he was recalled home. Back in Tunisia he was finally defeated in 202 BC by the Roman General Scipio at the Battle of Zama (near Le Kef), a defeat that signalled the end of the Carthaginian Empire. Cathage finally dumped its hero and forced him into exile in Syria, where he lived as a mercenary officer. Chased by the Romans even there, he poisoned himself at Libyssa in modern Turkey at the age of 65.

Hannibal is coming! Hannibal's fiery legend lived on for many years, and Roman mothers would get their children to be quiet by warning 'Hannibal is coming'. Despite this, until recently Tunisian children hardly heard his name mentioned in school as history teachers concentrated on the era beginning with the 7th-century Arab conquest. Now, however, the government has decided to promote historical pluralism in which the country's Berber, Phoenician (Punic), Hellenistic, Roman and Christian roots are being dug up. More funds are needed for excavation and conservation of Punic and Roman sites all over the country, many of which need urgent attention. Tourism is believed to be the answer, so it now remains to be seen whether the romantic Carthaginian hero will win this last battle, namely attracting people to Tunisia.

Above: General Scipio obtains Carthage's surrender and orders it to be razed to the ground Right: Scipio defeats Hannibal at Zama in 202 BC during the Second Punic War

Tour **Carthage**

See map on page 63.

A pleasant excursion by train from Tunis, across the Lac de Tunis, to the archaeological remains of the city of Carthage. Once there, walk or take a ride in a *calèche* (horse-drawn carriage) to the sites that lie scattered amongst the elegant residential areas. (In summer, the *calèche* may be a better choice as it offers some shade.) For more information on the sights, see pages 62–3. Allow at least half a day: a half-hour train ride followed by 2–3 hours by *calèche* or 3–4 hours' walking.

Leave Tunis from the Marine Station at the end of avenue Habib Bourguiba, and catch any TGM train going to La Marsa. The train runs at first along the spit of land that crosses the Lac de Tunis, with the port and industrial zone of Tunis to the right. Get off at Carthage-Hannibal, and from here walk or take a *calèche*, for which you must agree in advance the price for a two- or three-hour tour. Follow the signposts through the desirable villa areas for the **Thermes d'Antonin Pius (Anthonine Baths)▶▶▶**, Carthage's

Above: Roman villa interior

most impressive remains and now set in their own archaeological park.

After a visit to the baths, return the way you have come and cross avenue President Bourguiba to visit the much-restored 2nd-century AD **Théâtre d'Hadrian▶** and the **Parc Archéologique des Villas Romaines▶**. At the latter, do not miss the 3rd-century AD Villa des Volières, with its lovely floor mosaics.

Take the road beside the ruined site of the Thermes de Gargilius (Baths of Gargilius) and climb up towards the top of Byrsa Hill. Here is the imposing mock-Byzantine Cathédrale de St-Louis, now occasionally used for performances; there are excellent views from its terrace. Next door is another highlight, the **Musée National de Carthage▶▶**, including the Quartier Punique showing the layout of the early Punic (4th-century BC) houses. From here you can either make your way back to the TGM station Carthage-Hannibal or continue past Carthage-Dermech towards the sea and the **Punic Ports▶**, the **Musée Oceanographique** and the Salammbô **Tophet▶▶**.

EXCURSIONS

Sweet pleasures
There is nothing like a sweet pastry washed down with a hot mint tea; following are some of the best places to get them. Top of the range for Tunisian pastries is Patisserie Madame Zarrouk at 41–3 Rue Echam behind the flower market in Quartier Lafayette in Tunis (tel: 01 834 632), or opposite the TGM station in La Marsa (tel: 01 747 664). Chaouch, at 16 Souq el-Blat near Tunis's Jemaa ez Zitouna in the Médina, prepares pastries such as *makroud* (a fried pastry stuffed with dates) according to traditional recipes.

Despite the continuous flow of day-trippers, Sidi Bou Said has managed to retain much of its charm and character

►► Gammarth   83E2
Gammarth (24km north-east of Tunis) and Carthage are the smartest 'Tunis North' resorts. From La Marsa, a road signposted 'Hauts de Gammarth' climbs to the French Military Cemetery. Some 4,010 soldiers killed in World War II are buried here on Jebel Khawi, meaning 'Hollow Mountain', so called because it is riddled with the cavities of an early Hebrew necropolis. A lower road passes expensive villas and fashionable beach hotels. Gammarth's good beach gets crowded in summer, when many locals prefer to drive on a few kilometres to the north-west to Raoued Plage, a vast expanse of white sand, itself slowly being developed into another *zone touristique*.

►► La Goulette   83E2
The old walled town of La Goulette (15km north-east of Tunis), once a corsair stronghold with a large Jewish population, is a rundown neighbourhood of crumbling houses overlooked by a battered fort. But its location, where the Tunis canal runs into the sea (hence its name, meaning 'The Gullet'), means it still handles most cargo shipping and passenger ferries from Italy and France. La Goulette is very animated on summer evenings, when Tunisois come here with their families to eat in the fish restaurants (see page 200) and to stroll along the seafront promenade.

►► La Marsa   83E2
La Marsa (22km north-east of Tunis), a chic garden suburb, is far removed from the hubbub of Tunis. The beys held their summer court here and today the British and French ambassadors have their private residences in the old beylical palaces. Many holidaymakers from the capital follow their example, for life is easy and pleasant, although note that the large beach gets crowded in summer and can be polluted. At sundown, the smell of jasmine lingers in the air and well-dressed locals come out for a stroll, a flirtation, an ice-cream or a *fricassé* at the Café Saf-Saf (see panel on page 72 and page 200). The sunset view from the military cemetery for 1,200 French soldiers who fell during the Tunisia campaign (1942–3) is one of the most beautiful along this coast.

►►► Sidi Bou Said   83E2
'Sidi Bou' (20km north-east of Tunis), with its cobbled streets, white walls, blue studded doors and black *mashrabias* (wooden screens), is prominent on all tourist brochures and posters. Built on a hilltop, it became a beacon for early navigators, as well as an inspiring haven for affluent gentlefolk and early 20th-century artists – including Paul Klee, August Macke and Louis Moillet. Today, although regularly invaded by busloads of tourists, it still retains much of its charm and beauty and continues to attract a community of artists.

In the 10th century, Muslims built a *ribat* (fortified monastery) here to protect the coast against Christian raiders. The city takes its name from Abu Said Kalafa ben Yahia el Temimi el Beji, a 13th-century Moroccan Sufi who settled here on his way back from a pilgrimage to Mecca. He is widely believed to have been able to cure scorpion bites and rheumatism, but his mosque and *zaouia* (shrine), hidden in the centre of the village, are open only to Muslims. Although the *ribat* housed a Spanish garrison during the early 16th century, the whole village remained forbidden territory to Christians until as recently as 1820.

In 1912 an English baron, Rodolphe d'Erlanger (1872–1932), fell in love with the village and decided to build a sumptuous villa and to restore the old houses. In 1915 he obtained a decree to protect the village and insisted that all doors and woodwork be painted in the luminous blue now synonymous with Sidi Bou Said. His stunning Moorish palace, located 20m from the entrance to the municipal car park, is now **Le Centre des Musiques Arabes et Méditerranéennes (Centre for Arab and Mediterranean Music)▶▶** (*Open* summer Tue–Sun 9–12, 2–7. Rest of year Tue–Sun 2–5. *Admission charge* moderate), with an interesting collection of ethnic and international musical instruments and records of Arab music. In the garden of fragrant plants and flowers you will find the baron's simple tomb.

A visit to Sidi Bou Said is not complete without enjoying tea at the Café des Nattes or Café Sidi Chabaane (see pages 200–1).

Lac de Tunis
Originally a series of creeks, the Lake of Tunis was created in the 9th century by Arabs, who dredged a 10km-long canal out to the sea from Tunis and widened the sea mouth. It is now a rather brackish lagoon attracting flocks of flamingos and other waders, which come here to feed on mullet shoals.

Above: the splendid view from the Café Sidi Chabaane, favourite spot for a cup of mint tea and a water-pipe

Strange but true: the nail-studded blue doors that have become Sidi Bou Said's trademark were the inspiration of an eccentric English baron

■ **Tunisia today may be a quiet backwater on the Arab literary scene, with the best of its contemporary authors writing in French and often living in Paris, but it has over 2,500 years of literary culture and has produced writers of international fame. The most important of all was undoubtedly Ibn Khaldoun, whose work was described by the historian Arnold Toynbee as 'the greatest of its kind that has ever been created by any mind in any time or place'.** ■

Further reading 1
● Douglas, Norman *Fountains in the Sand* (1912). Entertaining account of travels in the south of Tunisia at the turn of the century.
● Dumas, Alexandre *Tangier to Tunis* (1847). Alexandre Dumas and his wife visited Tunis in 1846 on the invitation of the French government.
● Flaubert, Gustave *Salammbo* (1862). Flaubert visited Carthage in 1858 and read widely on the subject before starting a detailed reconstruction in this novel on the conflict between mercenaries and Hamilcar Barca, Lord of Carthage.

Phoenician and Roman writers The earliest example of Phoenician writing that has been found is on a 10th-century BC coffin, while the earliest Tunisian Phoenician is inscribed in a 5th-century BC pendant. Tunisian Phoenician literature, however, has only survived in translation, most notably in the form of quotations in Latin from Mago's agricultural encyclopaedia (lost when Carthage's library was destroyed) and a passage in Greek describing Admiral Hanno's exploration of Africa.

The well-known comic dramatist Terence (185–160 BC), who wrote comedy adaptations in Latin of Greek plays such as *The Mother-in-Law*, *The Eunuch* and *The Self-Tormentor*, was a young Berber slave who, because of his talent, was freed by his Roman master.

Christian writers The theologian and moralist Tertullian, born in Carthage *c.* AD 160, created a new form of ecclesiastical Latin, livelier and user-friendly, which was the language used by Christians in the West until well into the Middle Ages. Many of his sayings have become proverbs, as for instance: 'The blood of the martyrs is the seed of the Church'. The bishop St Cyprian (*c.* AD 200–58), also born in Carthage, wrote the influential work *On the Unity of the Church*. He was beatified after being beheaded by the Romans. The extensive literary works of another bishop, St Augustine (AD 354–430), born in Numidia but educated at Carthage, helped to shape the spirit of the early Church. His two most famous works are *Confession* and *The City of God*. Apuleius is the most famous satirist to have come out of ancient Tunisia. Born in Numidia and educated at Carthage, he used his inherited wealth to travel widely. The knowledge he gathered of religious mysteries was used in *The Golden Ass*, an attack on the vices of his age.

St Augustine: leading light of the Church

Arab writers Early Arab literature in Tunisia had little character of its own and was largely influenced by Middle Eastern writers. Early Arab writers were often travellers who moved between the princely courts. As a result, some of the best literature was devoted to eulogising the qualities of rulers, or to arguing theological matters.

Abu Zaid Abdel Rahman Ibn Khaldoun was born in the Khalduniyah quarter of Tunis in 1332 to a family of scholars and politicians who had fled from Spain during the Christian reconquest. He received a traditional education at the Jemaa ez Zitouna mosque before travelling through North Africa and Spain in the service of kings and sultans. In 1375 he retired to Algeria for four years to write his *Universal History*. Later on his entire family was drowned and his library lost at Alexandria. During the siege of Damascus in 1400 he was let down the walls on a rope to discuss a treaty with the Mongol conqueror Tamerlane. He died in Egypt in 1406.

Ibn Khaldoun's major work, the massive *Universal History*, is the principal source on the history of North Africa. His fame, however, rests not on the narrative, but on the 'Muqaddima', the introduction to that history. In this he considers the nature and development of society and creates a philosophy of history. In the process he established the basic principles and working tools of modern sociology. For modern Tunisian writers, see page 25.

For modern Tunisian writers, see page 25.

Freed slave and literary lion, Terence

Further reading 2
● Gide, André *Amynthas* (1906). More turn-of-the-century impressions of Tunisia.
● Manton, E Lennox *Roman North Africa* (1XXX). This history of North Africa, with large sections on Tunisia, is a good read and very comprehensible. *Rome in Africa* by Susan Raven (1969) is also recommended.
● Memni, Albert *La Statue de Sel* (1953). A semi-autobiographical account of the main character's childhood in Tunis' Jewish ghetto until 1945. Wonderfully written.

69

Shopping

Above: Tunis' saddle-makers were famous until the 19th century; today only a few artisans work the leather

Souqs and bargaining Wherever you are in the country, but in Tunis especially, the best places to shop are in the *souqs* (see also pages 58–9). The *medina's* main artery, rue Jemaa ez Zitouna, is almost solely geared towards busloads of tourists making their way to the Zitouna mosque, but in the specialised *souqs* it is still possible to find a bargain. However, you will have to haggle for almost everything you set your eyes on, even when the price is marked. In Tunisia, as in other Arab countries, bargaining is a way of life. You may find it awkward at first, but it's great fun once you get going. The golden rule is not to be bashful. To some extent, bargaining is like a game and the winner is the one who plays it to the fullest. So when a shopkeeper opens with a price that seems exaggerated if not downright preposterous, do not dismiss him; instead, take it as an 'invitation to treat'. A third or so of the price asked is your best opening offer. He will then come down while you go up a bit, so that eventually you will probably settle at half the original offer. If you aren't making progress, just pretend to leave. If your offer was fine, the shopkeeper will call you back; if it was too low he will let you go.

ONAT shops To get an idea of what is on offer or if bargaining gets the better of you, in the bigger cities head for the government-run **Offices Nationales de l'Artisanat Tunisien (ONAT)** shops, with their fixed prices. Prices are a little higher than in the *souqs* but the quality of the goods is usually good. In Tunis the ONATs are **Magasin Mohammed V** on avenue Mohammed V (tel: 01 346 479) and **DEN-DEN** on avenue de l'Indépendance (tel: 01 512 400).

Carpets Carpet-making is a time-honoured craft in Tunisia, as the carpet formed the focus of a household until quite recently. In every bazaar you will find girls on low benches working at high looms for eight hours a day, although on Jerba carpets in 'short nap' are made by men. The

DEN-DEN workshops in Tunis produce some excellent 'Kairouan' carpets, which are also found in other places in the Sahel. The *zerbia*, with its discreet geometry and subdued natural hues, evolved in Kairouan in the 1830s, as did the *mergum* when the Zarrouk family started using Berber embroidery patterns. The red *kilim* or natural-coloured *hanbal* originally come from Gafsa and Gabès. Remember that duty and VAT are payable on the full value, so it is essential to present the receipted invoice to customs authorities on your return home.

Clothes and jewellery Traditional dress designs have been updated and are available from the ONAT stores or from **Boutique Fella** in Hammamet, while cotton jellabas are available in various colours in the *souqs*. Silverwork is often *métal argenté* (silver-plating), the most popular designs being the lucky Fatima's hand or fish. Beware that Tunisian gold is often only 14 or even 12 carats.

Other crafts The two main centres for pottery in Tunisia are Nabeul with its Arab- and Andalusian-influenced pottery, and Guellala in Jerba, with Berber and Graeco-Roman influences. Both styles are available at good prices in shops all over the country. Leatherware is another good buy in Tunisia. Traditional-style wallets, handbags and the like are still made in green or red shades and incised with gold, but a whole range of fashionable European-style leatherware is also available at reasonable prices. Pouffes are as popular as ever, but check that the seams are strong. Colourful *babouches* can easily be worn as slippers back home, while the attractive white and blue birdcages from Sidi Bou Said and Raf Raf also make unusual souvenirs. Two 'antique' lines have been actively revived in recent years: old-fashioned soldier puppets and industrial samples of the now-vanishing handicraft of 'reversal' painting on glass, usually taking old Arab epics as a theme.

A water-pipe makes a great souvenir, but find out how to use it

Good bookshops
● Alif: 3 rue de Hollande (tel: 01 347 148. *Open* Mon–Sat 9–1.30, 3–7). Lovely books, mainly on Tunisian history, arts and culture, plus excellent fold-out books for children. Great postcards too!
● Espace Diwan: 9 rue Sidi Ben Arous, Médina (tel: 01 572 398. *Open* Mon–Sat 9–7). Good selection on Tunisian arts, culture, history and politics, mostly in French.
● Librairie Carlton: 31 avenue Bourguiba, in the Carlton Gallery (tel: 01 336 750. *Open* Mon–Sat 9–1, 3–7.30). Lots of translated Tunisian writers and Ceres publications; mainly art books.

A treasure trove
Ed-Dar, at 8 rue Sidi ben Arous and 7 Souq et Trouk in the Médina, is a 15th-century house/museum/shop, tastefully arranged by an antique dealer. It is well worth a visit for its collection of tiles and ceramics and for its view from the roof over the Médina, but also for the range of beautiful objects and textiles on sale at reasonable prices.

Roughly hewn wooden puppets of the Arab hero Antar

Spices and pulses are everyday essentials

The spice of life Tunisians love spices and home cooking: almost everything comes accompanied by very hot green peppers or mouth-warming *harissa* sauce, made from red peppers. Despite the excellent local cuisine, most restaurants and hotels seem to have decided that Westerners don't like hot food and often omit all spices, producing bland and uninteresting dishes. Although the best Tunisian food is undoubtedly that cooked by locals at home, beach hotels do offer the occasional 'native' dish and there are a few excellent up-market Tunisian restaurants in Tunis. If you are looking for some authentic flavour it is worth trying out *gargottes*. These are small and very cheap eateries serving the nearest thing to home cooking, where single men eat in a hurry. They never have an alcohol licence.

Tunisian specialities

Brik A very thin fried pancake (*malsouka*) filled with egg, tuna and parsley, or with prawns. Hold it by the corners and bite the stuffed part. Cheap and delicious.

Chakchouka/ojja Chakchouka is a delicious mixture of tomatoes, pimentos and garlic with a poached egg on top. *Ojja* is more like scrambled egg with the addition of the same ingredients, served with brains, *merguez* (spicy sausages) or prawns.

Couscous A semolina of hard wheat steamed above a boiling fish, meat and/or vegetable stew. The finest couscous is kept for special occasions like weddings or the end of Ramadan, the month of fasting. It is served with an extra bowl of *harissa* sauce. *Mesfuf* is a sweet couscous made with nuts and raisins. Home-made couscous is by far the best.

Fruits de mer Tunisia has delicious seafood, including lobsters (*homards*), oysters (*huîtres*), clams (*clovisses*), shrimps (*crevettes*) and king prawns (*crevettes royales*).

Harissa Hot red pepper sauce.

Kaftaji (dyari) Fried meatballs served with cubes of liver, peppers and onions.

Le sandwich
Sandwich bars and pizzerias are popular all over Tunisia, most being particularly crowded late in the afternoon. The most common sandwich is a *cassecroute*, a baguette spread with *harissa* and stuffed with boiled potatoes, tomato, egg, tuna, lettuce and olives. In Tunis, some of the best *cassecroutes* are sold at the Club Sandwich (see page 199). The delicious *fricassé*, perfect as a little snack before a late dinner, is a small fried roll or *beignet* (fritter) stuffed with more or less the same ingredients. The best *fricassé* we found was at dusk outside the Café Saf-Saf in La Marsa (see page 200), although we had to queue.

Kamounia A popular dish of slowly stewed meat in a thick cumin-flavoured tomato gravy.
Koucha Mutton roasted whole with chillies and potatoes.
Mechoui Roast lamb.
Mirmiz Stewed mutton with broad beans and a hot sauce.
Poisson complet Fried fish with fried egg, chips, tomatoes and pimentos.
Salade mechouia A tasty mixture of cubed, chargrilled peppers and tomatoes with lemon and garlic, also topped with tuna, olives and a hard-boiled egg.
Salade tunisienne Finely chopped tomato, cucumber, pepper and onion salad topped with tuna and black olives.
Tagine A tasty dish of left-overs, served hot or cold, in heavy squares or rounds and with the chunks of meat set in a solid centre of egg and cheese. The Tunisian *tagine* has nothing to do with its Moroccan namesake.

Tunisian delights For those with a sweet tooth, Tunisia is paradise. Numerous patisseries make both good French pastries and honey-soaked Tunisian sweets. Tunisians will tell you the best pastries are made at home, which may be true, but as a visitor you will easily be contented with what you find in the better patisseries (see panel on page 66). Baklava is a filo pastry filled with nuts or almonds, while *makroud*, a speciality of Kairouan, is stuffed with dates. Most pastries are made with almonds or almond paste. Deglet en-nour dates are delicious on their own, though Tunisians like them stuffed with marzipan.

The way to eat At mealtimes you will see men, women and children carrying several baguettes or flat Tunisian breads (*hubz*) back home, having first touched every stick in the grocery to find the crunchiest one. Bread is eaten with every meal, and is often used instead of cutlery. When eating with their hands, Tunisians use only their right hand as the left is reserved for ablutions. Alcohol is rarely served with food, apart from in tourist or up-market restaurants.

A fish against the evil eye Fish takes an important place on most menus, and restaurants pride themselves on serving the freshest catch, letting the client choose from a tray. Fish is expensive in restaurants and marked prices are per 100g. Apart from being a favourite food, fish are considered good-luck charms. The museum in El Jem (see page 115) has a Roman gladiatorial charm showing five fish and five Roman numerals, which is what Tunisian parents still buy for a newborn baby. Fish are also painted on walls, and embroidered cushions in a fish shape are presented to newlyweds.

73

*Above: fiery chillies
Below: makroud, stuffed with dates*

Nothing is more refreshing on a hot summer afternoon than a delicious cup of mint tea

74

The tea ritual
Sipping a digestive glass of strong mint tea is very much an acquired pleasure. Gunpowder tea is boiled with sugar and fresh mint until it forms a thick syrupy brew, and is then served in tiny glasses. In cafés a lighter tea is served with fresh mint in a bigger glass, while in the south mint is sometimes replaced with peanuts, almonds or verbena. For a European tea with milk, ask for a *thé anglais* or *thé au lait*.

A cup of coffee
Visitors often comment on the habit Tunisian men have of sitting for hours on a café terrace, watching the world go by while sipping a small glass of coffee. Coffee is indeed a popular drink here. Hotels usually serve a tasteless brew, but happily it is possible to find a bar with an espresso machine almost everywhere in the country. Coffee is usually good and relatively cheap, be it a strong cup of espresso, a cappuccino or a *café au lait*. Turkish coffee is usually served with sugar and cardamon, but can be ordered without the sugar.

Non-alcoholic drinks Tap water is safe to drink in most cities but can taste bad, so even locals have taken to buying bottled mineral water. Most international-brand soft drinks (*gazousa*) are available, as is the local Boga, a clear lemonade. *Sirops* mixed with water are also popular, especially the red grenadine, white almond milk and green mint varieties. Better patisseries sell freshly squeezed juices of whatever fruit is in season at very reasonable prices (note that some will automatically add sugar, so speak out if you don't want any).

Tea and coffee are both extremely popular in Tunisia, and are available in both the local and Western styles – see panels for more details.

Alcoholic drinks Even though alcohol is forbidden according to Islam, Muslim Tunisia produces some good wines. The best ones are rarely seen in restaurants as they are often kept for export to Europe. Sidi Saad is a heavy red bottled in a green-glass amphora. Better reds are La Bonne Bouteille and Château Feriani. Also very palatable are red Lamblot and Château Mornag, red or rosé Magon and Thyna and a rosé Gris de Tunisie. Most hotels and restaurants will offer red, rosé and white wines, the standard ones usually being Haut Mornag, Domaine Karime, Carthage and Koudiat. The cheaper but much coarser Sidi Naceur, Rossel, Grombalia, Naceur and Zarrour remain the village tipplers' favourites but might not be yours. All wines are medium dry, apart from the dry Muscat sec de Kelibia, a fine apéritif wine. Celtia is the common beer, sold either in bottles or in cans. And to round off a meal try Boukha, a fig liqueur.

Nightlife

Discos and nightclubs Nightlife in Tunisia is more or less restricted to nightclubs and discos in the hotels and cultural festivals in summer. A few restaurants in Tunis offer a cabaret show, of which **Monseigneur** (2 rue de Marseille), **Le Palais** (8 avenue de Carthage) and **Le Malouf** (108 rue de Yougoslavie) are popular. Real belly-dancers are a rare sight. The best discos are found out of the centre along the north coast. **Galaxy**, by the Hotel Tour Blanche (tel: 01 271 697) at Gammarth, and **La Baraka**, in Sidi Bou Said, are the two trendiest clubs, but all larger beach-hotel discos are popular in summer.

Smoke a *chicha*
Smoking is one of the most popular ways to spend an evening, staring at the stars or chatting to friends. Foreigners often assume that the pretty water-pipe is filled with hashish, but narcotics are illegal and most often it is *tombac* that is smoked. *Tombac* is a plant related to tobacco but is stronger and, reputedly, less harmful. Before being smoked it is first boiled, then mixed with honey and some lemon. The *tombac* is put on top of the water-pipe and a very hot piece of charcoal placed over it. The smoke is then filtered through the water in the pipe before being inhaled. For a more potent (and expensive) mixture, the water can be replaced by Boukha (fig liqueur) or whisky.

75

Follow the locals Locals spend the evening visiting friends and family, strolling up and down a promenade or window shopping. Men often sit with friends in cafés. To escape the summer heat, many Tunisois drive to Sidi Bou Said (see pages 66–7) for a breath of cool air, a tea and a *chicha* (pronounced 'shee-sha'), or water-pipe, in one of the town's wonderful cafés (see pages 200–1). The more affluent hang out in Gammarth or La Marsa, while the fish restaurants in La Goulette tend to be more popular with families.

Above (left) and left: try a traditional culture show at one of the more up-market hotels

Cinemas and theatres The staple diet of cinemas, popular with mainly male Tunisian youths, is American trash violence, kung fu and sugary Indian love stories in which the couples are thwarted by families and fate, although of course love triumphs in the end. The best movies, usually in French, are screened at the cinema of **Hotel Africa**. The **Théâtre Municipal** (avenue Habib Bourguiba) stages concerts of Arabic and Western classical music, while the **Maison de la Culture Ibn Khaldoun** (16 rue Ibn Haldoun) has regular one-off performances by foreign touring companies. Listings of all cultural events can be found in the daily French-language newspapers *Le Temps* or *La Presse*, or in the English-language weekly *Tunisia News*.

Tunisia has no shortage of modern, up-market hotels

Prices in hotels

Beware that prices are usually calculated per person and not per room, with a 30 per cent or 50 per cent discount for children. Hotel prices are fixed by the Ministry of Tourism and vary according to the three price bands during the year (see main text). A price list is usually hung on the wall at reception. Prices in low season can be half or less those in high season. Beach hotels are best booked as part of a package or through your local travel agent as walk-in rates for individuals tend to be much higher.

The *zone touristique*

Most beach hotels usually lie in *zone touristiques* (tourist areas), outside town centres in complexes that often lack local flavour. Small trains leave regularly from *zone touristiques* for shopping in the nearest town, although in major resorts someone will always be trying to sell you camel rides, stones or palm-tree shoots.

Hotel standards Tourism in Tunisia really took off in the 1960s, so many hotels are modern and quite well designed. Business-standard hotels are confined to Tunis and Sfax, while all along the coast the resorts are crammed full of beach hotels designed for package tourists. The north coast is still being developed, particularly the smaller resorts of Gammarth, Bizerte and Tabarka. Most hotels are privately owned by a handful of Tunisian tycoons or by state-backed syndicates of local businessmen. A few are managed by international chains. Some years ago the Office National du Tourisme Tunisien (ONTT) introduced a classification programme allotting one star to 'four stars luxe', but in recent years standards have dropped considerably. One reason for this is that the authorities took into account only physical criteria, such as room dimensions, equipment and numbers of personnel, and not the quality of services or friendliness of the staff. There are three main price bands, according to season: high is July to mid-September; middle is April to June; and low is November to March.

De luxe hotels In Tunis, Hammamet and Port el Kantaoui there are now a few five-star hotels, but most of these would still only rate four stars or sometimes even three in other countries. Top-grade hotel rooms are equipped with minibar and satellite TV, while the hotel will offer the usual range of services from hairdressing and conference facilities to swimming-pools and sports facilities. A few five-star hotels, such as the Hasdrubal Thalassa in Hammamet and the Abou Nawas in Sousse, offer thalassotherapy, an invigorating cure of sea water and algae for relaxation and health.

Mid-range hotels Most hotels on the Sahel coast have three or four stars, and many are designed so that guests need not leave them. They are totally self-contained with sports facilities, souvenir shops, bars and restaurants, car-hire agents and excursion offices. Large does not necessarily mean ugly, although some of the complexes are imposing. The majority of Tunisia's hotels are no taller than a palm tree, most are set in landscaped gardens and some are designed in traditional Tunisian style. However, the drop in tourist numbers in recent years has left some hotels unable to afford necessary maintenance or renovations. As a result, they may feel rather the worse for wear. The inland hotels at the oases of Tozeur, Nefta and Douz are of equal standards, but are usually cheaper than those at the beach resorts.

Low budget Cheaper hotels are usually found in the *medina* or *ville nouvelle*. Accommodation ranges from filthy flea-pits at the bottom end to pleasant and spotlessly clean rooms for a few dinars more. Unlike in huge holiday complexes, staff are often more friendly and helpful (especially in family-run places) and the buildings have more character. Cheap hotels in the centre of Tunis, such as **La Maison Dorée** (see page 194) and **Transatlantique** (avenue de Yougoslavie), are in old art deco buildings that date from the French protectorate. Inland, there are basic rooms in troglodyte dwellings which are worth staying in for the atmosphere (see page 199). In Jerba the hotels in Houmt Souk, such as the **Dar Faiza**, the **Sables d'Or** and the old caravanserai that has been converted into the **Marhala** (see page 199), offer a perfect alternative to hotels in the *zone touristique*.

Food in hotels Many beach hotels insist on selling a room with half or full board, especially in high season. Hotel food is rarely the best, and can seem rather bland. Most hotels offer a buffet breakfast, which in cheaper hotels often means picking up a roll, jam and coffee. Coffee is always the watery American variety and even in better hotels the juice is rarely fresh. Dinner is a set menu or buffet with international dishes and the occasional cooled-down version of a Tunisian speciality. The food in hotels inland can sometimes be of very poor quality, and in general we would recommend that you take only bed and breakfast.

Marhalas
The Touring Club of Tunisia runs a chain of *marhalas* (cheap, traditional hotels) in the south of the country. With prices slightly higher than at youth hostels, they offer basic but clean rooms in buildings of typical southern Tunisian architecture. There is also usually a very friendly welcome. *Marhalas* are either in troglodyte dwellings, as in Matmata, or in old Arab buildings like the Marhala in Houmt Souk, Jerba (see page 199).

Spending the night in one of the basic troglodyte dwellings in Matmata is an unforgettable experience

To ensure an amicable end to a taxi ride, make sure that the driver uses his meter

Transport from the airport
The airport lies 7km outside the centre of Tunis. The easiest way to reach the city is to take a meter taxi, allowing a little more than the usual fare to cover luggage, or 50 per cent more after 9am. Beware of unofficial taxis (see main text) which operate from the airport; if you must take one, agree on a price before you get in. The regular bus No 35 goes from the airport to avenue Habib Bourguiba. A more expensive airport bus (Transtours) runs to the railway station on place de Barcelone (departures every half-hour 6am–midnight and every hour midnight–6am).

Buses The main bus station in Tunis is on the place de Barcelone in front of the railway station. Buses are cheap but the lack of an official bus map makes them hard to use. Bus numbers and destinations are usually written in Arabic. Tickets are bought on board. For information on bus routes in town check with the office SNT, 1 avenue Habib Bourguiba (tel: 01 259 422), or at the Parc Thameur. A private company also operates green and white buses; these are slightly more expensive but are also more comfortable as they only take seated passengers.

Metro An efficient tramway system recently introduced in Tunis to ease traffic congestion seems to be a success. There are now five lines and the system is still expanding. The most useful lines are No 4 to the Musée du Bardo and No 3 to the bus station at Bab Saadoum. The central station is at the Barcelone train station.

Taxis The easiest way to get around town is by taxi, a relatively cheap form of transport. Taxis in Tunis are numerous, but make sure you use yellow cars with a taxi sign as these are official taxis equipped with a meter. Always insist that the driver uses the meter, or fix a price before leaving. Prices go up 50 per cent in the evening. It can be quite difficult to get hold of a taxi during the rush hour; try along avenue Habib Bourguiba or in front of the railway station.

TGM The TGM (Tunis–La Goulette–La Marsa) train leaves Tunis for the northern suburbs, including Carthage and Sidi Bou Said, from the end of avenue Habib Bourguiba, near Tunis Marine (metro station line 1). Tickets must be bought in advance. The less crowded first class is only marginally more expensive than second class. Trains, which run every quarter of an hour during the day and every hour at night until 3am, can be crowded at rush hours and on Sundays, when everyone heads for the beach.

Intercity buses Tunisia has a good bus system, with services to most towns and prices slightly cheaper than the train. Some local buses fill up quickly and so seats are as rare a commodity as curtains. Buses between major cities are now becoming more comfortable and many are air-conditioned. For information, call SNTRI in Tunis (tel: 01 247 368). Timetables for SNTRI services between major cities are listed in the daily French newspapers *Le Temps* and *La Presse*. The 'North' bus station (tel: 01 562 299/532), for buses to the north coast, is at Bab Saadoum. The 'South' bus station (tel: 01 495 255), for all other destinations and for services to Libya, is at Bab El-Fellah. In summer, try to book in advance as seats are in demand.

Trains The main train station is on place de Barcelone (for information, tel: 01 244 440/427). There is a network of more than 2,000km of railway, and although trains are slow they are also cheap and quite efficient. The most crowded is second class. For comfort there is *confortable* class, more expensive than first class but offering more leg room and a bigger seat – essential for a longer journey. Some fast trains require a supplementary payment.

Louages These are large communal taxis that run between cities, leaving only when all five seats have been sold. In Tunis the *louage* stations are located next to the bus stations – at the front of the North station and to the left of the South station. In summer most *louages* operate during the cooler hours of the day. They tend to be slightly more expensive than the train, but are a lot faster – usually because the drivers often behave like maniacs.

Internal flights Tunisair operates flights to Jerba (one hour), Monastir, Sfax, Gabès, Tozeur and Tabarka. The smaller companies Tuninter and Tunisavia run more services to the same cities. In summer it is essential to book well in advance as the small aircraft fill up fast.

Useful bus routes
● No 3 from avenue Habib Bourguiba in front of Tunis Air or from the Hotel Majestic on avenue de Paris to the Musée du Bardo.
● No 5 from place de l'Indépendance to place Pasteur near the Parc du Belvédère.
● No 35 from the airport to avenue Habib Bourguiba.

Car parks
A car is useful if you want to get out of Tunis to visit the northern coastal resorts, but in the city centre it can be a nightmare. Apart from chronic congestion at peak times, there are very few parking spaces. If possible, it is advisable to use only the rare pay car parks. Hotel Africa has an underground car park open to non-residents; there is another public car park near the tourist office.

Tunis' brand-new metro system, a modern tramway, is both fast and efficient

THE NORTH

81

THE NORTH

A woman's work is never done

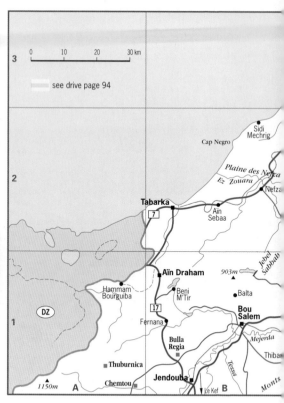

see drive page 94

The Mejez el Bab front line
The main road from Tunis to Jendouba/Bulla Regia largely follows the Mejerda Valley, turned into a bloody battlefield during the Tunisian Campaign (Nov 1942–May 1943), when British and American troops fought the Germans in the area of Mejez el Bab, about 40km east of Béja, and also at Mareth in the south of the country (see page 174). The large Commonwealth war cemeteries at Mejez el Bab and Massicault (28km south-west of Tunis) are a sad reminder of how many lives were lost.

Previous pages (main photo): Bulla Regia's wonderful Roman theatre

The north The north coast is the least developed in Tunisia, although all that is about to change and with good reason. It is wilder but also more varied than the southern coasts, and as well as ancient ports and long sandy beaches it offers wetlands, lush farmland and the foothills of the Tell to explore.

Ancient history The Berbers established themselves along the coast before the arrival of the Phoenicians, but it appears to have been the latter, looking for resting places along the route from the eastern Mediterranean to Spain, who first settled places like Utica and Bizerte. These offered much-needed protection from the sea, for the coast here is more exposed than Tunisia's east-facing shore. They also had the virtue of being easily defended from inland.

The Romans went further, as always, developing Utica, Thabraca (Tabarka) and Bizerte (which they called Hippo Diarrhytus) into significant settlements, linked by road to Carthage and the Algerian coastal towns.

Shipping news The two main ports of the north are Bizerte and Tabarka. Bizerte in particular has been prized throughout history, especially since a canal was cut by the Phoenicians to allow passage from the sea through the vast Lac de Bizerte. Barbary pirates reinforced Bizerte, knowing that they could have their fleet ready and waiting inside the lake to attack passing ships. One of the first

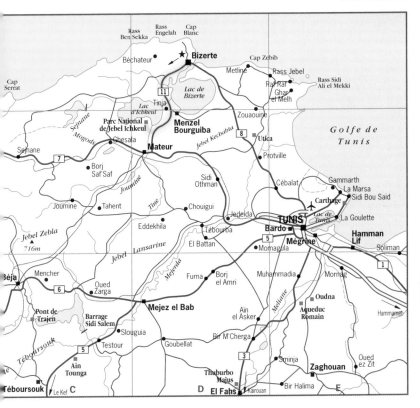

things the French did under the protectorate was to build a huge naval station at Bizerte, which they managed to hold on to for some years after independence. Tabarka was also prized, though perhaps less so: the pirate Barbarossa was prepared to hand it over to the Spanish in return for the release of his protégé, Dragut.

Below: the splendid forests around Aïn Draham

The natural beauty of the northern coast is a magnet for visitors

Getting there
Transport links to northern Tunisia have improved since 1899, when Herbert Vivian complained that the 'ramshackle light railway' took more than 3 hours to cover the 65km from Tunis, 4½ hours by mule. The road is now in good condition and passes rich farmland and surviving colonial villas; it takes just an hour by car or *louage* (shared taxi) to make the same journey today.

Wildlife The wetlands of the north coast are one of the finest places in the Mediterranean for birdwatching, particularly at the Jebel Ichkeul National Park, North Africa's most important bird sanctuary. From October to February Tunisia is home to a wide variety of birds escaping the European winter. Many of them will winter in the northern wetlands and hills, while others continue their journey further south.

The French writer Alexandre Dumas called this region a 'sportsman's paradise' after its abundance of wild animals. In the forests that cover some of the hills leading up to the Tell a few still exist – jackal, fox and wild boar, for instance – but as there is still hunting in season they don't hang around when they see humans.

The interior Another factor also attracted Phoenicians and Romans to the region: its fertility. Inland from the coast is some prime farmland, the sort of landscape that reminded French colonists of home. Béja and Bulla Regia were both wealthy towns in antiquity, and Béja remains

as such today. The road inland from Tabarka to Aïn Draham runs through more extreme countryside of hills and forests whose names still carry the memory of the Berber tribes who lived here long before the arrival of the Phoenicians and Romans.

A sporting chance In 1899, an English traveller remarked that 'with a little effort, [Bizerte] may soon become a tourist resort on a small scale'. A century later Bizerte and Tabarka are poised for the big time: a new development drive is under way, concentrating on the sporting opportunities offered by the northern region. There are some excellent, relatively untouched sand beaches, from Raf Raf Plage and Sidi Ali el Mekki to Rass Engelah and Zouiraa Plage, and the waters around Tabarka are clear enough to support coral, earning the stretch the name 'Coral Coast'. In the hills there is excellent hiking and, in the cork forests around Aïn Draham, hunting in season. At the moment, the scarcity of big hotels makes the north an ideal destination for independent travellers.

Coral diving
Unlike the northern Mediterranean coast, Tunisia has some fine coral beds. Tabarka has the best and, not by chance, is also most popular for diving. Coral has been fished from these waters since antiquity, though these days you can only look and not touch. The sea-bed around the La Galite islands (60km out from Tabarka, and also accessible from Bizerte) is considered the most interesting dive zone (see panel on page 96).

THE NORTH

Boar hunting
The pine forests around the village of Aïn Draham are a popular boar-hunting ground (the season is from October to February). The Les Chênes hotel (see page 195) offers weekend and one-week packages, including hunting and transfers to and from the airport. It is recommended that you book as far in advance as possible (tel: 08 655 215/315; fax: 08 655 396).

▶▶ **Aïn Draham**   82B1

The approach to Aïn Draham from Tabarka through the valley of the Oued el-Kebir is nothing short of dramatic. Surrounded by magnificent forests and mock chalets, the mountain village, whose name means 'Spring of Money', is something of a rarity in North Africa as it could easily be taken for a hamlet in the foothills of the Alps. Built on a col between two mountains, it was a popular hill resort in colonial times, and today busloads of Tunisians come looking for cooler temperatures and a change of scenery.

Aïn Draham now feels suburban but makes a good base for hikes in the area. The walk up to the summit of Jebel Bir (1,014m), starting behind the mosque, is easy and has rewarding views over the region. The other mountain, Jebel Fersig (also known as the Col des Ruines), can be approached from a path 500m north of Aïn Draham, off the Tabarka road. The path winds through a lovely cork wood with some chalets, ending at a terrace with breathtaking views over the region.

Aïn Draham's forests, popular with walkers

▶   **Béja**   83C1

Béja is the main town of the fertile Mejerda Plain. Before the Romans arrived it was a rich corn market, but when the Béjans rebelled against their invaders, the latter destroyed the wealthy town completely. The town was sacked several times again throughout its history, but each time it rose from the dust so that today it continues to be an important corn market.

The picturesque *medina* and *souqs* are rarely visited by tourists, even though they are more authentic than most. In the centre of town stands a strange French colonial church, with, to its right, the main thoroughfare of the *medina*, **rue Kheireddine**▶▶. This busy shopping street is at its liveliest in the morning and early evening, as are the café terraces on the shady **place Abdel Kader**▶▶ to the left. The **rue el Attarine**▶ has a good food and spices market, while the merchants in **Souq en-Nehasach**▶▶ sell wonderful handwoven blankets at what are usually the lowest prices in the country. The **Bab el-Ain**▶▶, on the left of the main street, is the water gate with a cool spring and a *marabout* (shrine). The 7th-century **kasbah**▶, built on the site of an earlier Byzantine fortress, is still occupied by the army and is therefore closed to the public.

Bizerte's *ville nouvelle*
The modern town has little of interest apart from some well-preserved examples of colonial architecture. For a pleasant late-afternoon stroll, head along the quai Tarik ibn Ziad up to the Club Nautique and then down avenue Habib Bou Guetfa towards the corniche. Look out for some grand buildings in art nouveau style. To the left, the animated avenue Habib Bourguiba leads to the centre of town, with its many café terraces, shops and little squares.

▶▶ **Bizerte**   83D3

The town of Bizerte, the largest on the north coast after Tunis, is expanding fast as a tourist resort, with hotels along the corniche road overlooking dunes and sandy beaches. Bizerte was already an important port under the Phoenicians, who dug the canal connecting the Lac de

The colonial church still stands proudly in the centre of Béja

Bizerte with the sea. Under Turkish rule Bizerte was a feared corsair port, but the French made it an important naval base as soon as they arrived in 1881. After independence the Tunisian army moved in.

The **Vieux Port (Old Port)**►►►, harbour to multi-coloured fishing boats and overlooked by the white and blue houses of the *medina*, is the town's star attraction. From the waterfront it is but a short walk to the **kasbah**►►, the old Byzantine fortress, with pleasant strolls through the maze of narrow streets. From the ramparts there is a good view. The Old Port is enclosed by the winding streets of the newer *medina*►►►, with covered *souqs* and a few medieval forts; the Sidi el-Hanni fortress houses a small **Oceanographic Museum**► (*Open* hours vary). There are good sandy beaches to either side of the town: the best one to the south is Remel, while the corniche beach to the north is more crowded and lined with hotels. Further north is Cap Blanc, a popular picnic spot with a ruined fortress and white rocks set in the middle of scrubland.

Bizerte's picturesque Vieux Port (Old Port) is the town's star attraction

■ **The Roman passion for decorating public buildings and private houses with mosaics has provided us with a major source of information about their lives. Mosaics were one of the principal art forms of Roman Africa, and remained so even during the Christian period until the 6th century AD.** ■

A Hellenistic tradition
Tesserae mosaics were first developed in Greece from an older tradition of pebble paving. The earliest figurative pebble mosaic in Greece was found in Macedonia, dating from the 4th century BC. The form caught on and by the 3rd century BC the use of tesserae mosaics was widespread across the Hellenic Empire. As in wall paintings, the subjects were mostly taken from mythology. As techniques developed so it became possible to create finer designs, called emblemata, from tiny tesserae and little slices of stone.

Many Roman villa ruins still retain fragments of their magnificent mosaics

The early mosaics The Phoenicians were already partial to well-paved floors, which early Roman writers praised for their elegance. Excavations at Carthage and Kerkouane have revealed floors in plain white mosaics and also 'terrazzo' flooring of crushed terracotta with specks of shiny marble and glass. Here and there the marble formed simple designs such as the symbol for the moon goddess Tanit. The earliest coloured figurative mosaic in Tunisia was found in the Baths at Acholla, and is now displayed on the second floor of the Musée du Bardo in Tunis (see pages 54–6). Dating from the early 2nd century AD, it was created by Greek craftsmen, who used tesserae in a sophisticated art form (see panel).

Roman African mosaics Once the North Africans discovered tesserae mosaics there was no stopping them; in fact, workshops struggled to meet the demand. As men spent most of their lives out of doors, on the land, in the forum or market-place, in the baths and amphitheatres, they tended to lavish money on public, not private, buildings. Soon mosaics were used to cover walls, domes and the floors of public baths, adding opulence to the already impressive architecture. Decorative themes were taken from the Hellenistic tradition, incorporating mythological images such as the Birth of Venus or Triumph of Dionysus. The output of the workshops of the major cities was often identifiable by recurring patterns.

By the 3rd century AD mosaics were used in private houses, and this was where a distinct African style developed. Some 'nouveau riche' landowners may have imported or commissioned mosaics in the 'international' style, but African patrons wanted hunting and circus scenes to commemorate the games they gave at the amphitheatre. Soon local craftsmen developed a style of their own, not found anywhere else in the Roman Empire and distinguished by a lively naturalism. Understandably, agriculture was another popular theme, and the large numbers of marine mosaics found even inland suggests that many a rich landowner owed at least some of his prosperity to investment in shipping.

With such a large output, techniques improved and larger areas of fine and detailed mosaics could be composed, as could circular compositions which were meant to be viewed from different angles.

Mosaics

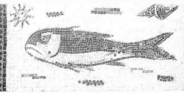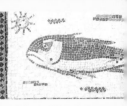

The Christian mosaics By the 4th century AD, with city life becoming harder, many rich landowners preferred to live in large countryside villas. The decorations reflected their lifestyle and showed country scenes and country houses. With the steady advance of Christianity in North Africa at this time came the first purpose-built churches, with mosaic flooring. Until late in the 5th century, Christians followed the Jewish tradition of avoiding images, instead using geometric patterns and certain Christian motifs such as fish, the Greek letters alpha and omega or the 'PIX' monogram. For the first time, burials were allowed in religious buildings (many of the Christian mosaics in the Musée du Bardo are tomb mosaics, definitely the most important art form at the time). A mosaic from Tabarka, in Room V of the Musée du Bardo, shows a representation of a 4th-century church and gives a clear idea of what these early places of worship were all about. Remarkable as well from this period are baptismal fonts like the one found in Sbeïtla, vulva-shaped baths covered in mosaics to symbolise a second birth after baptism.

The Byzantines encouraged a renaissance of the art of mosaics and reintroduced fine figurative designs into church mosaics. They also started using cut glass. However, their revival was short lived in Tunisia and after the Arab conquest the use of mosaics more or less died out, with the exception of some fine marble floors.

Spending your money
For successful North African businessmen, administrators or professionals, there were only a couple of ways to spend profit. Either it went back into land, ships or cargo, or, as was often the case, it was spent on conspicuous consumption. 'All the natural competitiveness of the rich second-century African frustrated by the pax Romana from its traditional expression in war, was poured into the improvement of his native city' (From *Rome in Africa* by Susan Raven, 1969). So it was that rich citizens vied to outdo each other, whether in rank or in prestige.

Mythological themes were popular (this is the sea god Oceanus)

89

Above: Bulla Regia's villas were partly built underground
Below: headless statue in the Memnian Baths

▶▶▶ **Bulla Regia** 82B1

In 2 BC, Bulla Regia (*Open* summer 8–7. Rest of year 8.30–5.30. Closed Mon. *Admission charge* cheap) was the capital of one of three small Roman kingdoms in Numidia. After the Emperor Hadrian annexed it to the empire, it became one of the wealthiest cities in Roman Africa. It is now a remarkable Roman site, all the more so for being rarely visited by tour groups .

The ruins cover the terraces of the Jebel Rebia, overlooking the Mejerda Valley. To escape the blistering heat in summer and withering cold in winter, houses and villas were partly built underground, not unlike the troglodyte dwellings of the south (see page 172). Because of their unusual architecture, most have been remarkably well preserved despite a few earthquakes. In traditional Mediterranean style, the living and sleeping areas – often with stunning mosaic floors – open around a central courtyard, this reached by an open staircase. The best mosaics have been taken to the Musée du Bardo in Tunis (see pages 54–6), although a few remain, notably in Maison de la Pêche (House of Fishing), the Maison d'Amphirite (with a mosaic of Venus, Marina and Neptune riding a centaur) and the Maison de la Chasse (House of the Hunt). Above ground are the ruins of the theatre, the forum, the imposing Memnian Baths and a Temple of Apollo.

▶▶ **Chemtou** 82A1

Founded in the 1st century BC under Augustus's rule as the Roman colony of Simitthus, Chemtou (*Open* always. *Admission* free) was famed for its dark yellow marble (antico giallo), which was considered the third most precious stone in the empire after Egyptian purple porphyry and Spartan green serpentine. The blocks of marble were each marked with the name of the emperor in power at the time, the quarry manager and the proconsul for Africa. Beside the quarries are the remains of a slaves' camp, baths and a theatre.

▶▶ Ghar el Melh 83E3

Ghar el Melh, Arabic for 'Salt Cave', is famous as the site where Charles V landed his troops in 1535 to fight the corsairs, and where the siege of Tunis was planned. The port, no longer connected to the sea, was one of the main pirate bases along the Barbary Coast (see panel on page 95). Once impregnable, it is now just a sleepy village.

▶▶▶ Jebel Ichkeul, Parc National de 83D2

The most important of Tunisia's six national parks encompasses the Lac d'Ichkeul, covering over 12,600 hectares. More than 150,000 waterfowl use it as a winter resting place after their migration from Europe (see also pages 92–3). Peak occupancy is from October to April, with November, March and April the best months for watching water-birds and waders. Beside the thousands of birds, there are about 70 species of mammal such as otter, jackal, porcupine, water buffalo (see panel) and boar.

The small but interesting **Ecology Museum** (*Open* daily 9–12, 1.30–4.30. *Admission charge* cheap) covers all aspects of the park; the view over the lake from its terrace is excellent. The lake is too shallow to be navigable and water-levels have been so low in recent years that they threaten the lake's viability as salt water has been flowing in from the Lac de Bizerte. The reason for this is that the dams take more and more water from the lake's feeder rivers to supply the ever-expanding tourist complexes and irrigation projects. Various tracks lead over Jebel Ichkeul, an impressive limestone mountain standing 511m above the south side of the lake.

Story of the water buffalo
The water buffalo has become a common sight again in the marshes near Lac d'Ichkeul, but this was not always the case. The king of Sicily gave a pair of water buffaloes to Hussein Bey in 1729, when Ichkeul was a beylical hunting ground. Ahmed Bey encouraged their breeding as the animals were strong enough to haul his artillery carriages, but they were always used for 'sport' as well – visiting dignitaries loved to shoot them and take the heads home as a trophy. In 1963, when only three females remained, a bull was brought over from Italy. Today, their offspring are thriving once again.

Before it silted up, the calm, shallow lagoon at Ghar el Melh used to be open sea

Birdlife

■ **Like many tourists, birds flock to Tunisia for its mild climate, lakes and beaches. The limited population of resident birds increases dramatically in winter when European birds settle near the country's coast and lakes. Migrants fly through in autumn and then return northwards in increased numbers after breeding in the spring.** ■

A desert inhabitant
Sandgrouse are extremely well adapted to the rigours of desert life. Their flocks will fly for up to 65km to reach a known watering spot, and when their chicks have hatched the parents soak their breast feathers at the drinking pools and carry the water back to the nest scrape. Coronated and spotted sandgrouse manage to find shoots and seeds even in the most arid desert areas, these making up their diet. They are difficult to spot, but the best clue to their presence is the liquid, gurgling calls they utter during flight.

Below: the rare marble teal duck
Bottom: Lac d'Ichkeul is a key bird sanctuary

Lac d'Ichkeul Jebel Ichkeul National Park is the most important bird sanctuary in North Africa. Between October and February huge flocks winter here, having migrated from Europe. Ducks and geese account for the largest numbers, and in the marshy parts there are waders such as grey and purple herons, egrets, black-winged stilts, Kentish plovers, black-tailed godwits, redshanks and sandpipers. Several races of yellow wagtail actively catch insects from the drying mud, while marsh terns, pratincoles, swallows and martins hawk insects in the air above. The rarer birds to watch out for on the lake are the marbled teal duck, the white-headed duck and the purple gallinule (see panel opposite). The black-headed bush shrike also breeds here in very small numbers. Smaller birds include reed warblers, nightingales and bee-eaters. The mountain scrub of Jebel Ichkeul attracts striking Moussier's redstarts, found only in North Africa, and Sardinian warblers with their glossy black caps.

Birds of prey are common all over Tunisia, the dominant species being marsh harriers. Peregrines, lanner falcons and kestrels all breed on Jebel Ichkeul, along with long-legged buzzards, Bonelli's eagles and short-toed eagles.

Coastal sanctuaries The salty lagoon of the Lac de Tunis attracts gulls, egrets, herons and waders, as well as flamingos and cormorants in winter. In spring, thousands of birds of prey pass over Cap Bon on their way north across the Mediterranean. The wildlife information centre near the village of El Haouaria on the peninsula is worth a visit (see page 104).

One of the most important sites in the whole Mediterranean for wintering waders is the Gulf of Gabès. The saltpans stretching south from Sfax to Thyna in particular attract enormous numbers of birds for the winter, amongst them egrets, herons, flamingos, spoonbills, gulls and terns. Many species also stay on to breed.

Desert and desert oases In the steppes, desert and dry stream beds, it is easy to overlook an enormous range of birds, especially larks and wheatears, including crested and hoopoe larks, desert wheatears and trumpeter finches. A rare bird to spot is the sandgrouse, most likely to appear early in the morning around the oases (see panel opposite). Chott el Jerid (see page 130) is a vast salt lake with seasonal flooding whose birdlife depends on the season and level of the lake. Flamingos can be seen in the lake in large numbers at times, but larks, bustards, wheatears and birds of prey can also often be seen close to the road between Kebili and Tozeur. Crossing the Sahara has become increasingly difficult for many species as the desert is gradually encroaching southwards, so many more now winter in the Sahel instead.

City life Although modern resorts on the coast are not really attractive to wildlife, the inhabitants of Tunisia's traditional towns and villages have a more harmonious relationship with the environment. In the skies over towns throughout the country, common, pallid and alpine swifts scream through the air in search of insects. Shrubs and bushes in gardens are host to numerous wintering chiffchaffs, and to migrants such as willow and Bonelli's warblers. Residents throughout the year are the common bulbuls that abound wherever shrubby vegetation is encouraged. Bulbuls are a truly African species and make up for their rather sombre appearance with a loud, flute-like song.

Pink flamingos are common on most of Tunisia's lakes

The purple gallinule
Found in Lac d'Ichkeul's reedbeds, the purple gallinule is one of Tunisia's most colourful birds, looking something like an outsize moorhen. In certain light, its purple and blue plumage is almost iridescent, and its bright red beak and frontal 'shield' are conspicuous. The quiet observer may see the bird picking its way through the reeds with surprising agility, flicking its tail as it goes.

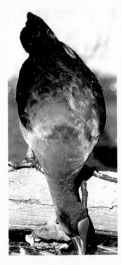

Above: the colourful purple gallinule
Left: lanner falcon

Drive **To the lakes**

See map on pages 82–3.

An unusual outing for Tunisia, away from the coast of Bizerte and along the shores of Lac d'Ichkeul (see also page 91). Take a picnic, and allow half a day (approximately 35km one way).

Leave Bizerte on the Mateur road, passing Bizerte airport and skirting the Lac de Bizerte. Although this lake is marred by military installations and belching factories, it none the less performs a vital role in the ecology of neighbouring Lac d'Ichkeul, to which it is joined by the shallow Oued Tinja river. The village of Tinja► sits astride the river; fishermen throw hundreds of nets in here to catch eel and mullet as they pass from Lac d'Ichkeul to the

Above: the shores of Lac d'Ichkeul

sea. The river also has a complicated system of dams, designed to keep the water-level sufficiently high.

A few kilometres past Tinja is **Menzel Bourguiba**, the former Ferryville, created by the French to receive European immigrants at the end of the 19th century. Once nick-named 'Petit Paris', or 'Little Paris', it is now a characterless industrial town with more than 60,000 inhabitants.

Continue along the Mateur road until the road forks, then take the right fork, signposted to Lac d'Ichkeul. In the marshland to the right look out for water buffalo, intro-duced here in 1729 (see panel on page 91). The gravel road passes a quarry at the foot of Jebel Ichkeul, where workmen keep their sheep and cows in stone huts roofed with marshland reed. The road climbs to a wooden ridge on a peninsula to end at the **Ecology Museum**►►. Beside the museum is a good viewing point over the lake and a track leading off to the shoreline north of the mountain Jebel Ichkeul, with more viewing points and some wonderful picnic spots.

▶▶ Raf Raf
83E3

Raf Raf Plage, 38km east of Bizerte, is a magnificent crescent-shaped beach of fine white sand facing the small rocky island of Pilau, which resembles some sort of battleship. The beach is backed on one side by the village of Raf Raf and further on by dunes and shady pine woods. In summer the beach is often strewn with seaweed, and suffers with discarded litter. However, the rocky shore is a delight for snorkelling and underwater fishing. The village is of little interest, apart from a few café-grills and a good patisserie providing food in summer. Most women in town still wear traditional dress, and the local embroidery is well known. The view over the Gulf of Tunis from Jebel Nadour, crowning the village, is wonderful.

▶▶ Rass Engelah
83D3

This excellent, long sandy beach, usually fairly empty, lies 16km west of Bizerte on a headland crowned with an attractive Moorish lighthouse. Nearby Béchateur is centred around the shrine of Sidi Daoudi, and the entire hilltop is covered with unexcavated Roman ruins.

▶▶▶ Rass Sidi Ali el Mekki
83E3

The isolated beach of Sidi Ali el Mekki is one of the finest in the country. Despite being close to Bizerte and Tunis, it is rarely crowded even at the height of summer, and a handful of cafés and straw huts for camping so far remain its only facilities. The beach takes its name from the tomb of Sidi Ali el Mekki, more like a fortress than a burial place: the thick walls hide a network of caves and tunnels to the saint's tomb, hidden inside the mountain. This *marabout* attracts many pilgrims, and although non-Muslims are not allowed inside it is worth climbing up to the terrace for the view. On the Cap Farina headland, 2km further on, is the *marabout* of Sidi Haj Bareck, where a shepherd–guardian does admit visitors to the tomb, covered in plastic flowers and shell pictures.

> **Perfect for pirates**
> Ghar el Melh, 6km west of Rass Sidi Ali el Mekki (see also page 91), was one of the chief bases for the Barbary pirates. It was perfectly situated, just off one of the narrowest and busiest shipping lanes in the Mediterranean, from where captured merchant ships were easily dragged into the lagoon. The British Admiral Blake bombarded the port in 1654, but the town continued to thrive on piracy until 1834, when the corsairs' arsenal exploded, flattening most of the town.

95

The still largely undeveloped northern coast offers some of Tunisia's best beaches: vast stretches of white sand, crystal-clear waters and not a hotel complex in sight

The photogenic Les Aiguilles and the Genoese fort across the water are Tabarka's main sights

La Galite

About 60km from Tabarka out into the Mediterranean is La Galite, a volcanic archipelago of seven islands inhabited by a few families of wine-makers and fishermen. There are some Roman and Punic tombs here and a classified nature reserve, home to colonies of monk seals. There is no regular boat service, but enquire at Tabarka's diving club (tel: 08 644 478), in the harbour or at the tourist office at 32 avenue Bourguiba (tel: 08 670 111).

▶▶   **Tabarka**   *82B2*

The meeting of the Khroumiria Mountains, covered with pine and eucalyptus forests, with the clear blue sea provides a stunning setting for the fishing village of Tabarka. The jewel of the Coral Coast is fast becoming a trendy resort; the new marina, an 18-hole golf course, a casino and several hotel complexes have taken away some of the town's sleepy charm.

The Phoenicians founded Thabraca, meaning 'Place in the Shade', as a trading post. The port gained importance under the Romans as vessels came here to pick up antico giallo, the precious yellow marble quarried in Chemtou (see page 90), as well as grain, oil and metals from the interior. Grand villas and public monuments kept a whole crowd of artists busy, and Thabraca's school of mosaics was famed throughout the empire. In the 5th century AD the town prospered as one of Africa's main dioceses, and it flourished even after the Arab conquest. In the 16th century the pirate Barbarossa gave Tabarka away to the Genoese in exchange for his protégé Dragut (see panel on page 160), but the army of Ali Pacha took it back. It was used as a French army base during World War II.

The main monument is the fine Genoese **fort** on a hill which is now joined to the mainland by a causeway. The view from the top is well worth the climb. The **Musée Archéologique** (*Open* summer Tue–Sun 9–1, 3–7. Rest of year Tue–Sun 8.30–5.30. *Admission charge* cheap), housed in the old basilica, has a fine collection of 4th- and 5th-century mosaics, but was closed for restoration at the time of writing. At the end of avenue Habib Bourguiba are the much-photographed Les Aiguilles ('Needles'), a dramatic rock formation. About 20km towards Tunis is Chott Zouiraa, a vast and beautiful sandy beach but with extremely dangerous offshore currents. The main street in Tabarka is lined with shops and stalls selling the corals the town is famous for (see panel on page 85). Note that coral is endangered and protected in Tunisia, so the items on sale may have been gathered illegally.

► **Thuburnica** 82A1

The remote Roman town of Thuburnica (14km along a gravel track from Chemtou) was founded in the 1st century BC by the Roman General Marius. It is reached via the site's main monument, a 10m-high Roman bridge in such good condition it almost looks new. The driveway to the colonial house used by archaeologists is scattered with Punic and Roman stelae; inside are more Punic artefacts. Little else remains apart from the scant ruins of a mausoleum, a triumphal arch, a temple to Juno and Concord and another to the Four Seasons, and several houses with cisterns.

► **Utica** 83D2

Little remains of the old Roman city of Utica (*Open summer Tue–Sun 8–6. Rest of year Tue–Sun 8–5. Admission charge* cheap), which is still partly buried in a 5m-deep coating of alluvial mud from the Mejerda river. Like many other towns in Tunisia, it was originally a Phoenician settlement before becoming an important Roman port, even though nowadays it lies 5km away from the sea. It is hard to imagine that this was once the capital of the 'Provincia Africa', boasting many grand public buildings. The city collapsed under repeated invasions by Vandals, Byzantines and finally Arabs.

The best-preserved monuments are the Maison de la Cascade (House of the Waterfall), which still has a fine mosaic floor depicting fishing scenes, and the Roman baths. Unfortunately, one of the site's most beautiful mosaics, of cherubs playing with dolphins, is now in the Musée du Louvre, Paris. The small museum contains funerary furniture, jewellery, mosaics and Punic sarcophagi of children who may have been sacrificed here.

An evening stroll
Two tourist routes in Tabarka, perfect for an evening stroll, offer panoramic views over the village and gulf. The first was recently created and heads from the centre towards Annaba. The other goes eastwards towards Tunis to the *zone touristique* and lovely golf course.

Diving in Tabarka
The underwater world near Tabarka is pretty amazing and the local diving club, Club de Plongée du Yachting Club, based at the marina, is very active. This was the first centre of underwater sports in Tunisia, and organises diving courses and excursions, rents out equipment and provides information (tel/fax: 08 644 478).

97

The massive ruins of the public baths at Utica give an idea of how splendid they must have been in their heyday

CAP BON AND THE SAHEL

see drive page 109

100

Previous pages (main photo): Nabeul is nationally renowned for its pottery, stone-carving and wrought ironwork

Cap Bon and the Sahel The Cap Bon peninsula and the Sahel, or coastal plains, contain some of the most popular resorts in Tunisia, for glorious sandy beaches, lush countryside, towns with tourist facilities and Roman architecture are all close at hand. What's surprising is that so too is a taste of a less developed Tunisia.

The lie of the land The Cap Bon peninsula, joined to southern Europe long ago and today lying only 140km from Sicily, looks familiar to anyone coming from the north. It has lush coastal plains, where vines, corn and wheat have always grown well. The mountainous spine that runs along the peninsula and into the sea breaks Cap Bon in two and also shelters some fine old Tunisian villages where life is less disturbed than one might expect, considering international resorts lie only an hour's drive away.

The Sahel is another country: the coast around Hammamet has one of the Mediterranean's finest stretches of beach (though others around Sousse and Mahdia are equally desirable). Between Hammamet and Sousse, where there are no beaches worth lying on, the flat and dull inland plains are home to hundreds of thousands of olive trees. Trade in olives – both the fruit and the oil – has long provided the Sahelis with profit enough to build, hence the large number of significant towns here.

Ancient beginnings The main coastal towns were once overnight stops for Phoenician boats following the southern shore of the Mediterranean on their way to Spain and its silver. Kerkouane, Nabeul, Hammamet, Sousse, Monastir, Mahdia, Sfax and many other towns and villages along the coasts have histories that go back at least to the 2nd century BC. Inland lies El Jem, a perfect example of what could be accomplished if there was enough money to be made, in this case squeezed from olives. The magnificent Roman amphitheatre here is one of the country's greatest archaeological attractions and is proof of the sophistication of ancient Tunisia.

Historic encounters You encounter history in many ways in the Cap Bon and Sahel: in the continuity of

Above: Nabeul potters were greatly influenced by lead-glazing techniques introduced by Andalusians in the 17th century
Below: Korbous spa, on the Cap Bon peninsula, known in Roman times as Aquae Calidae Carpitanae

101

CAP BON AND THE SAHEL

Cap Bon tour
The circuit of Cap Bon from Hammamet takes about seven hours and passes some splendid scenery inland: Kelibia's castle, Kerkouane's Punic ruins, El Haouaria's Roman quarry and the spa of Korbous.

Right: the modern town and harbour of Port el Kantaoui
Below: in the peaceful Cap Bon hinterland the call to prayer still rules farmers' lives

agriculture, in traditional crafts like pottery at Nabeul, the drying of chillies, cumin and other spices at Lebna, and in the cutting of limestone near El Haouaria. The Arabs neglected agriculture to begin with and the arrival of migratory tribes from the east is blamed for a crisis on the land which was only rectified with the arrival of refugees from Andalusia. There are more obvious historical reminders in the towns, with their *ribats* (fortified monasteries) built soon after the Arab conquest, and the monumental walls and fortresses from the age of the corsairs, when the struggle between Christianity and Islam spilled out of Spain and across the Mediterranean.

Cap Bon and the Sahel today At the end of the 19th century, Hammamet must have looked very much the way Barbarossa would have remembered it when he used to hang around the harbour nearly 400 years earlier. It was that sense of timelessness, as well as the beautiful sweep of the bay, the lushness of the ground and the perfection of the beach, that attracted a group of wealthy European holidaymakers. Where the people of Hammamet counted foreigners in their dozens in the 1920s, today they count them in the tens of thousands. That long swathe of beach has now been infringed upon – although nowhere near as intensively or insensitively as

Old wine
The Phoenicians were skilled wine-makers and the Romans were happy to continue that tradition. The arrival of the Arabs, banned by Islam from drinking alcohol, brought the industry to an end, although grapes continued to be grown in quantity in Tunisia. The French revived the tradition, and both profit-oriented colonists and zealous missionaries helped improve the quality. Although the vines suffered an attack of phylloxera virus earlier this century, cuttings were grafted onto New World imports. Cap Bon continues to produce the bulk of the country's average annual output of 30 million litres.

Quintessentially Mediterranean
'Nearby is the town Enfidaville, where the youthful André Gide had a remarkable initiation into amatory experience, and came to Hammamet on the sea, which the Romans called Pupput. Here is a modern house often called by connoisseurs the most beautiful in the world. Hammamet, like Taormina, is a minor capital for sophisticated ex-patriates. Everything about this part of Tunisia is quintessentially Mediterranean. We passed on to Sousse, where many Maltese live today, and which was the Roman Hadrumetum; Caesar landed here in 46 BC. Further south is Sfax, which the novelist Robert Firbank thought was the most beautiful city in the world.' From *Inside Africa* by John Gunther (1955).

at many other major Mediterranean resorts. Damage has, however, been done elsewhere along the coast, in places like Sousse, where back-to-back hotels have overwhelmed what was until recently a sleepy town centred around a picturesque *medina*. But in spite of this – and the fact that many people in this region are dependent on tourism for their livelihood – go slowly, talk to people, get as far from the well-trodden track as you can and you may catch a glimpse of the qualities that first attracted foreigners to Tunisia early in the 20th century.

Kelibia's fishermen set out at night to catch fish, attracting them with lamps

The wild beauty of the Roman quarry caves near El Haouaria makes them worthy of a detour

▶▶   **Cap Bon**   *100B5*

Tunisia's north-eastern peninsula reaches out to nearby Sicily (only 140km away), to which it was linked long ago. With soft landscapes of vineyards, citrus groves and rolling green fields, it feels in many ways more like southern Europe than North Africa. Phoenician nobles possessed large farms and vineyards on the peninsula and Rome depended heavily on its produce. Even today the region relies as much on its agriculture as on the tourism concentrated along its southern edge at Nabeul (see pages 118–19) and Hammamet (see pages 106–11).

The setting of the Roman quarry caves at El Haouaria▶ (*Open* summer daily 8–7. Rest of year daily 8.30–5.30. *Admission charge* cheap), on the sea's edge opposite the island of Zembra, is wild and truly spectacular. Some 24 caves provide the orangey brown limestone that was used for decorative carving in Carthage, El Jem and throughout the empire. Local guides usually point out the main cave, Ghar el Kebir, where a camel has been sculpted out of the rock. The village itself is famous for falconry. Villagers capture young peregrine falcons on the cliffs in March or April and train them for competitions that take place during the Falconry Festival in June. It is said that the birds are released after that, but many people keep at least one all year round.

The dull road north from Nabeul to Kelibia passes Korba village, on the site of Roman Curubis, and Lebna, which smells of hot *harissa* and spices thanks to the Warda spice factory. Barrel-vaulted farm buildings hide hot red peppers, tomatoes and other vegetables, while flamingos and other wading birds go about their business in the lagoons and marshes near the road. The small village of Kelibia▶▶ offers some welcome peace and quiet after the crowded resorts. The 7th-century **Byzantine fortress** (tel: 02 296 318. *Open* summer daily 8–7. Rest of year 8.30–5. *Admission charge* cheap) has been well restored and commands stunning views over the region. The popular Café Sidi el-Bahri (see page 201) on the western edge of the harbour is perfect for a cup of tea and a water-pipe as you sit watching the bigger fishing boats tow the smaller ones out to sea late in the afternoon. The fishermen work at night, using power lamps to catch sardines, anchovies and mackerel.

Kerkouane▶▶ (tel: 02 294 033. *Open* summer Tue–Sun 9–7. Rest of year Tue–Sun 9–4.30. Closed Mon. *Admission charge* cheap) is an impressive example of a purely Punic town. Thought to have been founded in the 5th century BC, it has probably been particularly well preserved because it was abandoned after the fall of Carthage. The whole site is beautifully tended, with pretty gardens lining the approach path and the sign of the moon goddess Tanit laid out in flowers. The town plan and house foundations are clearly visible, and it is easy to imagine what life must have been like. The houses, with central courtyards, show a remarkable degree of sophistication – some have well-preserved bathrooms in pink cement. It is estimated that around 2,500 people lived here, mostly involved in manufacturing a precious purple dye from decomposed shellfish. The small yet interesting museum has good Carthaginian pottery and jewellery. The site is right on the sea, which is too rocky for swimming, but makes a scenic spot for a picnic.

The scenic road from El Haouaria is probably the best thing about a visit to the spa town of **Korbous**▶▶. After rolling fields the road suddenly descends to the coast, where the hot sulphurous spring of Aïn el-Atrous gushes into the sea. The resort has four other springs, already in use during Roman times. The town has pretty white-washed houses and a relaxed atmosphere, although most visitors are attracted by the restorative qualities of the water.

Local markets
● Monday: Kelibia.
● Thursday: Hammamet, El Haouaria.
● Friday: Nabeul.
● Sunday: Korba, Beni Khiar, Dar Chaabane.

A sea of blood
The industrial fishing port of Sidi Daoud, facing the islands of Zembra and Zembretta at the tip of the peninsula, is a desolate place for most of the year. Like Sicily across the water, Sidi Daoud is famous for the age-old but cruel tradition of La Matanza, held during the tuna's spawning season from May to the end of June. After trapping tunas in huge nets, fishermen bring the fish to the surface to harpoon them, turning the sea red in the process. The tuna, which can weigh up to 250kg, are loaded onto the boats and canned within hours.

105

Kelibia's fortress encapsulates a summary of the town's history: Roman capitals and bastion, Byzantine walls, Turkish barracks and a French lighthouse

Hot love
'Those peppers! An adult Arab will eat two pounds of them a day. I have seen a native woman devouring, alternately, a pepper, then a date ... and so on for half an hour.' From *Fountains in the Sand* by Norman Douglas (1912).

A view of old Hammamet – although these traditional houses are now mostly hidden by large hotels

Tea at the kasbah
The kasbah museum has little to offer, but the Moorish café on top of the ramparts is one of the most relaxing places in town to while away the afternoon drinking tea as you watch the sea and the fishermen at work.

▶▶▶ Hammamet 100B4

The once sleepy fishing village of Hammamet is now one of Tunisia's leading resorts and is also arguably its most pleasant. Here, unlike in Sousse tourist development has been carefully controlled and efforts have been made to preserve the town's character. Nevertheless, this is a major resort that is swamped by European tourists in summer.

The Romans first settled nearby Pupput in the 2nd century AD (see page 110), and subsequently Normans, Hafsids, corsairs and others came and went with the usual battles and bloodshed. Hammamet became notorious in Europe, under the name of 'Mahometta', when in 1605 the Muslim population fled when they saw ten galleons from Sicily and Malta coming to land, only to send back 100 men, unseen, who massacred the 1,100 invaders.

When the French marched into town in 1881, the commanding officer was so enamoured with the place that he resigned and decided to spend the rest of his days here. In the 1920s the Romanian millionaire George Sebastian similarly fell in love with it and proceeded to build a sumptuous villa, now the Centre International Culturel (see opposite). Other wealthy Europeans and Americans then followed his lead, building and laying out exotic gardens, most of which have been incorporated into the bigger beach hotels. After George Sebastian invited his friends Paul Klee, André Gide and Bernanos to his house, Hammamet became a hang-out and inspiration for an influential artists' community.

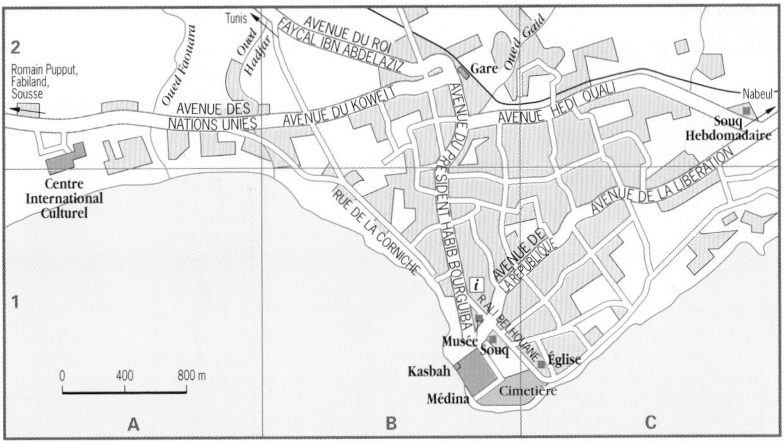

The map shows Hammamet with labels: Tunis, AVENUE DU ROI FAYCAL IBN ABDELAZIZ, Oued Feouara, Oued Hadjar, Gare, Oued Guid, Nabeul, Romain Pupput, Fabiland, Sousse, AVENUE DES NATIONS UNIES, AVENUE DU KOWEIT, AVENUE HEDI OUALI, Souq Hebdomadaire, Centre International Culturel, RUE DE LA CORNICHE, AVENUE DU PRESIDENT HABIB BOURGUIBA, AVENUE DE LA LIBERATION, AVENUE DE LA REPUBLIQUE, R.N. BEL HOUANE, i, Musée, Souq, Église, Kasbah, Médina, Cimetière, 0 400 800 m, A, B, C

The *medina*►►► sits on the headland, dividing Hammamet's beach areas in two. The ramparts were first erected in AD 904, but their present shape is attributed to the 13th-century Hafsid ruler Abu Zakaria. The Bab es-Souq (Market Gate), the main entrance to the *medina*, leads into the busy *souq* street, which is now lined with souvenir shops. The first turning on the left leads to a little square, now also taken over by the tourist trade, and from here left and off to the right are, respectively, the **Turkish bath►** (*Open* men: mornings; women: afternoons) and the **Great Mosque►** (closed to visitors). It is worth wandering off into the quieter alleys of the *medina*, where many doors are decorated with good-luck fish or the hand of Fatima, Prophet Muhammad's daughter.

For a closer look follow the signpost to **Dar Hammamet►►** (tel: 02 281 206. *Open* daily 8.30–7.30. *Admission charge* moderate), a traditional house with a collection of costumes and wedding dowries from all over the country. The **kasbah►►** (*Open* summer daily 9–1, 3–7. Rest of year daily 8.30–5.30. *Admission charge* cheap), entered via a colossal ramp, has commanding views over the *medina* and the sea. The beaches on either side are among Tunisia's best, although the southern ones are more sheltered.

The house of Hammamet's first millionaire, George Sebastian, has now been turned into the **Centre International Culturel►►►** (tel: 02 280 065. *Open* daily 8.30–7. *Admission charge* cheap), 2km from the centre on avenue des Nations Unies. The ground floor has an art gallery, and the centre hosts an annual summer festival of music and drama as well as cultural conferences. The gardens are worth exploring, full of little paths, hidden treasures and peaceful corners for a picnic, while a café opens in the summer next to the lovely pool.

Continued on page 110

Market day
A daily fruit, vegetable, meat and fish market is held near the restaurant de la Poste, on Hammamet's central square. The Souq el Khemis, the weekly market, is held on Thursdays in the El Haouanet district around avenue de la République. This lively, interesting and ever-expanding market, which actually starts on Wednesday afternoons, still feels fairly authentic.

107

The splendours of George Sebastian's seafront villa were enjoyed by the likes of Anthony Eden and Erwin Rommel, as well as by writers and artists such as André Gide and Paul Klee

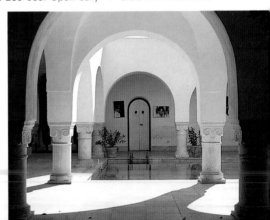

■ **The olive tree is both food and livelihood for many Tunisians, as it has been for thousands of years. The Phoenicians imported it, but it was the Romans who made it big business. Today there are olive groves as far as the eye can see from Cap Bon down to the Gulf of Gabès.** ■

Olive harvest
As olives need to be picked as soon as they are ready, labour is always in short supply at harvest time. Information about assisting in the olive harvest, which takes place around November, can be obtained from the Syndicat d'Initiative, place de l'Indépendance, Sfax (tel: 04 224 606).

108

Most of the land in the Sahel region is dedicated to olive groves, which stretch as far as the eye can see

Some history The Romans didn't rate olive oil for human consumption, but used it for oil lamps, heating, cooking and to oil wheels. It was Tunisia's second most important asset after wheat, but after grain production dropped it became one of Tunisia's largest exports, as it is today. The theatre of El Jem (see page 115), which could seat 35,000 people, suggests the value of the trade, for it was with profits from olives that it was built. The olive tree is also of great importance in Islam, where it is associated with the Prophet Muhammad, with light and with virility.

How it grows There are more than 50 varieties of olive trees in Tunisia, and some 21 million trees in all. New trees take 15 years to yield their first crop; after that, in a normal year, a tree bears 50kg of fruit. In years of drought, the trees usually survive but don't produce fruit, which spells disaster for the Sahelis.

Young green olives or mature black ones taste bitter straight from the tree, so they are soaked in water for one or two weeks, and then preserved in brine. After that they are usually kept in olive oil with herbs, garlic, preserved lemons or *harissa*. To make oil, the olives are packed into bags and pressed three times. The first pressing produces superior oil and the second common oil, while the third is used locally for cooking or making soap. There is no waste – even the olive stones are used to make soap.

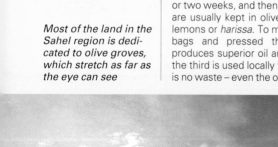

 **From Hammamet to Thuburbo Majus**

See map on page 100.

A relaxing drive inland, with fine rural scenery. Allow 4–5 hours, including time for visits and a picnic (approximately 150km).

Leave Hammamet on the main road out towards Tunis. At the motorway junction, where the Tunis sign points right, follow the Zaghouan sign and cross straight over the top of the motorway. A little further on, follow the sign towards Hammam Jedidi. Before long, the imposing hill-mountain of Jebel Zaghouan appears straight ahead.

   After arriving in **Zaghouan**►► (see page 111) follow the signpost to 'Centre Ville' and head for the picturesque centre of town. At 1.2km from the signpost, turn left at the pharmacy and drive up the steep hill through the old part of town. Once at the top, take the first street to the right and continue downhill as far as the crossroads. Go straight over the crossroads and climb again, following the signs for **Temple des Eaux**

Above: imposing Jebel Zaghouan

(Temple of the Waters). The site has a pleasant café-pizzeria as well as plenty of shade for picnics.

   Returning to the main road, follow the signpost for Tunis. After 4km take the fork marked 'El Fahs' and, once there, keep following the Tunis road. About 2.5km past El Fahs, follow the sign left towards the Roman site of Thuburbo Majus. After 1km another rusty sign on the right points to the site. After visiting **Thuburbo Majus**►► (see pages 110–11), return to the main road and continue northwards to Tunis. Soon after the fork back to Zaghouan, the road passes through the unmistakable arches of the well-preserved aqueduct that fed Roman Carthage with water from Zaghouan. After climbing in the aqueduct, continue to Muhammadia, where you will see more stretches of the aqueduct as well as the ruins of a 19th-century palace rising above the houses to the left. Follow the road towards Tunis, then return to Hammamet along the motorway.

Capitoline temple ruins, Thuburbo Majus

The Roman baths
During a visit to the baths, the cold room (frigidarium) was the first stop. Bathers then went via the tepid room (tepidarium) into the hottest room (caldarium) for a massage. Heating was provided by a system of pipes in the walls and floors (hypocaust). After ablutions, bathers returned to the frigidarium before getting dressed in the atrium.

Pegasus carving, Thuburbo Majus

Continued from page 107

Hammamet environs The half-day excursion on horse-back to the peaceful dry river bed of **Oued Faouara▶** can be a welcome alternative to another day on the beach. Horses can be arranged by hotels and the tourist office, or hired in front of Hotel Fouarti in Bir Bou Regba (guides also available). Several kilometres up the river bed is a small waterfall, where the spring-fed stream runs over some old Roman stones, thought to be the remains of an aqueduct. One of the spurs above the valley held the sanctuary of Thinissut, a Roman temple dedicated to the Punic gods Baal Hammon and Tanit. Several terracotta statues were found here, now on display in the Musée du Bardo in Tunis (see pages 54–6) and in the museum in Nabeul (see page 119).

Not much remains of the Roman site of **Pupput▶** (*Open* summer daily 8–1, 3–7. Rest of year daily 8.30–5.30. *Admission charge* cheap), now squeezed between the Samira Club and the Tanfous Hotel 6km south-west of Hammamet on the Sousse road, but it makes for a pleasant stroll along the beach. Pupput was just a small Roman settlement until the 2nd century AD, but by the time of the Byzantines it had become an important stronghold. The fine mosaics on display came from 4th-century Christian tombs, while the baths also have mosaic flooring. The Roman villas below have courtyards with fountains, dining rooms, some interesting mosaic floors and underground cisterns.

Thuburbo Majus▶▶ (*Open* summer daily 8–7. Rest of year daily 8.30–5.30. *Admission charge* cheap) 67km west of Hammamet (see also page 109), is rightly considered one of Tunisia's great Roman sites, with impressive ruins set in a lovely valley backed by hills. Probably founded in the 5th century BC by Berbers, the settlement was colonised by the Phoenicians before the Romans arrived in 27 BC. Like many other Roman towns in Tunisia, Thuburbo Majus reached its peak during the reign of Hadrian (2nd century AD) and started its decline with the Vandal invasion in 407.

Just beyond the entrance the colossal Corinthian columns of the Capitol temple appear. The temple, one of the largest in Africa, was dedicated to the three chief Roman deities: Jupiter, Juno and Minerva. Fragments of Jupiter's 7m-high decapitated statue are now in the Musée du Bardo in Tunis. Past the forum is the Temple of Mercury, the god of money and commerce, with eight columns set in a circle. Not much remains of the forum itself, but the vast Summer Baths had several pools and attractive mosaics. A line of columns flanks the Palaestra of the Petronii, an exercise courtyard where the famous mosaic of obese boxers was found, again now in the Musée du Bardo. Further uphill are the Winter Baths, with well-preserved black and white mosaic flooring. These baths provide about the only shady place on the site, making an excellent picnic spot. From the small temple of Baalat there is a panoramic view over the whole site.

Zaghouan▶▶ (see also page 109), a large agricultural centre built at the foot of Jebel Zaghouan (1,295m), has charm in the form of picturesque squares and narrow, cobbled streets. It was from here, ancient Zita, that the 100km-long aqueduct collected water for Carthage. Some arches are still visible along the Tunis road.

In the centre of Zaghouan is the white **Mosque of Sidi Azouz**, with a *zaouia* (shrine) next to it. Just above the road, a triumphal arch is surrounded by popular cafés. The main attraction, however, is the Roman **Temple des Eaux (Temple of the Waters)**, 1km out of the centre, built by the Emperor Hadrian in AD 130 to honour the nymph of the spring and to secure a steady flow of water to Carthage. This agreeable site has been badly restored, but it is a pleasant walk from town none the less.

Useful addresses
● Office du Tourisme: avenue du President Habib Bourguiba, opposite the beach (tel: 02 280 423. *Open* hours vary).
● Hertz: avenue des Hôtels (tel: 02 280 187).

More baths
Some 5km from Zaghouan on the road to Enfida is Hammam Zriba, with hot mineral baths said to cure skin conditions. Housed in a pretty domed building, the baths are popular with locals. The road leading up to them is lined with food and drink stalls.

111

The pleasant hill town of Zaghouan, with its cobbled streets, red rooftops and forested slopes

Roman Africa

■ For two or three centuries from 30 BC onwards, Africa Proconsularis was both the most politically stable province of the Roman Empire and one of its most important, providing two-thirds of the grain it needed and a third of its senators. ■

Tunisia's grandest Roman sites
● Carthage: the remains of the second city (see pages 60–5).
● Dougga (see pages 131–2).
● Sbeïtla (see page 153).
● Amphitheatre and excellent museum at El Jem (see page 115).
● Underground villas at Bulla Regia (see page 90).
● Thuburbo Majus (see pages 110–11).

Because of its sheer size and magnificent setting, the well-preserved Roman site at ancient Thugga (Dougga) is one of Tunisia's highlights

Africa Proconsularis After the victory over Carthage in the 2nd century BC, the Romans founded the province of Africa Proconsularis. In 46 BC Julius Caesar defeated an alliance of Cato and the Numidian king, Juba I, and annexed most of Numidia, calling it Africa Nova. Carthage was then refounded as a colony for destitute and landless Romans as well as decommissioned soldiers. During several bloody campaigns the frontiers moved progressively further south and west. At the height of the empire (AD 37–235) the province had over 8 million inhabitants.

Africa Proconsularis was ruled by a governor in Carthage, who travelled around the province to oversee the administration and collect taxes. A fifth of the fertile lands were taken as imperial estates, which were then run by their own curators. Continuous border problems were solved by creating a border region, or *limes*, on the edge of the desert where former legionaries were settled on farms. That way, trade could continue but if there was a problem an army was quickly gathered.

An African emperor Under the Roman Empire African citizens were free to work their way up to senior administrative positions, some of them even becoming Roman senators. One such citizen, Septimius Severus, became the first African emperor. Born in Leptis Magna, in modern-day Libya, he maintained an interest in the African province, and after his accession in AD 193 he steadily expanded the empire. However, all his

Roman Africa

achievements are now often overshadowed by the debate on how black his skin really was. Was it fair? Or was it as black as it is portrayed in African history books?

Opulent towns North Africa had hundreds of towns and cities, in which rich and powerful local landlords displayed their wealth by erecting grand public buildings in their name. Most of these towns were built to a set pattern, with the rectangular, paved courtyard of the forum acting as a centre. The major religious building was the Capitoline temple, always set above the forum. The Capitoline was dedicated to the three chief Roman gods: Jupiter (god of city and state), his wife Juno (protectress of the people) and Minerva (protectress of wealth and commerce).

All self-respecting towns had at least one set of baths, impressive structures with vaulted ceilings and elaborate mosaic flooring. Like the hammam (see page 120) they were not just for hygiene, but were also social centres where all levels of society would mix for a nominal fee. The towns were linked by excellent roads and bridges designed to facilitate trade.

Roman architecture The majority of the surviving Roman buildings in Tunisia were built or rebuilt in the 2nd and 3rd centuries AD, at the peak of Rome's imperial power. Imperial architecture was already well developed when the Romans arrived in Tunisia and it was very little influenced by Tunisian traditions. The only noticeable concession to the indigenous traditions of worship was the addition to temples of a small shrine in an open-air enclosure, as in Dougga (see pages 131–2). Most Roman buildings appear to have been built by local masons, since studies have shown that they were planned according to the Carthaginian ell (51.4cm) rather than Roman measurements. Artistically, Roman Africa's greatest legacy is its mosaics (see pages 88–9), which were of a higher standard than was reached anywhere else in the empire.

The gigantic amphitheatre at El Jem

Saturn worship
Saturn was an important cult figure in Tunisia – there are more than 100 known sites where he was worshipped. Very few of these sites have been excavated, but a dig at Aïn Tougga near Testour yielded over 500 stelae inscribed by worshippers, each giving details of their sacrifice. In front of the central sanctuary at the Temple of Saturn in Dougga (see page 131) is a pair of crudely carved footprints. These once held the god's footprints in metal, believed to be the marks Saturn left after visiting the temple.

By the end of the 2nd century AD most large cities in Tunisia had mosaic workshops

Beaches on Kerkennah
Most of the islands' hotels are on the beach in Sidi Frej, which is only sandy in front of the Grand Hotel. The most stunning beach is undoubtedly Sidi Fankhal, a few kilometres from Er Remla, but it is hard to reach as there are no buses. Bounouma (near Ech Chergui) and Berdimes (further on towards Kraten) are two great deserted beaches.

▶▶ Iles Kerkennah (Kerkennah Islands)   *100C2*

There are seven islands in the group, 20km east of Sfax and mostly covered in fields and palm groves. They are reached by Sonotrak ferries (tel: 04 222 216) from Sfax port: a minimum four departures per day in winter, with services almost every two hours in summer and more frequently during weekends (journey time is one hour). The ferry lands in Sidi Youssef on the island of Gharbi (Arabic for 'Western'), connected by a Roman causeway to the biggest island of Chergui ('Eastern'). Wonderful, underexploited beaches are the islands' main attractions. Tourism is only a recent development, concentrated mostly around Sidi Frej and Er Remla on Chergui. As the islands are small and flat (neither is higher than 10m), the ideal way to get around is to rent a bicycle from Hotel Farhat in Sidi Frej (tel: 04 281 240).

Cut palm fronds, used locally to make fish traps

Gladiators
Some of the most important shows at El Jem were of gladiators fighting each other or facing wild animals. Some gladiators were professionals at killing animals, not unlike today's Spanish matadors. Before a fight they paraded in their fine clothes and gave the famous collective salute to the presiding magistrate: *'Ave, morituri te salutant '*, or 'Hail, we who are about to die salute you.' Famous gladiators often came out alive, but most were thrown to the wild beasts at dawn.

The 15,000 islanders are reputed to be the friendliest people in the country, and their speciality fish and seafood dishes, especially those involving squid, are also excellent. Most islanders depend on fishing for their livelihood and still use some ancient techniques. The traditional method called *sautade* involves hitting the sea with palm-tree fronds to chase the fish (usually mullet) into baskets placed on the sea-bed in shallow water. It is quite an interesting spectacle to watch and for a small payment many fishermen will take you along for the ride.

Feluccas, or sailing boats, are another of the islands' typical attractions. Now restored to preserve the centuries-old tradition of boat-building, they are rented out with a captain for trips around the island (for more information, ask at the Grand Hotel or Hotel Farhat in Sidi Frej, in Er Remla or in El Ataya). Apart from this, there is little to do here apart from relax on the beach, indulge in a few watersports and enjoy!

▶▶▶ El Jem *100B2*

The small town of El Jem would be of little interest if it wasn't for its magnificent **amphitheatre** (*Open* summer daily 7–7. Rest of year daily 8–5.30. *Admission charge* expensive), which is better preserved than the building on which it was modelled: the Colosseum in Rome. El Jem was part of ancient Thysdrus, one of the richest cities in Roman Tunisia, home to some 40,000 people at its peak in the 2nd century AD. The olive tree created the city's wealth, but was also the cause of its destruction. Thysdrus went into decline in 238 when El Jem's citizens objected to high taxes on olive-oil sales; the emperor responded by having the city sacked. A couple of centuries later, invading Arabs set fire to the olive groves.

The theatre is 149m long by 124m wide, with seating tiers that rise 36m. In its heyday it could seat up to 35,000 spectators. Construction began in the 2nd century AD, probably under Emperor Gordien I, but due to political instability and a shortage of funds it was never completed. It is interesting to note that the amphitheatre's measurements correspond to the Punic unities, not Roman, which suggests that it was built by locals. The spectacles on show were pretty bloody, which was the fashion of the day: instead of gladiatorial combats, people wanted to watch slaves, Christians and criminals being thrown to the lions. Later, it was used as a fortress, and legend has it that for three years it became the stronghold of El Kahina, the woman who, in the 7th century, led the Berbers against the invading Arabs (see box on page 34).

It is worth staying overnight at the Relais Julius (see page 196) to watch the theatre glowing at dawn or at dusk. The ticket to the amphitheatre also allows entry to the museum on the outskirts of El Jem, a reconstruction of a Roman villa that houses some superb mosaics of wild animals, bringing the savagery of the theatre spectacles to life. The village of El Jem has a colourful market on Mondays and the theatre stages a music festival in June (for information, tel: 03 690 714/790).

The amphitheatre at El Jem was used as a fortress until 1695

Despite being raided by local builders for stone, the theatre remains in better condition than the Colosseum in Rome, on which it was modelled

Walk Mahdia

See route on map opposite.

Mahdia has a long history and, as yet, has not become too over-whelmed by tourists. Allow 1½ hours (approximately 1½km).

Begin the stroll on the broad prome-nade in front of the triangular fishing harbour with its hundreds of colourful fishing boats. Walk on to the main square and cross over to enter the *medina* by the massive gateway known as **Skifa el Kahla (Dark Passage)►►►**.

By carrying straight on from the gate you will reach a little street lined with souvenir and other shops and, after 100m, the atmospheric place du Caire. A refreshment stop in one of the cafés opposite the lovely façade of the **Mosquée Mustapha Hamza►** is a must here. Continue straight along the road to the next square

facing the **Grande Mosquée (Great Mosque)►►►**, then stroll out along the narrow coastal road towards the **Borj el Kebir (Big Tower)►►**. Just before the tower, look out on the left of the road for the scant remains of an excavated Fatimid palace.

Beyond the tower, the rocky head-land is covered with simple tombs, part of a Muslim cemetery that reaches towards the sea. The inden-tation in the rocky shoreline, where a few boats still bob, marks the old Fatimid port, originally closed off by a chain suspended between two small towers at each end of the curve. Out on the headland is the Phare, an attractive lighthouse on the site of a Fatimid tower. Near by are some rock-cut tombs, probably Phoenician in origin. Walk back towards the port along narrow rue Cap d'Afrique, passing some of the lovely houses of the whitewashed *medina*.

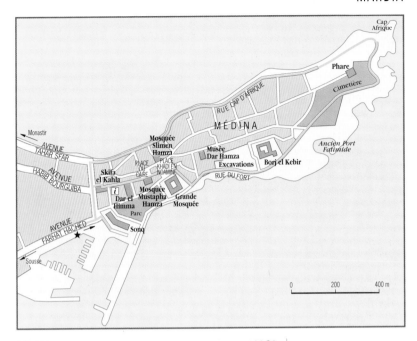

▶▶▶ Mahdia
100C3

Mahdia (see also walk opposite) is the most picturesque town on the Sahel coast, and has a lively fishing harbour. Although beach hotels are multiplying in the *zone touristique*, the town seems to have remained unspoiled and has preserved its traditional Tunisian character.

The Fatimids under Caliph Ubayd Allah built Mahdia on an easily defensible headland in 916 as the capital of Ifriqiya. In 945 the city survived an eight-month siege by Abu Yazid, who, when he was subsequently captured, was flayed, stuffed with straw and hung as a toy for the caliph's monkeys. In 969 the Fatimids moved to Cairo, leaving the Zirids as governors. In the 11th century the city changed hands between Christians and Muslims. Known by then as Cape Africa, for seven centuries it remained one of the wealthiest cities on the Barbary coast.

The gate known as **Skifa el Kahla (Dark Passage)▶▶▶**, part of the original 10th-century fortifications, guards the entrance to the *medina*. In the 1960s a perfect copy of the 10th-century Fatimid **Grande Mosquée (Great Mosque)▶▶▶** (rue du Fort; closed to non-Muslims) was re-erected, the original having completely disappeared. The monumental entrance gate in its otherwise plain façade was only used by the caliph and his family, while the austere interior is typical of early Fatimid architecture. The impressive 16th-century fortress of **Borj el Kebir (Big Tower)▶▶**, on rue du Fort (*Open* Mon–Sat 8–12, 3–7. *Admission charge* cheap), was built by the Turks. There are wonderful views from the tower over the town, old Fatimid port and cemetery.

The doorways, narrow streets and alleys of Mahdia offer a unique insight into traditional medina life

These days it's hard to find an empty space in the shade on Monastir's crowded beach

No expense was spared by President Bourguiba when building a sumptuous mausoleum in the town of his birth

▶▶ **Monastir** 100B3

The city where former President Bourguiba was born in 1903 has since become a major beach resort. Bourguiba wanted his city to be more beautiful than all others, but in the process, Monastir lost most of its charm and atmosphere. The beach hotels are mainly in Skanès, and although there is a good beach in town it is often crowded.

Monastir's history dates back to the Phoenicians, while under the Romans it was a major military base known as Ruspina. The *ribat*▶▶▶ (tel: 03 461 272. *Open* May–Sep, Tue–Sun 9–12, 2.30–6. Oct–Apr, Tue–Sun 2–5.30. *Admission charge* moderate), on route de la Corniche, was built in AD 796 by Harthema ibnou Ayyoun as part of the Arab coastal defence system against the Berbers inland and the Christians to the north (see page 143). More recently it was used as a film set for Monty Python's *Life of Brian* and Zeffirelli's *Life of Christ*. The prayer hall is now the small Museum of Islamic Art, with displays of calligraphy, Persian and Mogul miniatures, jewellery and lustreware.

From the tower there are good views over the town: note the yellow-stone Mosque of Sidi Ali el-Mezzeri (now closed), housing the tomb of a local saint who was reputed to cure sick children. Connected to the *ribat*'s southern gate is the 9th-century Great Mosque. North of the *ribat* is the lavish Bourguiba family mausoleum, topped with a large gold dome and approached by a processional avenue cut through the cemetery of Sidi el-Mezzeri. The *medina*, fronted by the grand Bourguiba Mosque (built in 1963), has definitely lost its soul, although its tidy streets lined with souvenir shops make for a pleasant stroll.

▶▶ **Nabeul** 100B4

Like nearby Hammamet (see pages 106–11), Nabeul has good sandy beaches that unfortunately are lined with too many beach hotels.

The town is rather dull and unattractive, its main draw being its pottery workshops, these offering a wide selection of items at reasonable prices. A small **archaeological museum**▶ (*Open* summer Tue–Sun 8–12, 3–7. Rest of year Tue–Sun 9.30–4.30. *Admission charge* cheap) at 44 avenue Bourguiba displays local finds, including Carthaginian sculpture and Roman mosaics. Little remains of the Roman city of **Neapolis**▶ (located near Club Aquarius. *Admission* free) except traces of a palace. On Fridays several streets in the centre of town are blocked off for the 'camel market' (*Admission charge* moderate), where tourists far outnumber the animals.

▶ **Port el Kantaoui** *100B3*

Meaning 'May Everything Go Well' in Arabic, Port el Kantaoui was created in the late 1970s as a beach resort centred around a lively and well-equipped marina. Most hotels at this elegant resort took their inspiration from Tunisia's traditional architecture, with the addition of sumptuous gardens and swimming-pools. Its white houses with their blue balconies are not unlike those at Sidi Bou Said. You'll either love it or hate it, but at least have a drink on a terrace facing the yacht harbour.

▶▶ **Sfax** *100B2*

Tunisia's busiest harbour and second-largest city is rarely visited except by those taking a ferry to the Kerkennah Islands (see page 114) or heading south. Most of the ever-expanding and polluted industrial city is unappealing, but the *medina* is one of the most relaxed in the country. Here it is possible to walk, without any hassle, around the entire inner circuit of the walls, passing some wonderful houses and palaces, workshops and delightful *souqs*

Continued on page 121

Nabeul's pottery
Tunisia's tradition of pottery dates back to antiquity, but in terms of decoration it owes its greatest debt to the Turks, Italians, Andalusians and Arabs. The two main centres of production, Nabeul and Guellala (on Jerba), produce very different styles of pottery. While the Jerbans specialise in amphorae and terracotta 'gadgets', many with Berber motifs, the potters of Nabeul, also originally from Guellala, were influenced by the Andalusians, who in the 17th century brought with them the art of lead glazing. Stone-carvers in the suburb of Dar Chaabane are famous all over the country for their finely carved limestone pillars and door lintels.

119

Despite being a major industrial town, Sfax has retained an animated medina *within its well-preserved walls*

■ In a country where private bathrooms are in short supply but where personal hygiene is taken seriously, the hammam, *bain maure* or Turkish bath plays an important role. Until quite recently a city was often judged by the beauty and grandeur of its hammam. And once again it all started with the Romans. ■

What to take

Going to the hammam is a unique experience and recommended for everyone keen to learn more about the Tunisians. Every town has its hammam: just ask the staff at your hotel where to find it. Take your own towel, soap, a hairbrush and flip-flops (although a few places rent these out). The following hammams are particularly recommended:

● Kachachine: rue des Libraires, Médina, Tunis. Men only; amazing décor.
● Halfaouine: rue Sidi Chiccha, near Bab Souika, Tunis. Women only.
● rue Ali Belhouane, Sidi Bou Said. Very clean.
● Sfaxi: rue du 7 Novembre, La Marsa. Excellent.
● Sidi Bouraoui: *medina* in Sousse.
● Sidi Brahim: 17 rue de Bizerte, next to the taxi station of Sidi Brahim, in Houmt Souk, Jerba.

Right: exotic hammam interior
Below: entrances are not always marked

Not just a bath Roman baths were the predecessors of the hammam, but where the prudish Judeo-Christian culture in the West considered them places of debauchery, Muslims found them useful to perform their total ablutions as prescribed in the Koran. The hammam was just as importantly a place to socialise. For many women it was the only outing allowed and, given the widespread use of haiks (veils) outside and the state of undress within the hammam, it was also the only way mothers could judge potential wives for their sons.

The works The hammam has two distinctive areas: the *mahras*, a central patio lined with *doukkanas* (benches), which functions as changing room and rest room; and another area consisting of three hot rooms. These are the Bit el-Barad (tepid), Bit el-Wost (medium hot) and the Bit el-Khum (hot with a hot-water pool). Men bathe in the morning 5 am–noon, women in the afternoon 2–7 pm. Men are sometimes also allowed to bathe for a few hours in the evening, as well as all day on Sunday.

Your turn now Most Tunisians visit the hammam once a week, for pleasure, relaxation and total cleanliness, despite having a bathroom in their house. Total nudity is not the norm and a *fouta* or *pareo* (towel) is worn after getting undressed. After you have built up a sweat in the hot rooms, a masseur (or masseuse for women) will rub off dead skin with a loofah or coarse glove (*tfal*). For delicate skins there is a total body mask and a clay soap, followed by several hot baths. Massages can be quite hard-handed, but your skin feels fantastic afterwards. You then wrap up in several towels and relax with a cup of mint tea.

120

Continued from page 119

(see panel). The 9th-century walls are well preserved, with the 14th-century Bab Diwan forming the main entry point into the *medina*. The interesting minaret of the **Grande Mosquée (Great Mosque)▶▶** (closed to non-Muslims) is not unlike that of the Great Mosque in Kairouan (see page 136).

The splendid 17th-century Dar Jellouli on rue de la Driba houses the **Musée des Arts et Traditions▶▶▶** (tel: 04 211 186. *Open* Tue–Sun 9.30–4.30. *Admission charge* cheap), one of the best such museums in the country. The excellent displays include explanations of Tunisian marriage and fertility rituals, furniture, jewellery and traditional costumes. The **Archaeological Museum▶▶** (tel: 04 229 744. *Open* Mon–Sat 8–1, 3–5.45. *Admission charge* cheap) in the Hôtel de Ville on the corner of avenues Bourguiba and Hedi Chaker merits a visit for its fine mosaics from ancient Taparura, its jewellery and its Roman glass.

▶▶▶ Sousse   100B3

No longer the picturesque whitewashed town George Curzon described in his *Tales of Travel* (see panel), Sousse is Tunisia's third-largest city. As well as being a major industrial port, it has managed to become one of the country's main tourist resorts. As a result, its attractive coastline has suffered from overdevelopment, and a fall in the numbers of visitors in recent years has meant that some hotels have been unable to keep up their standards. Despite this, the old walled *medina* facing the port still has plenty of charm.

Founded in the 9th century BC, Sousse was one of the main Phoenician ports and remained an important commercial centre under the Romans, who called it Hadrumetum. The town was destroyed by the Arabs in the 7th century, but flourished again in the 9th century as the port for Tunisia's then capital, Kairouan. Under the French it was the chief city in the region, and new road, rail and port facilities were built. It was badly damaged during World War II. One of the unusual things about Sousse is the way trains pass straight through the centre and big cargo ships sit in the port, just outside the *medina* walls.

The 9th-century walls around Sousse's *medina*▶▶▶ are still largely intact, except for the breach on place des Martyrs, caused by Allied bombing during World War II. This used to be the Bab el Bahr (Sea Gate), through which Aghlabid boats sailed into the interior harbour, which stretched between the Great Mosque and the *ribat*. With its thick stone walls and towers, the 9th-century **Grande**

Venture off the main streets to enjoy Sousse's medina

Sfax souqs
The Syndicat d'Initiative on place de l'Indépendance in Sfax (tel: 04 224 606. Closed Sun) proposes an interesting route through the *medina* and *souqs*, leaving from the kasbah. The Souq des Etoffes is one of the best places to shop for *kilims*, blankets and haiks (veils), with a very good selection at no 30 in Zribi Ahmed ben Taher's shop. For an idea of prices, visit the government Socopa shop on rue Hammadi Taj (tel: 04 296 826. *Open* summer daily 9–12, 4–7. Rest of year daily 9–12, 3–6).

Old Susa (Sousse)
'Susa ... lay in its glittering garb of whitewash – houses, walls, and roofs all drenched and crusted with the same unmitigated and blinding hue – looking like some great sea-mew preening its snowy plumage on the shore.' From *Tales of Travel* by George Curzon, Marquess of Kedleston (1923).

The simplicity of the architecture of Sousse's Great Mosque may partly be explained by the fact that it was probably converted from a kasbah

Sousse's simple yet impressive ribat

Mosquée (Great Mosque)►► (*Open* Sat–Thu 8–1. Closed Fri. *Admission charge* cheap. Only the courtyard is open; rental of a jellaba is compulsory for those in shorts or miniskirts) on rue el Aghlaba looks more like a fortress than a religious building. The courtyard is pleasingly simple, with a single colonnade of horseshoe arches, above which a line of stylised Koranic inscription is carved. In the corner, a wide stairway leads up to the walls, an octagonal sundial and the 11th-century minaret.

The oldest monument in Sousse is the 8th-century *ribat*►►► (*Open* summer Tue–Sun 8–7. Rest of year Tue–Sun 9–12, 2–6. *Admission charge* moderate) on rue el Aghlaba , a fortified monastery built to protect Muslims from invasion (see page 143). The simple, impressive interior uses materials scavenged from older sites – note, for example, the antique columns on either side of the door. The smaller rooms are the cells of the *murabitun*, or warrior-monks, the larger room on the first floor their prayer hall. The views from the watchtowers over the courtyard of the mosque, the *medina* and the sea are magnificent.

From the *ribat* the rue d'Angleterre leads into the *souqs* which, despite the tourist trade, still have charm, especially further away from the *ribat* and Great Mosque. To the right is Souq el Reba, with fabrics, perfumes and jewellery and a Moorish café; it leads to the lovely, covered Souq el Caïd. A 10th-century domed building on rue Souq el Reba was recently converted into the **Musée de Kalaout el Koubba►►** (*Open* Mon–Thu 9–1, 4–6.30, Sat–Sun 9–2. Closed Fri. *Admission charge* moderate), with displays on the traditional life in the *medina*, now all but disappeared.

At the south-west corner of the *medina*'s ramparts on rue Aboul Kacem ech-Chebbi is the **Kasbah Sousse Museum►►►** (tel: 03 233 695. *Open* summer Tue–Sun 9–12, 3–7. Rest of year Tue–Sun 2–5.30. *Admission*

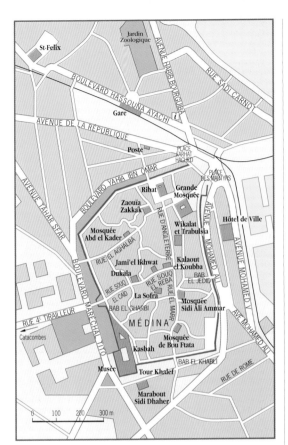

A Turkish bath
Sousse's *medina* has an excellent hammam run by a famous Soussi family: the Grand Bain Maure Sidi Bouraoui, located behind the Mosque of Abd el Kader on rue el Aghlaba. It is open to men from 6am to 1pm and for women from 1 to 7pm.

Burial place
Just 1.5km west of Sousse's centre, off rue Aboul Hamed el-Ghazali, are the Christian Catacombs (*Open* same hours as museum. *Admission charge* cheap), dating from the 2nd and 4th centuries AD. The 250 galleries extend for 5km and contain over 15,000 tombs. Most galleries are closed for repair, but a few reopened in 1996.

charge moderate), now one of the country's most pleasant and interesting museums. The kasbah was built during the 11th century and extended in the 16th century around the old Khalef, a *manar* or signal tower. The attraction of the museum lies in its splendid mosaics, mostly dating from the 3rd and 4th centuries AD and many depicting scenes of the sea. Exhibits, hung in airy rooms around a tranquil flower-filled courtyard, are better displayed than in the Musée du Bardo in Tunis (see pages 54–6). Particularly interesting is the 'Bacchus' Triumph' mosaic in **Room 3**, symbolising the victory over the forces of evil, and in **Room 11** a mosaic depicting the preparations for a gladiatorial battle with a gathering of ostriches, deer, gazelles and asses. On the side wall is a massive statue of Priapus, the male fertility god, his head and erect penis severed by zealous Christians.

If you only visit one museum in Tunisia, let it be the delightful Kasbah Sousse Museum, with a fascinating collection of mosaics displayed in bright, spacious rooms

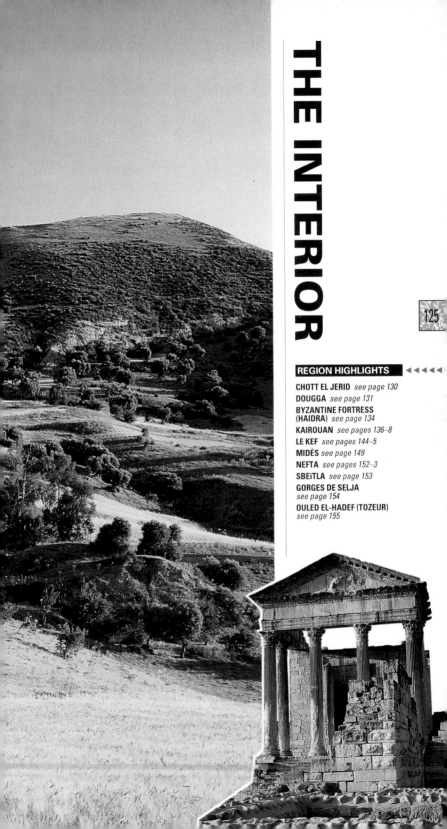

THE INTERIOR

125

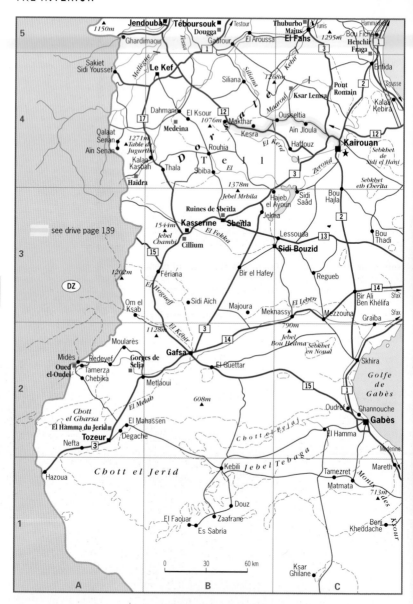

see drive page 139

Previous pages: Roman and Byzantine ruins are scattered across the Tell

Gafsa Man
The species of *Homo sapiens* known as Capsian Man takes its name from Roman Capsa (Gafsa).

The interior Tunisia's interior is a treat, in many ways the most rewarding and certainly the most varied part of the country to visit. The northern half contains Tunisia's spiritual heart, as well as fertile land that supported great cities in antiquity. In the south there are the great natural spectacles of gorges, salt lakes and the gateway to the desert.

Another granary Several parts of North Africa claim the title 'Granary of the Roman Empire'; the northern part of the interior, known as the Tell, is just one. Under the guidance of the Roman Empire, it enjoyed considerable wealth from the production of wheat. The spectacular remains of cities such as Dougga and Sbeïtla are proof of this, while the number of other Roman sites, including Haïdra, also suggests that in the ancient world the Tell was a very desirable place in which to live. As well as producing an abundance of food and drink, the elevation of the Tell meant that summers were usually more bearable than down in the desert. A number of water sources, which provided the means of filling baths in which to cool off, added to the attraction.

The northern part of the Tell has always needed a strong administration to flourish, so it went into decline with the fall of Rome and enjoyed only sporadic moments of revival until the late 19th century. One benefit to interested travellers of the centuries of neglect is that it is here that you are most likely to come into contact with a living past, whether a natural spring made into a bath by the Romans, or an ancient farmhouse that has been built upon but is still recognisable for what it once was.

Holy land The mosque of Kairouan plays a role of great importance in Tunisia. This was the first mosque to be built in Tunisia (by the conquering Arab general, Oqba ibn Nafi, in 671), and thereby gives the country a sense of its significance in Islam. Some Tunisian Muslims believe that by visiting Kairouan several times they will be excused the obligation of making a pilgrimage to Mecca.

Carpet land
Kairouan is the capital of Tunisia's traditional carpet manufacture, with an estimated 12,000 families producing 40,000 carpets a year – or a mere 170,000sq m of carpet. Pay a visit to the Artisanat to get an idea of the variety on offer and the prices to expect, but be aware that carpets are often cheaper elsewhere. Always check that the carpet or rug has an official stamp and try to buy directly from the weavers' souq. Also note that musées des tapis are not museums, just normal shops.

127

Business-minded Tunisians make the most of every opportunity – even in the less visited interior

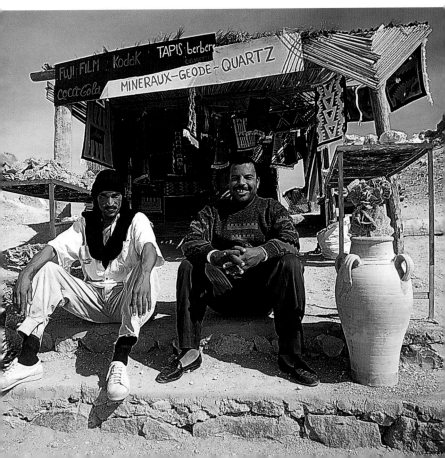

THE INTERIOR

The 'wild west'
The road from Chebika to Tamerza is wonderful, cutting through the mountains, running down canyons and passing an amazing array of landscapes and colours. About 2km before Tamerza, look out for the lovely Grande Cascade, the largest waterfall in the area, with a few cafés and souvenir stalls. The road was built during World War II by Rommel to get his troops out of Chebika, where they were hemmed in by the Allies.

National Sahara Festival
Usually lasting from 23 to 27 December is the National Sahara Festival, held at Douz (see also page 23). It attracts mainly Tunisians who come to see the camel races, camel fights, traditional weddings and Arab poetry competitions. Tourists get lost in the crowds, which is part of the attraction. Ask for information at the tourist office on route de Zaafrane in Douz (tel: 05 470 351. *Open* Mon–Thu 8.30–1, 3–5.45, Fri–Sat 8–1.30; Sun afternoons in summer). Make sure you book a hotel room in advance and be aware that the first day is always the best.

Grazing land The southern part of the Tell doesn't receive enough rain and doesn't have a river like the Mejerda to support regular farming. This is grazing land and was home to nomads. With the arrival of the Arabs in Tunisia, the farmlands of the northern Tell were neglected in favour of the grazing offered to the south, a state of affairs that continued until the French colonised Tunisia and recognised the potential of the north. Some of the grazing lands are being reclaimed thanks to new irrigation schemes, but most of the region remains barren and is sparsely inhabited.

Gorges and *chotts* South of the grazing land, the last of the mountains cut in from the west to create some of Tunisia's most spectacular scenery, from mountainside oases to dramatic gorges. Beyond the gorges, a series of *chotts* (salt lakes) spreads across the country from Algeria to the Mediterranean. The largest of them, the Chott el

Jerid, has given its name to this part of the region. Very little grows around the salt lakes, but several freshwater springs in the region support remarkable, lush oases. This is the beginning of the land of the palm tree, of desert culture and of more dramatic scenery.

'Real Tunisia' The interior has been visited by foreign travellers for as long as any other part of the country, but has never experienced mass tourism. That is until now. Improved transport is opening up the region and bringing its own problems: so many hotels have been built in Tozeur oasis, for example, that there is hardly enough water left to keep the palmery alive. But outside some of the *chott* oases, a lack of facilities continues to hinder tourism. Even in Le Kef, capital of the Tell and a great touring base, hotels and restaurants survive off Tunisian and not foreign trade. For as long as that is the case, this is the region to visit if you are looking for 'unspoiled' Tunisia.

Ignored for centuries, the once rich agricultural lands of the southern Tell are now only good for grazing sheep and goats

At the foot of Chebika's escarpment is a waterfall that flows into the palmery

A thermal bath
From the small town of Degache at the end of the Chott el Jerid, 10km before Tozeur, a road leads to El Hamma du Jerid, 5km away. The Romans recognised the virtues of these hot baths (38°C) and they are still popular with locals today. It is possible to bathe in one of the two baths – a perfect way to relax after crossing the *chott*.

As you drive the causeway across the Chott el Jerid, beware of mirages

►► **Chebika** 126A2

This is the southernmost of three oases near the Algerian border, the others being Midès (see page 149) and Tamerza (see page 154). The old village clinging to the mountainside was abandoned after the floods of 1969; since then, little by little, the houses have begun to merge with the rocky landscape. From the mausoleum there are superb views over the Chott el Gharsa, the oasis and the mountains. Behind the village is a small palmery with an *oued* (river) that leads to a small waterfall.

►► **Chott el Jerid** 126B1

Tunisia's *chotts*, Arabic for 'salt lakes', stretch for more than 300km from the Golfe de Gabès to the Algerian border, dividing the sand and stony deserts. The Chott el Jerid is the largest salt lake in Tunisia and, indeed, in all of North Africa. In summer, the hot air trembles slightly, making it impossible to define the exact outline of distant objects and turning the lakes into a shimmering white expanse where nothing survives except ghostly mirages. The extent of the lakes shown on maps is that found during the rainy season (winter), when certain areas turn into an inland sea.

The 90km-long crossing of the lake was once quite an adventure, but that ended when the army built a good causeway connecting Kebili and Tozeur. That said, mirages still make it an unforgettable and breathtaking experience: looking into the sun, an oasis or what appears to be a long caravan on the horizon disappears into thin air as you get closer. Along the road several stalls sell amethysts and coloured sand roses, the latter reputed to have gained their colour from the salt, although a bad paint job is a more likely reason.

►►► Dougga
126B5

If you only have time to visit one Roman site in Tunisia it should be Dougga (*Open* summer Tue–Sun 7–7. Rest of year Tue–Sun 8.30–5.30. Closed Mon. *Admission charge* moderate), the largest and definitely one of the most dramatic Roman towns in the Mediterranean, set on a steep 600m hill with magnificent views over the region.

Seeing the vast scale of the town (there are, for instance, more temples here than in any other site in North Africa), it is surprising that Dougga was only ever home to just 5,000 inhabitants. In the 2nd century BC it was a Punic trading town under a chieftain called Massinissa. Because Massinissa helped Rome against Carthage, Dougga was given some degree of independence after the fall of Carthage in 146 BC, only becoming a Roman colony in the 2nd century AD. After the decline of the Roman Empire, Dougga and its pagan temples were increasingly eclipsed. By the 6th century, when the Byzantines arrived, the town had slipped into oblivion.

The first building you come to upon entering the site is the heavily restored theatre►►, cut into the natural slope of the hill. It was designed to seat about 3,500 people and still draws crowds in summer when touring companies – including the Comedie Française – perform classical plays here. From the top steps a little path leads towards the Temple of Saturn►, built in AD 195 over a Punic sanctuary dedicated to the Carthaginian god Baal. Look out for curious footprints carved in the paving, said to belong to either the god Saturn himself or to a Roman emperor. Needless to say, the views over the green and purple plains are magnificent from this terrace.

Back at the theatre, walk along the paved street leading past the small Temple of Mercury to the Plaza of the Winds►, where a compass-like image has been carved into the paving, along with the names of the 12 Roman winds.

Guides in Dougga
Several 'guides' hang around the entrance to Dougga and at least one of them will offer his services as soon as you arrive. Most are not official and do not hold credentials issued by the Office National du Tourisme. As the site is large it may be useful to hire someone to point out the highlights, especially if you are in a hurry. But make sure you agree on a price beforehand and do not expect too much of the background information. A visit takes at least 1½ hours, but it is preferable to set aside a few hours more if you can spare the time.

131

Panorama of the site at Dougga from the top of the theatre

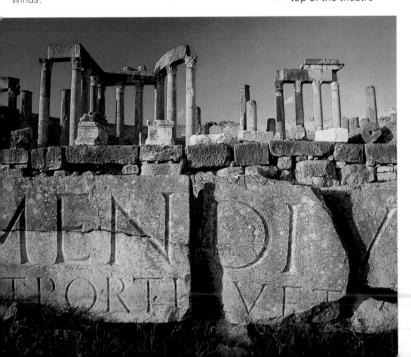

THE INTERIOR

The unusual 12-seater latrine at Dougga

Get lost
The site of Dougga spreads over more than 25 hectares, and although the monuments described in the main text are a must, it is just as interesting to stroll off the beaten track. Wander around the smaller temples west of the forum, examine the paved streets rutted by the passing of chariot wheels and try to visualise the market streets busy with merchants and clients.

Several cubicles lead off a central courtyard in the House of Trifolium, which is thought to have been Dougga's local brothel

Next to the Plaza of the Winds is the easily recognisable and lofty **Capitol Temple▶▶▶**. Built from golden stone, it is undoubtedly the best-preserved such temple in the country. The four frontal Corinthian pillars of the portico still bear the pediment, which has an eroded carving of the Emperor Antoninus Pius entwined with an eagle. The temple, as always with the Capitol, was dedicated to Jupiter, Juno and Minerva; three niches inside held statues of the gods.

From the temple, follow the broad paved street to the right of the small mosque, passing the **Temple of Concordia▶** on the left and the colonnaded courtyard of the **Temple of Liber Pater▶** on the right. Directly opposite are the high walls of the 3rd-century **Baths of Licinius▶▶**, a huge complex of hot and cold rooms and an attached palaestra or gymnasium. Slightly further downhill is the **House of Trifolium▶▶**, believed to be a brothel – prostitutes sat for hire in the cubicles around the courtyard. The huge phallus which would have advertised the service on offer here has long since disappeared.

Immediately beside the brothel are the **Baths of the Cyclops▶▶**, worth a visit to look at the communal latrines, a dozen seats set in a horseshoe shape, probably so occupants could chat together. The baths were named after a superb mosaic of the three giant Cyclops working in the forge of Vulcan, the god of Hell, now displayed in the Musée du Bardo in Tunis (see pages 54–6). Further still downhill is the **Triumphant Arch of Septimius Severus**, dedicated to the first African emperor (see pages 112–13), under whose rule the town reached the height of its wealth. At the foot of the site is a Libyo-Punic obelisk, the **Mausoleum of Ateban▶▶**, one of the few relics of the Punic era. Built around 200 BC, it combines Egyptian, Greek and Persian architectural features and is decorated with fine carvings. The British consul Thomas Read dismantled it in 1910 and took the inscriptions back to the British Museum in London; it was later restored.

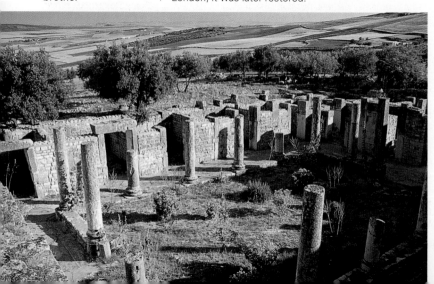

Many nomads of the M'Razig tribe, who live in outlying areas, come to Douz' colourful Thursday market

►► Douz   126B1

The drive through the desert past the Chott el Jerid (see page 130) and Kebili (see page 141) is a good preparation for the landscapes around Douz. Because of its location on the edge of the Great Eastern Erg, the tiny town of Douz has, much to its own surprise, become a major tourist centre for 'Lawrence of Arabia' experiences, with a rapidly expanding number of hotels to the north and now also to the south of the town.

Earlier this century, the hamlet was nothing more than a few buildings surrounded by tents. The nomads of the M'Razig tribe lived in Douz for the three hot months, but left with their herds as soon as summer was over. The otherwise sleepy town comes to life during its Thursday market, where business is done early (don't bother going after 9am).

► Gafsa   126B2

Gafsa is the regional centre of and the largest oasis in the Jerid. The town has little to offer tourists and lives mostly off its phosphate industry. Initially a Berber stronghold, the settlement became a prosperous Roman colony under Trajan's rule. The Byzantines evangelised here so effectively that in spite of the Arab invasion the population continued to speak Latin until the 12th century.

At the end of avenue Habib Bourguiba are the **Piscines Romaines (Roman Baths)**►► (*Open* summer Tue–Sun 8–12, 3–7. Rest of year Tue–Sun 9.30–4.30. *Admission charge* cheap), with two rectangular pools for swimming and a hammam. The oasis starts just behind the recently restored 15th-century **kasbah**► on the same street.

Desert trips
The Ofra sand-dune on the road from Douz to Zaafrane is one of the largest accessible sand-dunes in Tunisia, and is particularly attractive at dawn or sunset. It is possible to drive close by it and park at the Hotel Mehari, to walk or to take a camel ride. Douz is an important centre for desert trips (see also page 176). Another useful address in Douz is the Abdel Moulah Voyages tour agency at La Rose des Sables hotel (tel: 05 495 484; fax: 05 495 366).

Every December more than 50,000 locals, nomads and tourists flock to Douz for the spectacular National Sahara Festival

THE INTERIOR

The Numidian kingdom

The ancient Numidian kingdom was situated south-west of Carthage and occupied most of modern-day Algeria. The area was originally inhabited by Berber nomads, parts of it coming under Carthage's control around 300 BC. The Numidian leader Massinissa (see also page 131) sided with Rome during the Second Punic War (218–201 BC) and was rewarded with control over all Numidia. His grandson, Jugurtha, warred with Rome, and after his defeat in 105 BC the kingdom became a Roman client state. Juba I (reigned 60–46 BC) struggled for an independent state, but after Julius Caesar defeated him, Numidia became a Roman province.

134

The remote Roman ruins at Haïdra see more sheep passing through than tourists

▶▶ **Haïdra** *126A4*

Tunisia's most remote Roman site (*Open* always. *Admission* free) lies just a few kilometres from the Algerian border. Its excellent position, on a crossroads leading to Carthage, Tebessa, Gafsa and Sousse, and also close to the Oued (River) Haïdra, ensured the site was continuously inhabited from the 1st century BC by Carthaginians, Romans and Byzantines. The modern road cuts straight through the site of ancient Ammaedara, from where Augustus's Third Legion patrolled the southern frontiers of Roman Africa. Archaeological evidence of at least five churches is proof that there was an active Christian community here. The French established a small border post in 1880, but only a few huts remained until 1939.

The triumphal arch of Septimius Severus over the original paved road leading into town, and the Orange Mausoleum on the edge of the Oued Haïdra, its top floor built as a miniature temple, are the best-preserved Roman monuments here (most of the others have never been excavated). The site's main attraction is the 6th-century **Byzantine fortress**, one of the largest in North Africa. The northern wall has been restored, but the south-west corner and the Roman bridge which used to cross the gorge to the fort have collapsed after floodings. To appreciate its immense scale, enter the fort and climb up to the battlements. The 4th-century Basilica of Melleus was the largest church in Haïdra and the burial place of several bishops, including the Byzantine Bishop Melleus and possibly even St Cyprian, bishop of Carthage.

▶▶ **Jugurtha** *126A4*

The first sight of this gigantic table mountain rising out of the foothills near the Algerian border is unforgettable. The plateau is named after a Numidian king who retreated here with his troops in 112–105 BC. Its other name of Qalaat Senan (Fortress of Senan) refers to a local bandit chief who also made use of the mountain's natural fortifications. (See also Walk opposite.)

Walk **Jugurtha's table mountain**

An exhilarating experience in a unique mountain landscape, this walk involves a steepish ascent up rock-cut steps to the summit of the table mountain (see opposite). It can be very hot and there are no refreshment facilities anywhere in the area, so go fully equipped with water and food (allow approximately 2½ hours).

Start at the village of Qalaat Senan (see map on page 126), from where the mountain looks dauntingly unassailable, with apparently sheer sides all round. Towards the edge of town a blue sign points left to Aïn Senan. Follow the tarmac road as it winds up to the hamlet that sits at the foot of the mountain. At the hamlet fork left up another tarmac road which, after passing a smart house on its own promontory, turns into a stony track navigable only by 4WD vehicles.

The walk up this track is 4km long and takes about 1¼ hours, hugging the left side of the table mountain, whose sheer cliffs loom impressively

Above: formidable natural fortress

above. The views throughout this stretch of the track are breathtakingly beautiful. The last section of the ascent is steeper, the stones underfoot loose and slippery. The path ends at the rock-cut stairway, and the climb takes no more than 15 minutes. The steps are uneven and often require a bit of scrambling. Near the top is the Byzantine gateway built by the bandit Senan.

Once on the summit, you will find cows grazing among the ruins of houses, troglodyte caves and extensive Byzantine cisterns. The path from the summit of the stairway leads you directly to the white dome of a *marabout* (shrine), where the local saint Sidi Abd el-Jouad is buried. Unusually, visitors are permitted and even encouraged to enter the shrine, where candles are burned in memory of the saint. Local people often climb up to this *marabout* at weekends to ask special favours of their holy man.

The Great Mosque's cedar doors are closed to non-Muslims

▶▶▶   Kairouan   126C4

The spiritual and religious centre of Tunisia and first holy city of the Maghreb was founded in AD 671 by Oqba ibn Nafi, who brought Islam to Africa. Once renowned as 'the city of 300 mosques', it is one of the most visited cities in Tunisia: more than 3 million people come every year to admire its rich Islamic heritage. Even so, Kairouan is not easy to visit. It is invariably hot and dusty, people are sometimes unfriendly towards tourists, street names are rarely signposted and often change, and it is a haven for hard-sell carpet dealers and *faux guides* (unofficial guides). Despite all this, Kairouan is still worth the hassle. A guided tour may be the best option for those in a hurry (ask at the Office de Tourisme), but as ever it is better to wander around on your own to get a sense of the city's spirit.

Legend has it that when Oqba ibn Nafi arrived here a spring opened at his feet in which he found a golden cup he had lost in Mecca years before. Whatever the story, he soon made the site his capital as it had deep wells and was strategically placed between the coastal forces of the Byzantines and the Berbers in the hills. The name Kairouan, meaning 'Caravan' in Arabic, was appropriate as the city derived its wealth from the trans-Saharan trade. Kairouan flourished under the Aghlabids, who built several grand monuments, including the Great Mosque. It remained Tunisia's dominant city until the Fatimids left in 1057. Isolated from the more cosmopolitan coastal towns, and with Jews and Christians forbidden to enter before the French arrived in 1881, Kairouan has remained in many ways a more traditional, pure Arab and Muslim city.

The 9th-century **Bassins des Aghlabides (Aghlabid Pools)**▶ (*Open* summer daily 8–12, 3–7. Rest of year daily 8.30–5.30. *Admission charge* covered by joint ticket) on avenue de la République, north of the centre, were part of a more elaborate water system which collected winter rain and channelled water from the Tell Plateau to the city via a 35km-long aqueduct.

The holiest building in Tunisia, and one of the oldest mosques in North Africa, the **Grande Mosquée de Sidi Oqba (Great Mosque)**▶▶▶ (*Open* summer Sat–Thu 8–3, Fri 8–12. Rest of year Sat–Thu 8–2, Fri 8–12. *Admission charge* covered by joint ticket), on boulevard Ibrahim ibn el-Aghlab, was originally built by Oqba ibn Nafi in 671. Today's building is the restored structure built by the Aghlabids in 863. Its simplicity and size encourage a sense of peace and tranquillity. Across the *sahn*, or courtyard, non-Muslims are forbidden to enter the prayer hall, but you can still catch a glimpse through the heavy cedar doors of a forest of Roman pillars and a multitude of tiny lamps. Through the central door the superb mihrab (prayer niche) is visible, with, to its right, the world's oldest mimbar, or pulpit (9th century). The 128 steps leading to the top of the tall, sturdy

Just the ticket
Before starting a tour of the city's monuments, visit the Office de Tourisme (see panel on page 138). To visit the mosques you must sign an authorisation form stating that you are decently dressed and will not cause a disturbance. The office sells a single ticket covering seven of the major sites. Most monuments are open Sat–Thu 8–6, except for the Great Mosque, which opens summer Sat–Thu 8–3, Fri 8–12; rest of year Sat–Thu 8–2, Fri 8–12.

Great Mosque wellhead, incised by ropes

minaret can occasionally be climbed by non-Muslims for good views over the city.

The most magical time to explore the *medina*▶▶ is early in the morning when the traders open their shops. Surrounded by 7km-long, 11th-century ramparts, the *medina* is usually entered through the Bab et Tunis (Tunis Gate) or the Bab ech Chouhada (Martyrs' Gate), these connected by the main thoroughfare of avenue Habib Bourguiba. Immediately right of the Martyrs' Gate is the **Zaouia of Sidi Abid el Ghariani**, a 14th-century Sufi shrine now

open to non-Muslims as the saint's body has been moved elsewhere. Note the elaborate carved doors and the fine decoration of the floors and walls. In the middle of the avenue is a group of buildings including the Café el-Halfaouine, the Mosquée el Bey and the 17th-century **Bir Barouta**▶ (*Open* daily 8–5.30), where a blindfolded camel in an upstairs room turns a wheel to pump holy water from the well, believed to be connected with Mecca. According to local tradition, if you drink the water you will return. Apparently, Barouta was the name of Oqba ibn Nafi's dog,

The main thorough-fare of Kairouan's medina *is avenue* Habib Bourguiba, *which runs from* Bab et Tunis *to the* Bab ech Chouhada

137

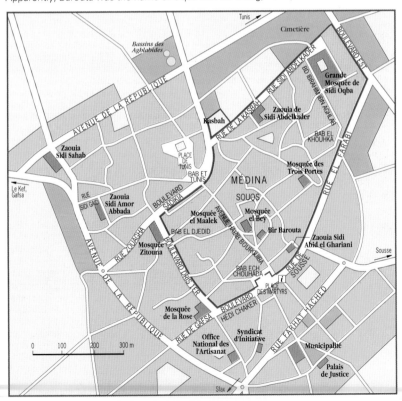

Top and above: the Zaouia of Sidi Sahab, place of pilgrimage and centre for ritual circumcision

which found the well. The 9th-century **Mosquée des Trois Portes (Mosque of the Three Doors)**►► is one of the oldest monuments in the *medina* (interior closed). Its stunning original façade has different doors for men, women and children.

Zaouia of Sidi Sahab (Shrine of the Companion)►►► (*Open* daily 8.30–5.30) on avenue de la République, where Abou Zamaa el-Balaoui, one of Prophet Muhammad's companions, is buried, is also known as the Mosque of the Barber as this holy man always carried three hairs of the Prophet's beard with him. His tomb is set in an elegant 17th-century complex of patios and corridors, with a superbly decorated main patio. The 19th-century **Zaouia Sidi Amor Abbada**►► (*Open* daily 8–5) on rue Sidi Gaid constructed by a blacksmith, was turned into a little museum displaying objects that belonged to him.

Useful addresses
● Office de Tourisme: place des Bassins des Aghlabides (tel: 07 221 797. *Open* Sat–Thu 8–6, Fri 8–1).
● Artisanat (Socopa): avenue Ali Zouaoui (*Open* summer Mon–Sat 7.30–1.30. Rest of year Mon–Sat 8.30–12.30, 3–5.30).
● Hertz: avenue Ibn el-Jazzar (tel: 07 224 529).
● Bus station: on the Sousse road (tel: 07 220 125).

A temple of carpets

Drive **From Kairouan to Makthar**

See map on page 126.

A drive through forests and extra-ordinary scenery in the interior of Tunisia, before reaching the impressive Roman city at Makthar. Take plenty of food and water, and allow half a day (approximately 180km, or 230km including Ksar Lemsa).

Leave Kairouan on the road to Le Kef, driving through deserted countryside. Between Aïn Jloula and Ousseltia you can make a diversion by forking north towards **Ksar Lemsa**▶▶, a beautifully preserved 6th-century Byzantine fortress. Its towers and battlements are still intact and architectural fragments are arranged in the custodian's garden.

Return to the main road to reach **Ousseltia**▶, founded by the French in 1927 as a centre for the surrounding olive and almond groves. Fork south after the town to cross more wooded country, then turn west at the T-junction towards Makthar. Where the road passes through a tunnel, **Dechrat el-Gharia**▶▶▶ appears, an amazing natural formation with dramatic needle-shaped rocks.

A few kilometres further you come to the **Forêt de Kesra (Forest of**

Above: amazing scenery en route

Kesra)▶▶, with Aleppo pines. From there take the signposted detour up to the village of **Kesra**▶▶. This Berber settlement, built into the hill-side, is quite different from the fortified hilltop Berber villages of the south like Chenini (see page 162). Several *koubbas* (domes) around the edge of the village indicate the tombs of local holy men.

The road between Kesra and Makthar passes through some of Tunisia's most beautiful scenery, with gorges and abundant valleys. If you turn off any of the sidetracks into the forest you will find plenty of lovely shady picnic spots. Back on the road, climb up from a valley to reach a high plateau and **Makthar**▶▶ (see page 145). Return directly to Kairouan via Haffouz (just over an hour).

■ **Indifferent to worldly concerns and not satisfied by merely worshipping God through prayer or obedience, mystical Sufi brotherhoods aspire to a direct experience of the divine. They get closer to God by meditating or by entering a trance through a repetitive action such as the recitation of the name of God, music or dancing, as in the case of the famous whirling dervishes.** ■

140

Repression of the Sufis
For centuries Sufi brotherhoods cultivated *maalouf* music (see panel on page 154) as a form of entertainment, mostly to calm entranced disciples at Sufi festivals. After independence, the Sufi brotherhoods fell out of favour and were either disbanded or had their activities seriously repressed by the government, who took control of the mosques, the wealth of the religious institutions and also of the *maalouf* tradition. Now, little by little, Sufis can once again resume their activities and recruit new members.

An Islamic sect Early on in Islam some of the Prophet Mohammad's followers, including his son-in-law Ali, became ascetics in their search for purity, perhaps inspired by eastern Christian monks. They believed that more than merely obeying God's command, their relationship with the divine needed to be one of pure love. They wanted to draw closer to God and in doing so become aware of God's love for men. Those who put this idea into practice became known as Sufis, a name derived from the Arabic word *suf*, meaning 'wool', as the first adherents wore woollen robes. Some souls could reach the desired union with God alone or guided directly by a dead teacher or by the Prophet himself. However, most people needed teaching and guidance from a *shaykh*, or master, who had advanced further on the path. Later on those who followed the same great master formed a spiritual family, or *tariqa*. Some *tariqa* have been going for hundreds of years and have expanded right across the Islamic world.

Sufism in Tunisia Tunisia's most important Sufi *shaykh* was Sidi Belhassen ech-Chadli. Born in the 13th century in Morocco, he stopped in Tunisia on his way back from Mecca and taught disciples from a cave near Tunis. About 15 Sufi groups still regard Chadli as their spiritual leader. Nefta is the country's centre of Sufism, and its most important *zaouia* (place of mystical studies) follows the teachings of 12th-century Abd el-Kader el-Jilani, who was the first *shaykh* to set up a brotherhood (the Qadriya in Nefta) and is considered the father of the Sufi tradition.

A typical Sufi marabout, Tozeur

► **Kasserine** *126B3*

This dusty administrative centre has palm-lined streets busy with heavy traffic, trucks and traders. The modern town, stretching 5km along the main road, with army barracks and a train station, is entirely French. It was the scene of a bloody battle in World War II, when the Allies lost more than 6,500 men to just a few German casualties.

The name Kasserine derives from the Arabic for 'the two *ksour*', referring to two surviving Roman mausoleums. The first is hardly standing and can be found just past the first dry river bed, but the second mausoleum – of Flavius Secundus and Petrouan – just after the river bed of Oued ed-Darb, is an impressive three-storey monument with Corinthian columns. On the hill south of town lie the scant remains of Roman Cilium, with a triumphal arch, a few rock-cut tombs, a 1st-century AD theatre and good views over the Oued ed-Darb. West of the town is Tunisia's highest mountain, Jebel Chambi (1,544m), popular with hikers and boar hunters.

► **Kebili** *126B1*

An old Berber town squeezed between a palmery and sand-dunes, Kebili is the main town of the Nefzaoua region and is the gateway to the oases. Until the 19th century it was also a well-known slave-trading centre, with caravans coming from Sudan (see panel). The town's other claim to fame is that Bourguiba was exiled here in 1934. There are several army barracks in Kebili, so taking pictures is not really the thing to do.

The vast palmery is irrigated from a spring at Ras el-Aïn to the north of the town, and there is a Roman pool in the centre of Kebili to the left on the road to Douz, where it is possible to swim. Most visitors to Kebili come for a stay at the charming Borj des Autruches hotel on the edge of the desert (see page 197).

Kasserine's Mausoleum of Flavius Secondus and Petrouan

The slave trade
Descendants of black Sudanese in Kebili's narrow streets are a reminder of the once-flourishing trans-Saharan slave trade. Kairouan was always an important centre for slavers, although in the 17th century the Souq el-Berka in the *medina* in Tunis (see page 58) was the country's main market for domestic slaves, selling Christians captured by corsairs on the Barbary coast and black Africans brought from the Sudan. Slaves were put up for auction on a stand known as 'the cage'. Prices depended on religion, nationality, beauty, family ties and so on. The slave trade was abolished in 1841 by Ahmed Bey, although the loss of the heavy tax on slavery provoked his bankruptcy.

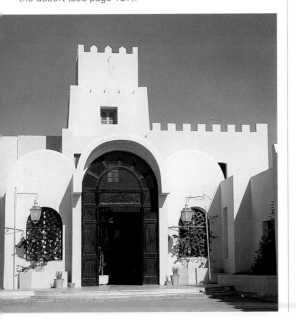

The cosy and pleasant Borj des Autruches hotel

■ As you wander through a *medina* the first things that catch your eye are elegant and slender minarets, white or tiled domes and perfect horseshoe arches. However, there is much more to Islamic architecture than this, as most of its delights and treasures lie hidden behind high walls. ■

142

Highlights of Islamic architecture in Tunisia
● Jemaa ez Zitouna and Sidi Youssef Mosque in Tunis (see pages 52 and 53).
● Skifa el Kahla, Great Mosque and Borj el Kebir in Mahdia (see page 117).
● *Ribat* in Monastir (see page 118).
● Great Mosque and Dar Jellouli in Sfax (see page 121).
● Great Mosque, Musée de Kalaout el Koubba and the *ribat* in Sousse (see pages 121–2).
● Great Mosque and Zaouia of Sidi Sahab in Kairouan (see pages 136–8).
● Mosque of Sidi Bou Makhlouf in Le Kef (see page 144).

The dark prayer hall of the Great Mosque in Kairouan hides the world's oldest mimbar (pulpit)

A different philosophy Islamic architecture has striven to create an indoor, inward-looking space where rooms and windows give onto a private internal courtyard. In Islam the house is a place where women can take off the veil and walk about freely, unseen by strangers; a place, therefore, where male visitors are rarely invited. Larger houses have a bench-lined hall, or *driba*, by the entrance to entertain male visitors, usually positioned so that the courtyard is not visible.

Mosques and *medresa* (Koranic schools) follow a similar pattern of rooms centred around an open-plan courtyard, enclosed by a high windowless wall. In the middle of the courtyard there is usually an ablution fountain for the ritual washing of hands and feet before prayers, and at the end is a carpeted prayer hall where shoes are removed before entering. The interior of the prayer hall is very simple, with the mihrab (prayer niche) and the mimbar (a pulpit on a staircase) as the main decorative features. The muezzin summons the faithful to prayer five times a day from the minaret, or mosque tower.

The Great Mosque The *medina*, or old city, always evolved around the Great Mosque. At first this also had a military purpose, the courtyard was a place of refuge in times of trouble and the colonnades were a place of assembly. Later it also became a commercial centre, surrounded by busy *souqs* like those around the Jemaa ez Zitouna in Tunis (see page 52). Each quarter in the *medina* has its own mosque, a bakery and often a *zaouia* (place of mystical studies) or *medersa*.

Fortresses of religion Some of the earliest Islamic buildings in Tunisia are the *ribats* (fortified monasteries) in Monastir and Sousse, built at the end of the 8th century for the holy warriors defending the North African coast. These fortresses are very simple, again centred around an open square with battlements facing both inwards and out, and with an added *nador*, or watchtower. The gateway, usually resting on pillars salvaged from antiquity, later developed into the horseshoe arch, so typical of North Africa.

A mixture of styles The inspiration for the model house, focused on its central courtyard, is more Mediterranean than Arab, while the domes of mosques and *zaouias* were drawn from Byzantine architecture. Places like Sidi Bou Said (see pages 66–7) still clearly show another element of Tunisian architecture: the Moorish influence, which began in the 12th century under the Almohads. From the 17th century the Ottoman style was imported and Italian baroque and rococo influences became popular, as in the mosque of Hammouda Pacha in Tunis (see pages 52–3).

The mosque of Sidi Bou Makhlouf, Le Kef

143

Islamic decoration
Decoration in Islamic buildings is always based on geometrical or floral patterns as the representation of humans or animals is forbidden. The idea is to forget about the real world and enter a divine one of pure geometric forms; the endless repetition of geometrical patterns is as much a part of Islamic philosophy as the repetitive chanting of Koranic verses and prayer five times a day. Floral motifs, meanwhile, are representations of the delights of paradise.

Architectural glossary
bab door, gate
bir well
borj tower, fort
dar house, palace
fondouk caravanserai where merchants spent the night, stored goods and rested their horses
ghorfa rock-cut or mud chambers
hammam public steam-bath (Turkish bath)
jami'/jemaa mosque
kasbah citadel of a town, or rural fortress
koubba dome, sometimes also a saint's tomb
ksar (pl ksour) fortified village

marabout a holy man, who is buried in a shrine that is also called a *marabout*
medersa Koranic school, often with rooms for students
medina old Arab town, once high-walled, with narrow alleys
mihrab niche in the mosque indicating the direction of Mecca
mimbar pulpit, used for the Friday noon sermon
nador watchtower
ribat fortified monastery
souq market
tourbet mausoleum
zaouia shrine or place of prayer and mystical studies

The Mosquée de Sidi Bou Makhlouf is a popular place of pilgrimage

Sidi Bou Makhlouf mosque
Le Kef has always been an important religious centre, and its nine *zaouias* (religious study centres) are still very influential in the region. The mosque of Sidi Bou Makhlouf was originally the *zaouia* for the 16th-century Sufi brotherhood of Aissouia, whose disciples believed in prolonged dancing as a way of getting closer to God and becoming insensible to pain (see page 140). To prove their point they would eat poisonous snakes and mutilate their bodies.

Le Kef's Turkish fort

►►   **Le Kef (El Kef)**   *126B4*

The name Le Kef (Arabic for 'the Rock') refers to the town's dramatic setting on a high escarpment overlooking rolling hills. Although the town lacks serious tourist facilities, the visitor looking for a bustling provincial town with Tunisian character will not be disappointed.

Le Kef's long history started with a prehistoric settlement. The Carthaginians exiled their mutinous mercenary army here and under the Romans it became an important trading centre known as Sicca Veneria, also famous for its temple of prostitution. The 6th-century Byzantine fortress fell to the Arab invasion, and from then on the town was always involved in border disputes. In 1942 it served as headquarters for De Gaulle's Free French; Habib Bourguiba's second wife was also born here.

At the heart of Le Kef is the spring of **Aïn el Kef►►►**, which has provided the town with water for more than 2,000 years. Beside it is a small altar to Lalla Ma, the Lady of the Waters (see also Walk on page 146). On summer evenings the courtyard becomes a popular open-air café. Past the mosque of Sidi Hamed Gharib and beside the spring lie the ruins of **Sicca Veneria►**, with an impressive Roman bath complex against which a Byzantine church was built, its altar and some mosaic paving still visible.

On the way up to the kasbahs, on place Bou Makhlouf, stands the **Jemaa el Kebir (Old Mosque)►►**, one of the oldest places of Muslim worship in Tunisia. The purpose of the original 4th-century building around which the mosque was built remains a mystery. Stairs lead to the **Mosquée de Sidi Bou Makhlouf►►**, with an octagonal minaret and elegant domes. Two **kasbahs►►** loom over the town, a Byzantine one constructed with stones from the Roman town, and a Turkish fort (1601) reached via the old Turkish drawbridge.

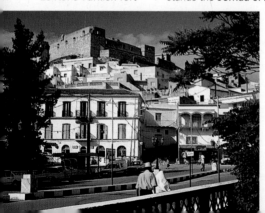

The **Tourbet d'Ali Turki**▶ lies downhill from the square and houses the tomb of the father of the Husseinite Dynasty (1704–1881). Further downhill again is the old Jewish quarter with a ruined synagogue. Off avenue Habib Bourguiba is the **Dar el Kouss**▶, a roofless 4th-century Christian basilica dedicated to St Peter, only open to the public during occasional open-air theatre performances. On place Ben Aissa is the **Musée Régional des Arts et Traditions Populaires**▶▶ (tel: 08 221 503. *Open* summer Tue–Sun 9–1, 4–7. Rest of year Tue–Sun 9.30–4.30. *Admission charge* cheap), housed in the attractive 18th-century Mausoleum of Sidi Ali Ben Aissa. The museum displays local Berber and farmers' clothes, jewellery and household objects.

▶▶ Makthar   126B4

The Numidians built a fortress here in the 3rd century BC to control the region's nomadic tribes. It was around this fort that Makthar grew, becoming an important city before being annexed to the Roman Empire in 46 BC. Most surviving monuments date from the 2nd century AD, when Mactaris, as it was then known, was at its most prosperous. The town was sacked by Vandals, Byzantines and Arabs, and then abandoned in the 11th century until French colonists founded modern Makthar.

Forming the entrance to the site (tel: 08 787 651. *Open* summer daily 8–6. Rest of year daily 8.30–5.30. *Admission charge* cheap) is an interesting museum. It has a small collection of Punic tombstones, small Roman sculptures and Christian grave mosaics. Climb up the pathway past the small amphitheatre and New Forum to reach the monumental Trajan's Arch, which offers splendid views over the site. Follow the paved road past the fine Church of Hildegun', named after the Vandal buried near its entrance, to reach the stunning 2nd-century baths converted into a Byzantine fortress.

Continued on page 148

Bathe like a Roman
From Le Kef take the road out to Sakiet Sidi Youssef and turn right to Hammam Mellègue. The last few kilometres plunge down towards the river in the Mellègue Valley. Hammam Mellègue consists of four original Roman baths, one of which is still in use – enter the stone bathhouse through heavy wooden doors. A dip in the Roman pool is definitely worth the tricky drive (*Open* women only until 1 or 2pm; men only in the afternoons).

Local markets
● Monday: Aïn Draham and Makthar.
● Wednesday: Jendouba.
● Thursday: Bousalem, Siliana and Le Kef.
● Sunday: Le Kef.

145

Below: Makthar's museum houses an interesting collection Bottom: Trajan's Arch

Walk Le Kef

A stroll through the centre of Le Kef (see also pages 144–5), dominated by its kasbahs, reveals a city like no other in Tunisia. Allow about two hours.

Start at **Aïn el Kef►►►**, the site of the old Roman spring, opposite the Hôtel Sicca Veneria on place de l'Indépendance. The Roman stonework and nymph is still visible, but the spring has been converted to the Islamic faith. In summer the hollow becomes a lively open-air café. Above the spring is the Hôtel de la Source, which despite dubious sanitation is famous for one beautifully decorated bedroom with splendid

Above: cannon guard the kasbahs
Below left: Hôtel de la Source

stucco and tilework. Near by is the entrance to a huge cistern which supplied the Roman baths. It is now closed, but if he is around the guardian will show you the 54 columns that still support the roof.

Follow the steep alleyway uphill to the right of the hotel for a taste of streetlife in the old town of Le Kef. Near the top, follow the great wall of the **kasbahs►►** round to the entrance gateway. There are two forts here. The first entrance is into the larger (lower) fort, built in 1601 and used earlier this century as a prison for Tunisian nationalists. A row of cannon lines the entry and the path leads round to the impressive hill gateway of the upper fort, built by the Ottoman bey in 1740.

Leave the kasbah and enter place Bou Makhlouf. Although the plain stone building has been used as a mosque without minaret since the Arab conquest, it was originally built in the 4th century probably as a market-place or brothel. Above the old mosque, stairs lead to the **Mosquée de Sidi Bou Makhlouf►►** and the pleasant Café des Andalous.

Walk or donkey ride

From Tamerza to Midès

One of the most scenic and romantic spots in the country, the river bed and gorge between Tamerza and Midès are the perfect background for a donkey ride or walk. Donkeys can be arranged from the Tamerza Palace Hotel or the Hôtel des Cascades (see page 198), with only a few hours' advance notice necessary. If you can't face the strong possibility of being sore for a few days, it may be wiser, although less fun, to walk this trip. Avoid the midday heat in the summer and take water. Allow two hours each way (5km).

Starting at the Tamerza Palace Hotel, the donkeys follow the trail over the ridge opposite the ghost town of old Tamerza▶▶ (see page 154). They then cut across a flat, open plain to approach Midès from the same direction as the tarmac road, reaching new Midès beside the customs post (Algeria is just over the next hill) at the opposite end of the oasis.

The walking route is more scenic as it is possible to follow the river bed. Where the tarmac road from Tamerza to Tozeur crosses the river bed, fork to the right into the gorge. This gorge is known as Oued el-Oudei and it becomes increasingly scenic and ever narrower, twisting and turning to give a wonderful sense of entering a separate, timeless world.

Your first sight of Midès▶▶▶ (see page 149), perched precariously on the ridge of a vertical rock-face and surrounded by the gorge on three sides, is breathtaking. Looking down into the gorge, you see a swirling, multi-coloured cross-section of browns, beiges and russet-coloured rock strata, with dots of green palm trees deep in the valley below. Until recently Midès relied entirely on a

The breathtaking gorge at Midès, dotted with palm trees

bartering system – that is until the villagers came into contact with tourism and learned the power of money. In the centre, a few simple one-room houses have been turned into souvenir shops selling local produce such as dates and oranges, together with petrified wood and mineral rocks. Behind the village sits the palmery, the villagers' lifeline, where everyone owns a small plot of land and the water from the springs is shared meticulously.

THE INTERIOR

Continued from page 145

As at most other sites in Tunisia, the impressive Capitoline temple and theatre at Medeina date from the halcyon days of the 2nd century AD

Behind the high walls, the structure of the baths and their colourful, wave-patterned mosaic floors are still visible. It is easy to imagine the comfort and luxury once enjoyed by Mactaris's Roman citizens. From the archway, another paved street leads past the Temple of Bacchus to the right and the Old Forum to the left, while the fork left at the next crossroads takes you to the Schola Juvenum. The élite young men of the town met in this tree-covered building, part of which was later converted into a church. Beyond are several graveyards, megalithic tombs and a new-Punic mausoleum with a pyramidal roof.

►► Medeina   126B4

Because of the perennial springs here there has always been a settlement in Medeina. The Roman site of Althiburos (*Open* daily dawn–sunset. *Admission charge* moderate), surrounded by modern Medeina, gives a sense of continuity, as villagers grazing their sheep and collecting water bring the monuments back to life. Ancient Althiburos was founded by Carthaginians in the 2nd century BC as an outpost on the military road from Carthage to Tebessa (in modern Algeria). As with most sites in the region, the majority of surviving monuments date from the 2nd century AD, when Medeina flourished under the rule of Hadrian (AD 117–38). The town declined quickly after the Arab conquest to become the sleepy village you see today.

A large triumphal arch dedicated to the Emperor Hadrian marks the entrance to the site, behind which two staircases lead to the vast paved forum, littered with richly carved Corinthian capitals and an inscribed pediment that contains footholes for a missing statue. Higher up are the

Geckos
You can often hear geckos shrieking at night in Tunisia. They are common residents in local houses, and sometimes in hotel rooms. With their suckered feet they can walk on walls and ceilings with ease. Tunisians don't mind their presence too much as they consume a good number of flies, mosquitoes and other unwelcome guests.

crumbling ruins of the Capitoline temple, although the steps leading to it are no longer there. By following the Roman street towards the precarious arches of the theatre you will reach a monumental fountain with four niches. Below the forum across the river are two interesting buildings: a palatial house whose mosaics are now in the Musée du Bardo in Tunis (see pages 54–6); and the building of Aesculapius, an elegant private house turned into a public bath in the 4th century, with fountains and pools galore.

▶ Metlaoui 126A2

The Frenchman Philippe Thomas, who discovered the first phosphate deposits here in 1885, began the transformation of Metlaoui from tiny village to industrial town. Most of its inhabitants now work in one of several factories connected to the phosphate mines. This is of little interest to visitors, who come here *en route* to the nearby Gorges de Selja (see page 154). The gorge is best seen from the little tourist train known as the *Lézard Rouge* (*Red Lizard*), which you can board in Metlaoui (see panel). The train was built in 1904 for the bey of Tunis, and although the original furniture and fittings have seen better days it still adds excitement to a great journey.

▶▶▶ Midès 126A2

The spectacular mountain oasis of Midès feels very much like the country's 'wild west' (the western movie *Fort Sagane* was actually filmed here and in the surrounding canyons), its proximity to Algeria adding to the atmosphere. The old village is perched on the edge of the gorge and seems to hang over a void. Most of the 120 villagers have moved to a new village, although a few have stayed on. Several years ago a Belgian company wanted to turn the entire village into a hotel complex, but the Tunisian tourist board refused and is itself restoring many of the mud-brick houses. A walk in the palmery, where pomegranates, oranges and figs grow in the shade of lofty palms, offers a cool escape. (See also page 147.)

The *Red Lizard*
The *Lézard Rouge* train leaves Metlaoui for Redeyef, another phosphate mining town, daily at 11am. The trip takes about two hours. The former beylical train, now run by Transtours (which has its office next door to the train station), can be crowded with tourists. The ordinary train from Metlaoui to Moularès or Redeyef, which leaves around 3pm, may be cheaper and less crowded but is also less appealing.

149

A marabout, or tomb of a local saint, near Midès. The blue door frame wards off the evil eye, but nothing can keep away the desert sands

FOCUS ON

Oases

■ **Few sights are as impressive or as pleasing as a green oasis lying amidst a barren, scorched landscape of sand and dust. The grass is always greener here, the water cooler, the fruits more plentiful: romantic imagery for the visitor, but not so for the local inhabitants, who must work hard to keep the water flowing.** ■

Date palms This region of the Sahara would not be habitable if it were not for the date palm and the fruit it bears. There are over 100 types of dates, all varying according to the climatic band in which they are grown, but the best and most highly prized of all is the deglet en-nour (meaning 'offspring or daughter of light'), which is harvested in November and is mostly found in Tozeur, Nefta and Douz. Each tree lives for 150–200 years and can produce up to 120kg of fruit a year. Of all the fruits, dates are the richest in protein and sugar. In addition to the dates, every bit of the tree is used: animal fodder is provided from the stones, rope and shoes are made from the fibre, the wood is used for building houses, bridges and fencing, the fronds are also used for fencing and for weaving baskets and mats, and the sap of old palm trees is tapped to make *lagmi*, a potent wine.

Gorgeous dates ready to be picked in La Corbeille, Nefta

Oasis life An oasis evokes thoughts of paradise, of lingering in the shade, swimming in freshwater pools and

150

Deglet en-nour
According to legend, the name of one of the highest-quality dates, Tunisia's deglet en-nour (meaning 'offspring or daughter of light'), came from the name of a Muslim saint, Lallah Nurah. This woman was so poor that she didn't even possess a rosary. When saying her prayers by the roadside, reciting the 99 names of God, she used date seeds to assist her. She died while she was praying and was buried on the spot. Seeds that were planted on her grave sprouted almost immediately into fine palms that bore the most delicious of dates.

indulging in fruits picked off the trees, but this is certainly not the view held by the oases' inhabitants. The irrigation system and husbandry that makes an oasis successful is extraordinarily complex. In the great oases like Tozeur (see page 155) and Nefta (see pages 152–3), water gushing from hundreds of springs is distributed equally to each and every plot. The system requires constant tending and maintenance, yet there is no formal method of enforcement, only mutual trust and dependence. Palm trees provide shade for smaller fruit trees such as apricots, pomegranates, figs, oranges, grape-vines and olive trees, and these in turn shade wheat, barley, lucerne and vegetables.

Tunisia's oases The most important groves are in the Balad al-Jerid, whose four oases of Nefta, Tozeur, El-Oudian and Hamma are all well protected from the north wind. While mountain oases such as Midès and Tamerza are small and dramatic, with clusters of palm trees bursting out from arid cliff faces and gorges, the desert oases are on a very different scale. About a million palms grow in these oases, and more than two-thirds of their dates are exported. Around every oasis, at a distance of about 300m, a rampart of piled-up earth crowned by a palisade of palm leaves encourages artificial sand-dunes to form as a barrier against shifting sand. In order to bind the sand, tamarisk, white broom and other desert species are planted on the dunes. No animals are allowed to graze.

The Jerid region has been cultivated with date palms since Roman times, and an Arab author of the 11th century praised its fertility and the beauty of its palm groves. No other region in Africa produces as many dates, these supporting almost the entire oasis population.

A late-afternoon calèche (horsecart) ride through the oasis at Gabès is a relaxing way to discover its secrets

The blessed tree
Several sayings of the Prophet Muhammad and suras from the Koran point to the special place the palm tree has in Islam:

'There is among the trees one which is pre-eminently blessed as is the Muslim amongst men. It is the palm.'

'Honour your maternal aunt the palm, for it was created from the clay left over after the creation of Adam, on whom be peace and the blessings of God.'

Some Islamic sects even believe that the valuable tree was created by the Prophet himself. The daytime fast during Ramadan is traditionally broken with a spoon of water and three dates.

Date palms have been cultivated in the Jerid since Roman times; today, no other region in Africa produces as many dates

The numerous white-domed marabouts (shrines) at Nefta point to its importance as a centre of Sufism

Local markets
● Sunday: Tozeur.
● Tuesday: Kebili.
● Wednesday: Gafsa.
● Thursday: Nefta, Douz.
● Friday: Tamerza.

Useful addresses in Nefta
● Tourist office (Syndicat d'Initiative): avenue Habib Bourguiba (tel: 06 457 236. *Open* daily 8–6). Official guides and tours by donkey or horse-drawn cart, all at fixed prices.
● Artisanat: next door to the Syndicat (*Open* mornings only).
● Hertz: avenue Farhat Hached (tel: 06 453 547).

The so-called 'Princess of the Desert' lies on the edge of the Chott el Jerid and is the closest town in the region to the Algerian border. Although not as picturesque as Tozeur (see page 155), its increasing popularity as a 'Sahara threshold' tourist destination has resulted in a boom of low-rise hotels. The palmery suffered during the devastating floods in 1989/90 and it may take several more years before the town regains its strength and all its charm. The government recently started the restoration of the old town, but unfortunately only for the cause of tourism, so more and more traditional architecture is making way for breeze-block structures.

The most important site in Nefta is the Qasr el-Aïn (Castle of Springs), better known by its French name **Corbeille (Basket)▶▶**. This natural, bowl-shaped depression, situated below the town escarpment, contains 152 wells that provide water for thousands of palm trees. The pools are traditionally used as a bathing place for women and children, while the men use a pool created by the Romans further downstream. However, the sight is not what it used to be as many wells have dried up and the palm trees are dying. The owners of the gardens no longer welcome individuals who come to peek around, so it is advisable to take an official guide (from the tourist office) who can explain the secrets of the oasis.

Few people venture into the old town, which is one reason to go. Other reasons include the houses here that are still decorated with traditional brick patterns, a lively *souq* and some white-domed *marabouts* (shrines). Nefta has a long spiritual tradition and is the second religious centre in Tunisia after Kairouan (see pages 136–8), with more than 20 mosques and 100 *marabouts*. The most revered shrines are the Zaouia el-Qadriya, up on the ridge above the Corbeille (see page 140), and the Koubba of Sidi Bou Ali, down in the oasis (both are closed to non-Muslims). It was Sidi Bou Ali who reputedly first planted deglet en-nour date palms in the 13th century (see page 150).

▶▶ Sbeïtla   *126B3*

This is the southernmost major Roman town in Tunisia, and is the most impressive Roman site after Dougga (see pages 131–2). Little is known of the history of ancient Sufetula, although the earliest-known inscription suggests that it was only founded in the 1st century AD. It achieved real fame in the 7th century when it became the capital of the Patriarch Gregory, who rebelled against Constantinople and proclaimed himself emperor. His glory was short lived, however, as the Arabs killed him a year later.

The site (*Open* summer daily 7–7. Rest of year daily 8.30–5.30. *Admission charge* moderate), located on the main road to Kasserine, merits a 2–3 hour visit and is best seen in the early morning or before sunset. The museum has a few good mosaics and sculptures excavated on site, although the best finds are in the Musée du Bardo in Tunis (see pages 54–6). From the impressive triumphal arch a path leads past two well-preserved 6th-century Byzantine forts into a main paved street. Take a right turn to explore the vast baths, with fragments of mosaic flooring, and continue downhill to the ruined theatre overlooking the gorge. Back up the paved street, past the Church of Severus on the right, is the magnificent 2nd-century AD Roman forum, marked by a monumental gate built by Antoninus Pius. Unusually, it has three Capitoline temples instead of just one dedicated to Jupiter, Juno and Minerva. The tunnel behind the temples leads towards the 6th-century Basilica of Vitalis, with a fish mosaic in the central basin and a well-preserved baptismal font covered in mosaics. The font is shaped like a vulva, symbolising the second birth through baptism. Most of the extensive area beyond is only of interest to specialists, although the scant remains of an amphitheatre are worth seeing.

Stelae depicting crudely carved men and women were found at the necropolis near Sbeïtla

Roman Sbeïtla was built of golden stone

Above right: the best way to enjoy the Gorges de Selja is from the Lézard Rouge *Below: tiled minaret of the Great Mosque at Testour*

▶▶   **Selja, Gorges de**   *126A2*

This impressive 15km-long gorge is best seen from the *Lézard Rouge* train (see panel on page 149), which runs from Metlaoui to Redeyef and back. Selja itself is at the half-way point in the middle of the gorge, and is a good place to stop for a walk and to view the remarkable bridges and tunnels built by the French for the phosphate trains. A local legend says that a princess ran off with a warrior who, with his sword, carved their nuptial bed into the rock, thus creating the gorge. Whatever the truth, the gorge is spectacular, particularly in the morning light.

▶▶   **Tamerza**   *126A2*

The derelict old village at Tamerza, the most attractive of the mountain oases, looks like a huge sandcastle slowly melting into the sea. Torrential rain and flash floods in 1969 washed huge chunks of the mud-brick village away, forcing its inhabitants to move to a new village. Conservation workers are now trying to save what remains from falling in the *oued* (river).

With its empty streets and excellent views, the old village makes for a picturesque walk during late afternoon. Tamerza's other attraction is the Cascade waterfall, reached by walking through the primitive bamboo huts and past the pool of the Hôtel des Cascades, which is located near the top of the cataract. While it is an enjoyable spot for a picnic out of season, in summer it can be covered with flies and teeming with young boys who try to sell you tacky souvenirs. (See also page 147.)

▶   **Testour**   *Arrowed from 126B5*

Testour was built in the 17th century by Moorish refugees who were expelled from Spain in 1609, and became a centre for silk-spinning and ceramics. These are still produced today, although on a much reduced scale. The few tourists passing through town are not really made welcome unless they arrive during the Friday market or the week-long festival of *maalouf* music (see panel), which is held at the end of June. Testour is dominated by the modern, tiled minaret of the 17th-century Great Mosque (closed to non-Muslims), as well as other minarets in a typical Andalusian style.

*The cooling Cascade
waterfall at Tamerza
keeps on flowing,
even through the
height of summer*

Too many tourists
Served by several
international flights,
Tozeur's *zone touristique*
has expanded rapidly in
recent years and, in the
process, is threatening to
destroy the town's *raison
d'être*. The people of
Tozeur, once renowned for
their hospitality, now
regard welcoming visitors
as a big business, while
the hotels have almost
destroyed the palmery by
taking up all the water
supplies. A conservation
project began in 1996 to
stop the building of new
hotels, repair the wells and
replant the palmery.

155

▶▶ **Tozeur** *126A2*

One of the most famous oases in the world, Tozeur is now
a major tourist centre trying hard to live up to its image.
The old quarter of **Ouled el-Hadef▶▶▶** makes for a
picturesque walk along its narrow alleys and streets. The
distinctive feature of the place is its brick architecture,
which uses similar motifs to those in Berber rugs. The
Musée des Arts et Traditions Populaires▶▶ (*Open* daily
8–12, 2–6. *Admission charge* cheap) on rue de Kairouan is
housed in the *koubba* (tomb) of Sidi Bou Aïssa and illustrates traditional life in the oasis. Note the courtyard door
with its three doorknobs – for men, women and children –
examples of which are still found in the old town.

More impressive is the **Musée Dar Cheraït▶▶▶** (tel: 06
452 100. *Open* daily 8am–midnight. *Admission charge*
moderate) on route Touristique, which shows in a grand
décor scenes in the daily life of Tunisia's upper classes.
There is also an art gallery for contemporary art. The
second part of the museum is more
confused, as well it might be, for it
attempts to retrace the history of the
Book of a Thousand and One Nights.
Near by is the **Belvédère▶▶**, a huge
rock with panoramic views over the
palmery, the Chott el Jerid and the
Chott el Gharsa, and hot springs
where women bathe in the morning
and men in the afternoon. Horse-
drawn carriages offer tours through
the palmery to the wonderful
Paradise Gardens▶▶▶, with palm
trees and fragrant flowers. Also here
is the **Zoo du Désert▶▶** (*Open*
dawn–sunset. *Admission charge*
moderate), housing an interesting
collection of desert animals.

*Old Tamerza is
slowly but surely
disintegrating,
becoming one with
its magnificent
surroundings*

JERBA AND THE SOUTH

REGION HIGHLIGHTS ◄◄◄◄◄

JERBA AND THE SOUTH

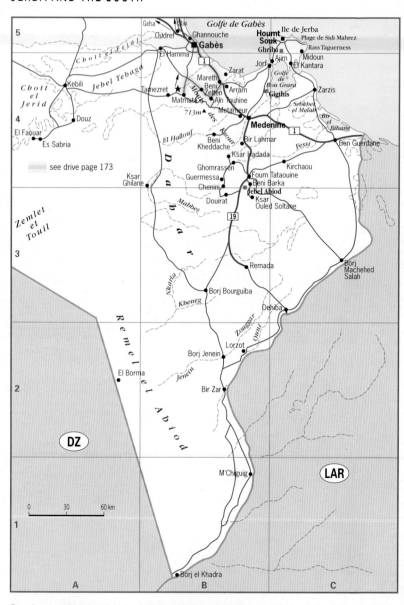

see drive page 173

0   30   60 km

DZ

LAR

Previous pages (main photo): restored ghorfas at the Ksar Ouled Soltane Opposite: Tunisia's most unusual pottery comes from Guellala on the island of Jerba

Jerba and the south Some of the most spectacular landscapes and striking architecture in Tunisia are to be found in the arid southern lands, far from the cosmopolitan influence of Tunis. Oases towns such as Gabès, the famous underground houses of Matmata, and the remarkable *ksour* (fortified Berber settlements) up in Jebel Abiod make this a region of memorable encounters. By contrast, the island of Jerba, joined to the mainland by an ancient causeway, has been drawing visitors for thousands of years to its flat, lush landscape. Today, it is one of Tunisia's main tourist destinations and also one of its most successful, for while making space for the

The barren, eroded landscape around Matmata hides many troglodyte dwellings

Honour amongst pirates
The pirate leader Barbarossa isn't known in the West for his concern for human life, but in 1540 he swapped the north Tunisian pirate base of Tabarka for one of his captains, Dragut, who had been captured by the Genoese and spent some years as an oarsman on their galleys. Dragut proved to be worth the exchange: in 1551 he saved the pirate fleet from a Genoese attack, and for the price of the single harbour he captured a significant slice of southern Tunisia and earned a reputation as one of the Mediterranean's bravest and most able captains.

ever-growing number of people seeking pleasure on its soft-sand beaches, it has also managed to preserve something of its original culture.

Island of the Lotus Eaters Jerba has always attracted foreigners, although not all have come for sea and sun. Separated geographically from the mainland long ago, it is culturally and climatically distinct. Jerba's tourist authority promotes it as a year-round destination, and although there are cloudy days – even in summer – it does enjoy a remarkably friendly weather system. But it was Jerba's position that attracted people looking for refuge, including the Jews fleeing the fall of Jerusalem in AD 70 and perhaps others as far back as 366 BC. Legend has it that long before then Odysseus, the Greek hero, was seduced by the island on his return home – the long way round – from the Trojan War (see panel opposite). The Phoenicians settled on the island and are probably responsible for the first causeway linking it to the mainland.

Pirate haven Jerba was often the first part of Tunisia to face attacks. The conquering Arab general, Oqba ibn Nafi, stopped here to convert the islanders to his new religion. After that, Kharijites, Ibadites, Hilali Arabs, Normans and Aragonese took the island. From the 14th century Jerba was a pirate base and in the first years of the 16th century it became home to the legendary Barbarossa. Originally from the Greek island of Lesbos, Barbarossa had earned a reputation as a skilful captain helping Muslims escape from Spain after the fall of the Moorish kingdom. At first he worked independently against Christian shipping, later becoming grand admiral of the Ottoman fleet and one of the closest advisers to the sultan in Constantinople, where he was buried with great honours.

The Berber south This has long been a region of conflict. After Julius Caesar took control of the Phoenician coast and the Pax Romana encouraged the farming of ever more remote pastures, settlers came into conflict with the independent Berber tribes who controlled part of the trans-Saharan trade. When Rome fell to the Vandals, the nomadic Berbers moved further and further north, closer to lush pastures, until the 11th century when they in turn were overwhelmed by the arrival of the Arab Beni Hilal and Beni Sulaym tribes, moving west from Egypt. From a position of having the run of the south, the Berber tribes were forced down into the Sahara or up into the Tunisian hills. Only in isolated Jerba and in the most remote southern places, where they lived an independent life in cave dwellings and mountainside fortifications, cut off from the rest of Tunisia, did Berber culture survive intact into the 20th century.

The deep south Unlike the south-western side of Tunisia, the deep south is problematic for tourists. The reopening of the border with Libya in 1988 made it possible to journey by four-wheel drive south to Remada and from there into Libya, but this is still a military area and you will need permission to enter it or to head further south still to Borj Bourguiba. There are few facilities and few welcomes, too, down in this part of the country, where the former leader Habib Bourguiba was exiled before independence. If your reason for going is to see the beauties of the Libyan Desert, then you might be happier crossing the border via the coast road and then heading south through Libya.

Tunisian proverb
'Rain is the best governor.'

Island legend
The history of Jerba reputedly starts with Odysseus, hero of the *Odyssey*. On his way back from Troy, he landed on a desert island which he found difficult to leave after discovering the lotus drink. Jerbans claim the idyllic island was theirs, and although no one knows what the lotus drink was, Jerbans claim it was their local *lagmi* date-palm wine.

161

Douirat was founded by the Moroccan saint and merchant Ghazi ben Douaieb

The view from the fortress at Chenini

A tall story
The room with the overlong graves in the underground mosque at Chenini is said to be the place where seven Christians were entombed alive by Roman soldiers during 3rd-century persecutions. According to legend, they slept for 400 years, growing to twice their original height; on awakening they were made to convert to Islam so they could die a normal, peaceful death.

Donkey work

►► **Chenini** *158B4*

Dramatically clinging to a rock, the village of Chenini is by far the most visited on the *ksour* (fortified village) circuit. At some times of the day the village's atmosphere is one of chaos as coaches and 4WD vehicles cause traffic jams as they try to squeeze themselves through the narrow alleys. But its mystery can still be savoured by going early in the morning or a few hours before sunset when all is quiet again. If you do go at the same time as the groups, take the unpaved track to the left (it forks off at the foot of the spur) before the tarmac road rounds the corner into the centre of the village. This track zigzags up through the village to the whitewashed mosque near the summit. From here there is a lovely walk to the highest point of the *ksar*, the *qalaa* (fortress), built in 1193, which commands excellent views over the palm-scattered valley and the village, whose cave houses are still inhabited. In old Chenini visit the underground mosque (see panel) and its cemetery of vast tombs, the communal olive press and a troglodyte bakery. The guardian here will show you around and point out the site of the original village, near the five springs in the mountain where children still come on donkeys or camels to collect water.

►► **Douirat** *158B3*

Less visited and smaller than Chenini is Douirat, another enchanting fortified Berber village, perched on a 700m-high peak. Long ago this was an important post along the caravan trade route, with over 5,000 inhabitants living in the caves, but the old village was almost completely abandoned in favour of a new settlement built down below in the 1960s. The few women who still live here keep to themselves and are very wary of visitors wandering around, so take care not to impose. The ruins are hauntingly beautiful and the panoramic views over the plains and mountain are worth the climb. The mosque is notable for the only known archaic Berber inscription, although no one knows what it means and non-Muslims are not allowed to see it. However, the mosque's basement is accessible, as is the small cemetery to the right.

► ### Foum Tataouine   158B4

The name Foum Tataouine is Berber for 'Mouth of the Springs', and with the recent construction of the four-star Hotel Sangho the town has declared itself Tunisia's southernmost tourist base. A good base it may be for exploring the *ksour* (fortified villages), but the town itself has very little to offer. Built by French administrators in 1892 it still feels like a colonial outpost, with a single, wide, palm-lined boulevard (called avenue Habib Bourguiba for the time being) and sandy streets leading off it. The French preferred Tataouine to Douirat, their original headquarters, and used it as a garrison town. It continues to serve as a base for a battalion of the French Foreign Legion. The fortress which dominates the town is now used as barracks for the Tunisian Army and is closed to visitors.

Tataouine was an important camel market for the Ouderna tribe from the 19th century onwards. The market held here on Mondays and Thursdays is still one of the most picturesque in southern Tunisia, with farmers selling their grain, olives and oil, Bedouin women displaying woven fabrics and blankets, and others bringing sheep, baskets, spices, food and second-hand clothes. On the edge of the town, past the Hotel La Gazelle, are two *ksour*, the Ksar of Megelba on the west of the road and the Ksar Degrah to the east, with two-storey *ghorfas* (rock-cut chambers) off the main courtyard. Look out for the local delicacy, *kab el-ghazal*, or *corne de gazelle* ('gazelle horns'), a delicious pastry horn filled with almond paste and honey.

In Phoenician footsteps
Douirat was founded by Ghazi ben Douaieb, a saint and merchant from the Moroccan oasis of Tafilet. He arrived amongst the local Beni Mazigh tribe about 500 years ago and was offered as much land as could be contained in a camel's skin. Like the Phoenician princess Dido (see page 61), he used his cunning, cutting the skin into fine strips and encircling the entire valley of Douirat. He soon established good trading links all over North Africa, so that Douirat became the most important market in the south.

163

The weekly market at Foum Tataouine brings together the different inhabitants of the region – Berbers, farmers and nomads

Calèche ride in Gabès
It may be a bit of a tourist trap in Gabès to take a *calèche* (horsecart) from the stand at the end of avenue Farhet Hached, but this is the most relaxing way to see the oasis. The price is set by the tourist office (check beforehand). Drivers will usually explain about the way the oasis functions and how the locals make the most out of the lovely gardens (see also pages 150–1). Try to end up near the Sidi Ali el-Bahoul Mausoleum, which has a tiny waterfall and is a pleasant place for a picnic.

The white-domed marabout *of Sidi Moussa Ben Abdallah is perched above the* ghorfas *of Ghomrassen to protect them from falling rocks*

▶▶   **Gabès**   *158B5*

Although it is often romantically described as Tunisia's only oasis on the sea, it would be more accurate to class Gabès as a major industrial centre. The palmery is impressive, but the air in town is quite smoggy and the beach suffers from chemical pollution. Nevertheless, the town has a laid-back charm and a distinctive African feel.

There are no Punic or Roman remains in Gabès, and little to show for the Berbers and Byzantines who are said to have settled here. In the 680s, Sidi Boulbaba, Prophet Mohammad's barber, built the town's first mosque. The Arabs, Spaniards, Turks and French came and went, but most of their monuments were destroyed either during the bombardments of 1943 or the devastating floods that hit the town in 1962.

Within Gabès' borders lie three villages: Menzel, Jara and Chenini (not to be confused with the village of the same name mentioned on page 162). **Jara**▶▶, near the riverbank, is the most picturesque, its market streets filled with baskets, palm-frond goods, pottery and cheap souvenirs (closed on Mon). On the road to Matmata at the edge of the town is the elegant **Mosquée de Sidi Boulbaba**▶▶ (*Admission* free. Only the inner courtyard may be visited), with lovely arcades around its entrance portal. Next door is the **Musée des Arts et Traditions Populaires**▶▶ (tel: 05 281 111. *Open* summer Tue–Sun 8–12, 3–7. Rest of year Tue–Sun 9.30–4.30. *Admission charge* cheap), set in a 17th-century *medersa*. The rooms illustrate traditional oasis life but the displays lack explanation, although one room shows the tools used in the oasis and there are local fruit trees in the small garden. The **palmery**▶▶▶, with more than 300,000 palm trees providing shade for pomegranate trees, vines and fruit trees, can be visited by *calèche* (see panel) or by driving to the village of Chenini, whose inhabitants specialise in basketwork.

► **Ghomrassen** *158B4*

This is the largest of the Berber settlements in this very picturesque region. The cave dwellings are still inhabited, although some are considered dangerous because of rock falls from the steep cliffs above. A little mosque perched on top of the cliff assures the town's protection and commands strange and fantastic views down below. The men of the town are reputed to be the best *beignet* (doughnut) makers in Tunisia. The *souq* is held on Fridays. Beyond Ghomrassen on the road to Foum Tataouine stands a prominent *ksar* (fortified village); its impressive courtyards are now deserted but are still in good condition.

►► **Guermessa** *158B4*

Guermessa, set in wild countryside, is probably the most attractive and haunting of the Berber villages. It is also said to be the oldest, built some 800 years ago. Most villagers now live in the modern settlement at the foot of the old one, but a few remain up on the clifftop despite the hardship and lack of sanitation and electricity. Villagers will assure you that it takes no more than 15 minutes to reach the top, but if you aren't fit then it may well take you a good hour. The difficult climb is rewarded with breathtaking views and a friendly welcome from the remaining inhabitants. The other advantage of the hard climb is that unlike Chenini (see page 162), Guermessa has not been invaded by tour groups.

► **Gigthis** *158B4*

One of Africa's biggest ports under the Romans, Gigthis (*Open* daily 8–6. *Admission charge* cheap) was destroyed by invading Arabs in the 7th century. The ruins, facing the sea and scattered over more than 100 hectares, were only uncovered in 1906. The most impressive remains are the large forum built during Hadrian's reign (AD 117–38), dominated by a temple to Isis and Serapis. Beside it are the baths, still with remnants of mosaic flooring. A stone-paved road leads down to the silted-up port, where the ancient jetty is still visible.

As elsewhere in Tunisia, there is no shortage of marabouts (shrines) in the south

Oudref kilims
The village of Oudref, 20km from Gabès on the road to Tozeur, is famous for its woven carpets, or *kilims*. A wide selection is on sale in the cooperative, often at half the price asked in the tourist bazaars, especially on Wednesdays (*Open* Mon–Thu 7.30–12, 2.30–5.30, Fri–Sat 7.30–12. Closed Sun). Note that although both dinars and foreign currency are accepted, credit cards are not.

The old ghorfas are slowly being abandoned as their inhabitants opt for housing with all the mod cons

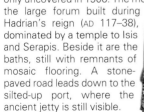

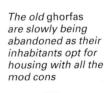

▶▶▶ **Ile de Jerba (Djerba)**   *158C5*

Legendary beginnings Idyllic but detached, Jerba is and always has been an outsider in Tunisian politics, religion and population. Its history begins with the legend of the *Odyssey* (see panel on page 161), after which the island became in turn Phoenician and Roman. It was then invaded by both the Vandals and the Byzantines before it was conquered by the Arabs in 667. By the 15th century Jerba was more or less ruled by pirates. Several attempts were made to overpower them, the most famous being in 1560 when papal troops joined forces with knights of Malta to crush the pirate Dragut and his corsairs once and for all. The 5,000–6,000 Christians who survived the first encounter fled into the Borj el Kebir, but Dragut massacred them a few months later and then made a pyramid of their skulls on the beach.

The Jerbans, who had welcomed the 7th-century Muslim invaders, supported the Kharijites in the 10th century when they sought refuge here from persecution by orthodox Islam, probably again to keep a certain independence. The Kharijite sect is known for its austerity, expressed also in the simplicity of its architecture, as can be seen in mosques on the island.

Crops only grow on the island with hard labour and the help of a complex irrigation system, and drinking water is piped in from the mainland. As the life of a farmer on Jerba is so hard, many men emigrate to earn money, very often working as grocers.

Capital sights Today, most islanders prefer living in isolated *menzels*, or family homesteads, which lie scattered all over the island, so **Houmt Souk**▶▶▶ is Jerba's only real town (see also Walk on page 168). Literally meaning 'the Market-Place', it is little more than that. At its heart lies a succession of white squares; here, it is delightful to stroll through the *souqs*, filled with traditional goods and souvenirs, or to watch the crowds pass by as you sit with a drink at one of the large café-terraces.

The imposing Borj el Kebir in Houmt Souk has seen it all before and is now the backdrop for an animated weekly market

Sunrise above Houmt Souk's harbour, where in winter the fishermen catch squid in pottery jars

The **Musée des Arts et Traditions Populaires**►► (*Open* summer Sat–Thu 8–12, 3–7. Rest of year Sat–Thu 8.30–4.30. *Admission charge* moderate) on avenue Abdelhamid el-Kadhi occupies the 18th-century Zaouia of Sidi Zitouni, a holy man who used to cure the mentally ill. Exhibits are well displayed but the explanations (in French or Arabic) are not always adequate. The first room tells the island's history and has a display of traditional costumes and jewellery. The next room shows a pottery workshop and explains how Jerban pottery is made. The most impressive room is the Qoubet el-Khiyal, or Ghost's Dome, once a place of pilgrimage. Not far from the museum is the Hanifite **Jami' et-Turuk (Mosque of the Turks)**►► (closed to the public) with a gorgeous Turkish minaret, and further on the **Strangers' Mosque**►► with its many white domes.

On the seafront stands the **Borj el Kebir (Great Tower)**►► (*Open* summer Sat–Thu 8–12, 3–7. Rest of year Sat–Thu 8.30–5.30. *Admission charge* moderate), a 15th-century fort later reinforced by the pirate Dragut. Inside the *borj*, the ruins of a 13th-century fort (built by the Sicilian Roger de Loria) are visible, while recent excavations show evidence of Roman occupation. In the northern wall lies the tomb of Ghazi Mustapha, who reinforced the fort for Dragut. Outside the fortress, on the way to the harbour, is a small white obelisk commemorating the 11m-high pyramid of skulls built by Dragut after he killed the Christians in the fort in 1560 (see opposite). The most remarkable thing about the skull pyramid is that it stood here for nearly 300 years until 1848, when the Jerbans finally buried the bones.

Rest of the island The ferry from the mainland docks at **Ajim**►, once renowned for its sponge fishing but now a crowded fishing port. The 6.5km-long **El Kantara causeway**►►, connecting Jerba to the mainland, was

Continued on page 169

Jerban Jews
Most of Jerba's Jews emigrated to Israel after Tunisian independence and only 1,000 still live here today. They form the last remnant of one of the oldest Jewish communities in the world, dating back to 566 BC and the fall of Jerusalem to Nebuchadnezzar. The Ghriba Synagogue at Hara Seghira (see page 169) is a place of pilgrimage for Jews worldwide and contains one of the oldest-known Torahs.

Unglazed pottery jars on display at the Houmt Souk pottery market

Shopping on Jerba
Woven baskets or typical Jerban straw-hats make pretty and cheap souvenirs, but for something a little more elaborate head for the Artisanat on avenue Habib Bourguiba in Houmt Souk (*Open* summer Mon–Sat 9–12, 4–6.30. Rest of year Mon–Sat 8.30–12.30, 3–6). Michèle-Art et Tradition on the rue des Antiquaires (tel: 05 652 532) has a wonderful selection of Tunisian crafts chosen by a French woman, as well as Berber crafts.

Walk Jerba

There is more to Houmt Souk than the tourist bazaars, too often filled with cheap souvenirs. As it is a tiny place, all of the sights lie within easy walking distance. Allow 2–3 hours (approximately 1km).

Start at the beautiful **Borj el Kebir (Great Tower)►►**; on Mondays and Thursdays a market is held on the square in front of it. From the *borj*, cross the road and take the left fork towards the town. To the right is the mausoleum of Mohamed Hioulou, a local wise man who died in 1925. At the end of the street turn left and left again, following the signs for the **Musée des Arts et Traditions Populaires►►**, housed in the Zaouia of Sidi Zitouni. As you leave and return to rue Moncef Bey, the **Jami' et-Turk (Mosque of the Turks)►►** is just on the other side of the street.

Facing the mosque, turn left into the little square and walk through the arched passageway in the left corner to reach the **Marhala Hotel►►**. The Tunisian Touring Club turned this old caravanserai into a simple hotel: the lovely courtyard, shaded by palm trees and bougainvillaea, is a pleasant place for an evening drink. Walk left

Above: Strangers' Mosque
Below: Mosque of the Turks

out of the hotel, then take the first street to the left, which leads to **place Sidi Brahim►**. To the left appears the beautiful dome of a hammam or Turkish bath, followed by the Zaouia of Sidi Brahim. Across the road is the **Strangers' Mosque►►**.

Return towards the café-terrace on the square and take the street containing the restaurant du Sud towards **place Hedi Chaker►►**. Walk left through several pleasant little squares and, before arriving at avenue Habib Bourguiba, turn left under the arcades to the covered **Marché Central►►**, the daily food market. Follow avenue Habib Bourguiba up to the end, where it leads to the tranquil little fishing port.

*The Ghriba
Synagogue is one of
the oldest holy
Jewish buildings in
North Africa, and
claims to have one of
the earliest Torahs in
the world*

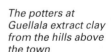

Flamingo excursion
Swashbuckling pirate-type
boats make day-trips from
Houmt Souk harbour to the
nearby Ile aux Flamants
(Flamingo Island) or the Iles
Borj Djilij. Trips
usually include a fish lunch.
For more information
head for the harbour or
tel: 05 650 488.

Continued from page 167

probably a Phoenician idea. The nearby hamlet of
Guellala►► lies hidden behind the clouds of smoke
produced from its kilns and by high piles of pottery.
Pottery is big business here, but there are also fun and
unusual objects for sale, such as various terracotta
'gadgets'. From Guellala, a road turns inland to Er-Riadh,
once known as **Hara Seghira**►►, or 'Little Ghetto', and
home to the Ghriba Synagogue (see also panel on page
167). It is believed that a holy stone fell from heaven to
mark the site and that a mysterious foreign girl, or *ghriba*,
appeared and helped the builders by performing miracles.
The present building dates only from 1920 and the interior
is unique more than interesting (cover your head during a
visit). **Hara Kebira**►, or 'Big Ghetto', was also inhabited
by a large Jewish community.

Sidi Mahrez►► is lined with beach hotels on either side
of the Rass Taguerness, with very little of Tunisia about
them, but the lovely white-sand beach is excellent. For
those staying in Houmt Souk, there is a good public beach
about 10km out of town just before these hotels.

In its attempt to re-create a traditional Jerban village
with a brand-new 'Old Town', nearby **Midoun**► sells very
expensive crafts and stages wedding processions every
afternoon for the tourists. Try to coincide a visit with the
pleasant Friday morning market or look for the *maasera*, a
300-year-old underground olive mill, off the road to
Taguerness near the hospital.

The **west coast**►►► of the island is rocky and
so has been spared from tourist development. A
track starts near the Princesse de Haroun
restaurant in the harbour of Houmt Souk, and
once you get beyond the rubbish tip
there are only palm trees, the sea,
absolute peace and a few
fishing huts.

*The potters at
Guellala extract clay
from the hills above
the town*

JERBA AND THE SOUTH

Ksar Ghilane
The only *ksar* for which a four-wheel-drive vehicle is essential is Ksar Ghilane, 90km west of Chenini. This magnificent oasis is set between a mountainous desert to the east and west and a sand desert to the south – the beginning of the Sahara. It is possible to hike or make camel treks to the Roman border fort to the north-east, or to head further out into the desert. The entrance to the village changes continually as sand-dunes move over the track.

The well-preserved ghorfas *at Ksar Ouled Soltane would make the perfect backdrop for a fashion shoot!*

►► **Jebel Abiod**   *158B3*

As the plains and mountains come together at the white mountain of Jebel Abiod, so do the nomadic herders and farmers. Their confrontations were not always peaceful, and the long history of tribal wars is illustrated in a wealth of legends and stories as well as in the defensive architecture of the numerous *ksour* in the area. A *ksar* was originally a fortified granary, with *ghorfas* (cells) centred around interior courtyards, the entrance being hidden in a well-protected gatehouse. Later on people started living in the *ghorfas*; until they abandoned them relatively recently for more modern housing, usually built at the foot of the old *ksar*. As a result, many *ksour* have fallen to ruin, but they are still fun to explore and usually give sweeping views over the surrounding landscape.

The Oued Zondag lies at the heart of Jebel Abiod; here are the villages of Beni Barka, with a remarkable ruinous *ksar* at its peak, and Maztouri, overlooked by three rectangular *ksour*, of which the one known as Kedim or Zenata has some beautifully decorated vaults with Berber, Jewish and Arab influences. The mountain is strewn with *ksour*, but the most beautiful is undoubtedly Ksar Ouled Soltane (see below).

►► **Ksar Hadada**   *158B4*

Also known as Ghomrassen-Hadada, this *ksar* was recently beautifully restored by a French architect who converted part of it into a basic but rather charming hotel, serving simple, traditional meals. The maze of little steps, courtyards and rooftops is a great place to explore. In its heyday the *ksar* was used for food storage by four local tribes: the Hadada, the Hamdoun from Ghomrassen and two others claiming Libyan and Moroccan roots.

►►► **Ksar Ouled Soltane**   *158B3*

The best preserved of Tunisia's *ksour*, this is also one of the few that is still inhabited, and tourists remain a rare sight. The four-storey *ghorfas* are centred around two courtyards, one dating from the 15th century and a later, 19th-century one. The local population prefers a traditional lifestyle to the comforts of the towns, and after Friday prayers the courtyards are used as a meeting-place for the semi-nomadic Ouled Chehida tribe. Grain and olives are still stored here. The views from the terrace at the top are stunning.

►►► **Matmata**   *158B4*

The road from Gabès to Matmata cuts across the Mountains of Matmata, strangely shaped hills with palm trees or patchy cultivation in every hollow. Matmata used to be famous for its surreal, moonlike landscape, but today probably the first thing you will notice is the modern whitewashed houses scattered all over the place. Nevertheless, the raw earth, pockmarked with some 700 pits dug by the Hammama des Matmata Berber tribe (half of which they still inhabit) never fails to impress. This tribe, cited in Roman chronicles for their raids, chose to live underground to protect themselves from the summer heat (see page 172).

Even before reaching Matmata you will see signs saying '*Visitez Maison Troglodyte*', and although some families resent the intrusion of tourists so much that they now hide behind barbed wire, quite a few make a good living out of inviting people into their homes. Since the town was used as a setting in the *Star Wars* movie, the influx of package tourists has rocketed, with tours arriving from the beach resorts in time for lunch. The invasion ends around 4pm, when the town returns to its normal pace – a good reason to spend a night in one of the local hotels. Sadly, the atmosphere is not what it used to be and some locals are even a little aggressive, having suffered one disrespectful visitor too many. Tour leaders sometimes make arrangements for a family to vacate their house while a tour group visits, although the old grandfather will stay sitting by the door waiting for his tip. There is an interesting market held in town on Mondays.

Visible reminder of a traditional way of life

So far most of the inhabitants of Ksar Ouled Soltane show no inclination to move

■ **Troglodyte dwellings may seem both bizarre and ancient, but the southern Tunisians chose to live in caves for the very good reason that they protected them from the baking summer heat above. Today, quite a few families continue to inhabit underground dwellings, although they may soon become a thing of the past as more troglodyte dwellers move into breeze-block housing with all the mod cons.** ■

Sleep like a troglodyte
In Matmata (see pages 170–1) a few of the largest troglodyte houses, each with several courtyards, have been turned into hotels. In the 1960s the Tunisian Touring Club converted a basic set of pits into the Marhala Hotel (see page 199). The Sidi Driss prides itself on having served as a base for the makers of the film *Star Wars* in 1976. The accommodation is basic, with candlelight in the evenings, but it is a memorable experience, giving a real feel of what it's like to live underground.

An ancient tradition The Tunisian troglodyte tradition is centuries old, even though the most famous caves at Matmata date only from the last century. Cave-dwellers are also found in the neighbouring Gharyan area in Libya. The troglodytes' ancestors originally took to the ground because it was easier to burrow into the crumbly, soft tufa rock than to use it for building bricks. Also, and equally importantly, the temperature underground was far more bearable than that above – cooler in summer and rather cosy in winter, with an average temperature of 17°C all year round. Unlike the *ksour* (fortified villages; see page 170) these dwellings were never built for defensive reasons, as has been claimed. Very occasionally, heavy rainfall can cause flooding and threaten the structures, but otherwise they are solid constructions, some of them more than 400 years old.

Designed like an Arab house The actual design of the houses, despite being underground, retains the typical Arab or North African ground-plan. The central courtyard, or *haouch*, is a hollow about 10m deep with a 10–15m diameter. Off the *haouch* are cut four to eight rooms, used for eating, sleeping, stabling and one for food and fodder storage. The walls are whitewashed, shelves and cupboards are cut out where needed and water is collected in cisterns. The rooms tend to be the same size – a richer man will simply extend the number of his courtyards and rooms rather than increase the size of each room. A gently inclined entrance tunnel, big enough to take a camel, connects the floor of the main courtyard to ground-level. Store rooms and stables often have holes in the ceiling for pouring supplies directly from above.

*Right: several stairways descend into the central courtyard
Below: many abandoned dwellings have been converted into hotels*

 **From Matmata to the coast**

See map on page 158.

Above: Beni Zelten

This interesting drive takes you through some of the less visited villages of the troglodyte south. There are no facilities *en route*, so go well equipped with water and food. Allow 2–2½ hours.

Start in Matmata▶▶▶ and head out of town on the main road to Gabès. After about 12km you reach Matmata Jedid, an unexciting breeze-block settlement where many Matmata troglodytes were relocated. Hopefully, the modern amenities of running water, plumbing, electricity and TV in these houses go some way towards making up for the soulless atmosphere and loss of tradition.

In town, watch out for a sign to the right marked 'Beni Zelten 16km', which doubles slightly back on the direction from which you have come. This tarmac road, leading through the outskirts of Matmata Jedid into flat rural landscapes, continues to **Beni Zelten**, a striking village ranged out over a hillside and lying beneath the ruins of a hilltop fort. Many of the

brownstone houses are now derelict, having been abandoned in favour of the breeze-block constructions in Matmata Jedid, but among them are several cave dwellings still in use.

The narrow tarmac road continues through increasingly attractive countryside, with surprisingly fertile, heavily wooded valleys contrasting strongly with the moonlike landscapes of Matmata. Drive slowly through Aïn Tounine▶▶▶ to appreciate the unspoilt nature of the dwellings and the lifestyle here. The road runs straight through the market square – just a vast mud courtyard surrounded by workshops, where trades are grouped together. A picturesque mud hut houses the café.

From Aïn Tounine follow the signposts to Mareth. Along the roadside you may see the black tents of local nomadic tribes who still roam across the pasturelands with their sheep, goats and camels. At Mareth, prepare for the shock of emerging on the busy road to Gabès. From here you can continue towards Jerba.

JERBA AND THE SOUTH

The Mareth Line
The small roadside town of Mareth, 40km from Medenine on the road to Gabès, was made famous by two battles. The first is celebrated in the epic *Johannides* by the Byzantine poet Corippe, and was won by John Trogliata over the Lawata nomads in 546. In 1938 the French built the Mareth Line against Mussolini's army, but it was later used by Rommel's Afrika Korps against Montgomery's Eighth Army. A British monument to Field Marshal Montgomery stands 3km south of Oued Zigzaou near Mareth.

▶ **Medenine**   *158B4*

In 1945 British government papers described Medenine as a village, and although it became the county town of the largest Tunisian governorate, it is still little more than that. It served the French as their southern headquarters and was the main market centre for the produce of the south. In the name of modernisation the town was bulldozed in the 1960s, so gone are 35 *ksour*, intricately connected with up to six-storey-high *ghorfas*, and the delightful arcaded market-place. Medenine means 'Two Towns' in Arabic as it is divided by a wide *oued*, or river bed. The southern part is dominated by modern administrative buildings, but the other side, along rue des Palmiers, has more charm. The remains of three *ksour* are run as souvenir shops, and although robbed of their traditional character the passageways, various levels and vaults are still impressive. These days, grain is stored in conventional silos on the outskirts of town.

▶▶ **Metameur**   *158B4*

Unlike in Medenine, the 600-year-old *ksar* at neighbouring Metameur, set on a flat plain, has been much better preserved. It rises elegantly above the little town, its three courtyards lined with three-storey-high *ghorfas*. Part of it has been converted by a Berber family into a basic hotel. The semi-nomadic population still uses the other courtyards on Fridays to chat and gossip after the noon prayers.

▶ **Remada**   *158B3*

Tunisia's southernmost town is the small oasis of Remada, watered by wells on the edge of the Oued Dhib. The Romans constructed a minor fort here, which the French subsequently incorporated into their garrison town. The place is still dominated by the military, as it is on the first line of defence against Libya. The centre of town, the place de l'Indépendance, is where everything or nothing happens, and is a good place to drink a few mint teas in the shade. The strangest sight is on the southern edge of town: a building with 15 *koubbas* (domes) which once housed the slaughterhouse. Borj Bourguiba, to the south-west, was named after its most famous prisoner, who was held here in internal exile for a year in the early 1950s. Dehiba, to the south-east, is the southernmost crossing post for civilians into Libya. The vast tracks of desert further south are a military area, for which visitors require a special permit to enter (such permits are rarely granted).

Not much is left of the old ghorfas at Medenine, which once stood up to six storeys high

▶▶ **Tamezret**   *158B4*

Tamezret, together with Taoujout and Zeraoua, were the only three villages where pure Berber was still spoken in the 19th century. It is a tiny village with stone houses built around the *marabout* (tomb) of the local saint Sidi Haj Yusuf. The café at the top of the little hill commands good views from its roof and serves excellent almond

tea. Typically for this region, the villagers wait for rain, which only falls every few years, before sowing grain. When the rains do come the village empties, guarded only by the old men, and everyone takes his pick of the land in the plain. Only when the crops are harvested and the animals are ready to eat do the villagers come back, their return generally followed by a season of trading, feasting and marriage.

The Berber family that converted some of Metameur's abandoned ghorfas into a basic hotel also organise trips to more remote ksour

▶ Zarzis   *158C4*

Apart from being a tax-free zone, Zarzis is, above all, a beach resort. Most of its beautiful sandy beaches lie in front of the hotels in the *zone touristique*, quite far from the centre of town. The town itself was created by the French as a garrison town (still occupied) and has little of interest to the visitor except for a signpost announcing 'Cairo 2,591km'. The 1970s Great Mosque was built on the site of the old Turkish fortress, and a fine market is held in the town on Fridays. From Zarzis it is but a 20km trip through olive groves to the El Kantara causeway, which connects the island of Jerba (see pages 166–9) to the mainland.

Long stretches of fine white sand make Zarzis a popular beach resort

Camels and camel treks

■ A brief camel ride on the beach can be a tacky tourist trap, but provided you are in good shape a longer trek in the absolute calm of the Sahara Desert will be an unforgettable experience. And although saddlesores are to be expected, most people don't take too long to get saddle-hardened! ■

The modern desert safari
For some, a desert safari in a four-wheel drive may seem more alluring than a camel trek. However, be aware that these excursions cover a huge amount of terrain in a short period, and tend to involve 5.30am departures with long spells of driving cooped up in bumpy, uncomfortable Land Rovers filled to capacity. The time actually spent at any of the destinations can be short, so those in search of a deeper experience of the interior may be disappointed. Hiring a four-wheel drive independently may be a more satisfying option, but don't consider driving yourself unless you have experience of this sort of terrain (see also 'Car rental' on pages 183–4).

Go for that 'Lawrence of Arabia' experience!

The ex-ship of the desert
The Arabic language has more than 100 words to describe camels: she-camels, camels of different ages, camels with long legs, aggressive camels and so on. Camels can live up to 25 years, ample time for its master to get to know its foibles – a camel owner can even distinguish the footprints of his own camels. Extraordinarily well adapted to their environment, camels can go for two weeks with no water as long as they find pasture instead. When they finally get the opportunity to drink they can consume up to 130 litres in one go. In addition to their role as a beast of burden, the camel's milk is much valued, although in the sub-Sahara today they are mostly bred for their meat.

A wobbly ride For a desert experience there is nothing like a camel trek. Tourist offices at Douz (see page 133), Nefta (see pages 152–3) and Tozeur (see page 155) organise trips which range from one hour to ten days. Camping Nomade el-Nouail, 5km south of Douz, in particular organises excellent camel treks (tel: 05 495 584). Douz and Ksar Metameur (see page 174) offer the most adventurous expeditions, led by experienced local guides, in which you ride from well to well, pitching nomad tents and cooking on camp fires. Some routes offer the option of moving from one *ksar* (fortified village) to the next and camping in small *ghorfas* (rock-cut chambers) for shelter.

The best time for a trek is between November and April, when warm clothing will be needed for the evening as temperatures in the desert can drop below 0°C. The summer should be avoided as travel is restricted to the early morning and evening (daytime temperatures exceed 40°C).

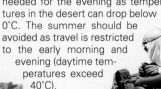

Getting there

By air Tunisia has six international airports: Tunis; Monastir, Jerba, Tozeur, Tabarka and Sfax. Tunisair and GB Airways run regular scheduled flights from London to Tunis. Tunisair has regular flights to all European cities, and all major European airlines fly to Tunis, but there are no direct flights from the US. The cheapest way from North America is to fly to London and look for a reduced-price scheduled flight. In summer there are various charter flights, which have restrictions on the length of stay and which legally must include accommodation.

All foreigners are issued with landing cards on board the plane, requiring passport and other details; these will be checked at passport control. Keep the card with you throughout your journey for surrender at passport control on departure.

Tunis-Carthage International Airport is 6km north of the city and has 24-hour exchange facilities. For getting into town, see panel on page 78. Monastir Skanès International Airport is 12km south of Sousse, a 20-minute taxi ride from the city centre. Jerba's international airport, to the west of Houmt Souk, is also approximately 20 minutes from town.

By sea Regular car/passenger ferries sail to La Goulette, the port of Tunis,

The majority of visitors to Tunisia come on a package tour

from Marseille (France), and Genoa and Trapani (Italy). The Marseille crossing is pleasant, but it isn't cheap and takes 24 hours. For information and bookings contact **Companie Tunisienne de Navigation (CTN)** in Tunis (tel: 01 242 775) or **Société Nationale Maritime Corse Mediterranée (SNCM)** in Marseille (tel: 91 56 32 00). The London agent is **Southern Ferries** (tel: 0171 491 4968). For information on the Genoa line (24 hours), call SNCM. The crossing from Trapani takes 7–8 hours on Tirrenia Line; for information in the UK call **Serena Holidays** (tel: 0171 373 6548). In summer, a jetfoil service runs between Trapani and Kelibia.

By train There is a daily train from Algeria to Ghardimaou in Tunisia, but the same difficulties may occur at the border as mentioned below.

By road It is probably easier to get out of the neighbouring countries of Algeria and Libya than to get in. If you did make it in, you will know that your documentation needs to be in perfect order and translated into Arabic. Both countries' customs officials do not make life easy for tourists, so be prepared for long waits. There are regular buses from Tunis to Annaba

(Algeria), Casablanca (Morocco) and
Libya, as well as the local buses near
the border.

Customs regulations
You are allowed to import 1 litre of
spirits or 2 litres of wine, 400
cigarettes or 100 cigars or 500g of
tobacco, 25ml perfume or 1 litre of
eau de toilette, two cameras, one
video camera, 20 films and a portable
typewriter. There is a well-stocked
duty-free shop upon leaving Tunisia,
but no Tunisian currency is accepted
beyond passport control.

Weapons cannot be taken in/out of
Tunisia, but permits for hunting
weapons can be obtained on organised visits. It is illegal to export
genuine antiques.

Travel insurance
Good travel insurance is vital.
Comprehensive travel policies cover
accidents, illness, delays, theft, flight
cancellation and so on. In the case of
medical care, keep all receipts and
ask for a full medical report. In the
event of loss or theft, register with
the police and ask for a report giving
details of the loss and stating how it
happened, even though this will be
in Arabic. The police will issue a
case number, which will allow your
insurance company to follow it up.

Inter-city buses are often excellent

Evening rush hour at Douz

Visas
At the time of writing no tourist visa
is required for nationals of the EC,
USA, Canada or Japan, but regula-
tions do change, so check all passport
and visa requirements with your
nearest Tunisian embassy. For stays
over six months (four months for US
nationals) a residence visa is required.
Tunisian embassies abroad:
- **Australia** 27 Victoria Road, Belvue
Hill, Sydney (tel: 363 5588).
- **Canada** 515 O'Connor Street,
Ottawa (tel: 237 0330).
- **Germany** Godesberger Allee 103,
53 Bonn 2 (tel: 228 276981).
- **UK** 29 Princess Gate, London SW7
(tel: 0171 584 8117).
- **USA** 1515 Massachusetts Avenue
NW, Washington DC 20005 (tel:
202/862-1850).

When to go

If you want to swim in the sea or in unheated hotel pools, your visit must take place between April/May and October. The sea is quite cold during the winter, and most hotels drain their pools at this time, although many up-market resorts now have heated or indoor pools that are open year round. For touring the interior, spring (March–May) and autumn (late September–November) are excellent, although it can rain in April. The sun can be hot and strong all year round, so always take suncream, sunglasses and a hat. A pullover is necessary in the evenings, even occasionally in the summer. Winter nights can be very cold and damp, so check if your hotel has heating before you book.

The greener north offers a pleasant Mediterranean climate of hot, dry summers and cool, wet winters

Climate

The northern coast of Tunisia has a Mediterranean climate, with hot, dry summers and wet winters, while the south is subject to a desert climate with extreme temperatures – very hot during the day, and often cold at night. In the winter, the climate is unpredictable: it can get pretty wet in the north or along the coast, but it is usually mild and warm in the south around the oases. This is the perfect time to explore the Sahara, although the nights are freezing. The summer can be extremely hot, especially in the interior and desert areas, but on

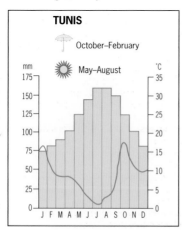

TUNIS

October–February

May–August

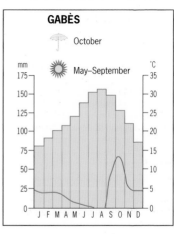

GABÈS

October

May–September

the coast temperatures are made much more bearable by the presence of sea breezes. In spring it sometimes rains in the north, but everything is green, the hills are covered in wildflowers, and the temperatures are mild and pleasant.

National holidays

Banks and businesses close on the following public holidays:

- **New Year's Day** 1 January
- **Anniversary of the Revolution** 18 January
- **Independence Day** 20 March
- **Youth Day** 21 March
- **Martyrs' Day** 9 April
- **International Labour Day** 1 May
- **National Day** 1 June
- **Republic Day** 25 July
- **Women's Day** 13 August
- **Anniversary of the Events of 1987** 7 November

In addition to these secular holidays there are the Muslim feasts which follow the lunar calendar, and therefore move backwards in the Gregorian calendar by about 11 days a year. Exact dates are determined by the religious authorities in Mecca, Saudi Arabia, according to sightings of the new moon. The Muslim calendar starts from AD 622, the year in which Muhammad left Mecca for Medina. As a visitor to the country during the fasting month of **Ramadan** (see page 15) you will not notice much difference in the resorts, but inland, away from tourist destinations, you will find that most cafés and restaurants and many shops close for the day. If you eat, drink or smoke publicly in such places, you risk offending local people. The end of Ramadan is marked by a three-day national holiday, the **Eid es-Seghir**. The **Eid el-Kebir**, 40 days later (see also page 22), is a three- or four-day holiday. The Islamic New Year, or Muharram, and the Mouled (Birthday of the Prophet Muhammad) are the two other Muslim holidays.

Time difference

Tunisia is always one hour ahead of GMT. When Britain is on British Summer Time, there is therefore no time difference between London and Tunis.

Tunisian dinars can only be bought when you get there

Money matters

The currency is the dinar (D), which equals 1,000 millimes (mill). Coins are in denominations of 5, 10, 20, 50, 100 and 500 millimes and 1 dinar, while banknotes come in 1D, 5D, 10D and 20D denominations. Prices over a dinar are often still quoted in millimes, which can be confusing – for example, 1500D is 1.5D and not 1,500D.

Tunisian dinars can only be bought in Tunisia and cannot be taken out. There is no limit to how much foreign currency you can bring in, but if it is over £300 you should complete a currency declaration upon arrival so you can take it out again. Change only what you need as you can only convert a limited amount of dinars back into foreign currency at the end of your stay. As you will also need proof of official exchange you should keep all bank receipts.

Credit cards are accepted in the better hotels and restaurants in Tunisia (check beforehand to avoid surprises), but not at petrol stations. In larger towns it is possible to withdraw money from cash dispensers with a credit card. Travellers' cheques are exchanged everywhere, including hotel receptions. Most banks do not charge a commission for exchanging cash, but do to change travellers' cheques.

Public transport

By bus Buses are the cheapest and most popular form of transport, but although there is an extensive network it can be hard to track down the right information. Local buses are usually crowded and filled to the brim – especially on market days, when you may find yourself sharing the journey with chickens, the occasional sheep and crates of fruits and vegetables. Inter-city buses, on the contrary, are generally modern, fast and comfortable. Air-conditioned buses are slightly more expensive but definitely worth while in summer. Avoid travelling during the midday heat at this time of year. Bus stations and tourist offices can provide information about buses, or you can call the **National Intercity Transport Companie (GRT)** in Tunis: Bab el-Fellah station for buses to the south (tel: 01 495 255); or Bab Saadoun station for buses to the north (tel: 01 562 299). The French-language daily

A new, fast motorway connects Sousse with Hammamet and Tunis

newspapers give a timetable for inter-city departures from Tunis. Advance booking is a good idea in summer, when buses are often overbooked, and make sure you arrive early as they often leave before schedule.

By train Tunisia has a good network of trains, which are efficient but slow, giving you ample time to admire the landscape. Timetables are available at train stations and from tourist offices. A timetable for trains leaving Tunis is published in the daily French-language newspapers. For all information, call Tunis **SNCFT station** (tel: 01 244 440). *Confortable* class is the most expensive and obviously the most comfortable, although both this and first class lack the excitement and crowds of the much cheaper second class. Trains usually leave on time.

The most important lines are: Tunis–Bizerte (1h 50min); Tunis–Hammamet (1h 25min)–Nabeul (20min longer); Tunis–Sousse (2h 20min)–Sfax (2h more), stops at El Jem; Sfax–Gabès (3h)–Metlaoui (11h from Tunis); Tunis–Gaafour (3h), with buses to Dougga (30km);

Do like the locals, and enjoy a chicha (water-pipe)

The French-language dailies list the main bus and train timetables

Tunis–Jendouba (3h), with bus to Bulla Regia (9km).

Train–museums ticket
It is possible to buy a combined train and museum pass that is valid for a week from major railway stations. This can be a considerable saving if you are planning on moving around and visiting numerous sites and museums.

By *louage* (communal taxi) Within towns and cities taxis are cheap and the best way to get around (see also page 78). For longer distances between towns, shared taxis, or *louages*, are fast – sometimes too fast – and only slightly more expensive than the train. They leave from *louage* stations, usually located next to the bus station, and take five people, departing as soon as they are full. If you are taking one just for yourself and your family be sure to fix a price in advance – this should be

equivalent to five or six times the fixed rate for one person.

By plane TunInter and Tunisavia (reservations via Tunisair) run regular internal flights between Tunis, Monastir, Tabarka, Gabès, Jerba, Sfax and Tozeur. Flights are cheap, but as the planes are tiny space is limited. Small planes can be hired from Tunisavia. **Tunisair** avenue Habib Bourguiba, Tunis (tel: 01 285 387).

Car rental
Car hire is very expensive, mostly because cars are expensive to buy in Tunisia. In summer and at Easter (the peak seasons) it is best to arrange car rental before departure as the rates will be cheaper. Out of season it is possible to bargain on the spot, especially for longer periods and at the last minute. Most major car-hire companies are represented in Tunisia (phone numbers for the main Hertz agents are provided in the 'Useful addresses' panels in the A–Z section of this guide). Mattei is one of the cheapest local firms, and has representatives in major towns. Four-wheel-drive vehicles for desert safaris can be hired locally, usually with a driver.

To hire a car you must be over 21 and have held a full licence for over a year. Make sure you have Collision Damage Waiver (CDW) and a full insurance cover: check the small print carefully! Always check water and oil levels and the state of the spare tyre before setting off in a hire car, and make sure the seat belts work. Very few companies have child seats, so it is safest to bring one with you.

Always keep car documents and passports to hand as police patrols are frequent. Failure to produce the right papers can result in you being sent back to where you started from, or to the nearest police station.

Car breakdown In case of breakdown call the hire firm for advice or find the nearest mechanic. The patrolling Garde Nationale may also help out or give you some advice. If you plan to go off the main road in the southern desert, only do so with a four-wheel-drive vehicle equipped with a full tool kit, a handbook and a spare-parts kit provided by the manufacturer; spare tyre(s), a tyre pump and tyre-repair kit; spare fuel can(s) and spare water; comprehensive first-aid kit; and emergency rations, maps and compasses.

Driving tips In Tunisia vehicles drive on the right. The roads are usually in

Some knowledge of Arabic is useful as not all signs are bilingual

good condition, but can be slow because of heavy truck traffic and general bad driving. Be careful when driving through villages and small towns as children, animals and older people have little road sense and may cross the road, or play on it, without paying attention to any vehicles. It is particularly dangerous around sunset, when villagers return home from the fields with their cattle and young people walk to the centre for the evening promenade. Avoid driving at night outside cities.

Safety belts are compulsory and petrol is very cheap. Speed limits are 50kph (31mph) in urban zones, 90kph (56mph) on the open road and 110kph (68mph) on the motorway. Speed traps are common on the outskirts of towns and on motorways, and speeding can result in an on-the-spot fine. Avoid parking illegally in major towns, especially in Tunis and Houmt Souk where cars are clamped or towed away. Fines are cheap compared to Europe but the wait can be tedious. Road signs are in French and Arabic.

Hitchhiking
Hitchhiking is easy, particularly along the coast, in the north and in the centre of the country where there are

good roads and plenty of traffic. In the south and deeper in the interior it becomes more difficult. Hitchhiking is definitely not advisable for women travelling alone.

Maps
The map supplied by the Tunisian Tourist Office is probably fine for most visitors' purposes and also has town plans of the major resorts. If you are driving around the country in your own car, the best map is Michelin 972. The Hildebrand's Travel Map is good for roads and has town plans for the major towns. As the place-names are transcriptions of the Arabic, spellings may differ from one source to another.

Student and youth travel
Students under 32 with a student card may get reductions at historical sites and museums, and on internal flights and trains. There is a network of Auberges de Jeunesse (youth hostels) open to all holders of an International Youth Hostel Card. They are cheap and clean, and close doors at 11pm. There is a strict segregation between boys and girls, and alcohol is not allowed. A card and information can be obtained from the **Association Tunisienne des Auberges de Jeunesse** 10 rue Ali Bach Hamba, BP 320, 1015 Tunis (tel: 01 246 000) or from **Tourisme et Jeunesse** 11 bis, rue d'Espagne, Tunis (tel: 01 242 693).

Women travellers
As in all Muslim countries, crime against women is rare. However, some Tunisian men are convinced that foreign women travelling alone in Tunisia do so looking for sex. This doesn't make it easy for women who genuinely want to explore the country without being verbally abused or stared at. The best advice for lone women is to dress modestly in loose cotton clothes, covering as much flesh as possible, and to stay close to women or families on public transport. Walk confidently, try to avoid eye contact with strangers and ignore any abusive comments.

Calèche (horsecart) driver, relaxing in the heat of the day before the evening rush

Media

The major tourist resorts of Tunis, Hammamet, Sousse and Jerba sell European newspapers the day after publication. There are three Tunisian French-language daily papers – *La Presse*, *L'Action* and *Le Temps* – and an English-language weekly – *Tunisia News*. There are two local TV channels, one in Arabic with lots of Egyptian soaps and one in French, both pretty poor in quality of programme. Most Tunisians watch the French TV channel Antenne 2 or the Italian RAI, which can be received throughout most of the country. Radio Monte Carlo is the most popular radio station for music, while the BBC World Service can easily be received on 15.07MHz from 5am to 11pm GMT.

Post offices

Tunisia's PTT (Poste, Telegraph et Telephone) system is well represented throughout the country and is efficient. Post boxes are small and yellow, but it is probably easier to drop the letters at your hotel reception. Letters to Europe take between one and two weeks to arrive, and those to the US two weeks or more. Stamps can be bought from post offices or, easier, from newsagents, kiosks or hotel shops. Post offices are open summer Mon–Thu 7.30–12 and rest of year Mon–Thu 8–12, 2–5, Fri–Sat 8–12.30. The main post office in Tunis is on rue Charles de Gaulle.

Telephone and fax

The telephone system is quite efficient, but public phone boxes are few and far between (usually in or adjacent to post offices) and queues are often huge. Calls from hotels are much more expensive, with a high minimum charge of three minutes. In between the two are taxiphones, kiosks with an attendant, which are springing up all over the country. It is easy to make inland or international calls from these kiosks, and often also to send a fax.

	Arabic	**French**
Greetings		
hello!	assálamu aláikum/ assláma	bonjour
how are you?	keef hálek?/la bés?	comment ça va?
well	kwáyyis/la bés	très bien
thank you	shúkran	merci
goodbye	bislémah	au revoir
please	min fádlek/birabbi	s'il vous plaît
God willing	inshállah	si Dieu le veut
never mind	ma'lesh	ne t'inquiète pas
(very) good	béhi (yéssir)	(très) bien/bon
bad	mush béhi	mauvais
go away	imshee/barra	va t'en
yes	naam/ih	oui
no	la'a	non
how much?	kadésh?	combien?
it's too much	yessir	c'est trop
Days		
Sunday	el-áhad	dimanche
Monday	el-itnéen	lundi
Tuesday	el-taláta	mardi
Wednesday	el-árba	mercredi
Thursday	el-khemées	jeudi
Friday	el-júma	vendredi
Saturday	es-sebt	samedi
tomorrow	búkra	demain
today	el-yóom	aujourd'hui
yesterday	ams	hier
later	ba'déen	plus tard

Phone services are easy to use

COMMUNICATIONS

Language guide

Arabic is Tunisia's official language, but French is still widely spoken. The most common of all, however, is 'Frarabic', a haphazard mixture of the two which most people speak in their own distinctive way, especially in the business community and wealthier classes. When Tunisians meet they do not just say hello, but ask about the other person's well-being, his family, his work and so on, interspersing these enquiries with blessings for the Lord. Although a foreigner doesn't have to go through these elaborations, it is only polite to greet someone properly and ask how they are. Below are some useful Arabic and French words and phrases.

Numerals

0	sifr	zéro
1	wáhid	un (m)/une (f)
2	tnéen	deux
3	taláata	trois
4	árba'a	quattre
5	kháms	cinq
6	sitta	six
7	sába	sept
8	tamánia	huit
9	tíssa	neuf
10	áshra	dix
11	ihdásh	onze
12	itnásh	douze
13	talatásh	treize
14	arbatásh	quattorze
15	khamstash	quinze
16	sittásh	seize
17	sabatásh	dix-sept
18	tmantásh	dix-huit
19	tissatásh	dix-neuf
20	ishreen	vingt
30	tlaatéen	trente
100	mía	cent
200	miatéen	deux cents
300	tláata mía	trois cents
1,000	alf	mille

187

	Arabic	French
General		
left/right	yassar/yameen	gauche/droite
straight on	ala tool	tout droit
enough	ízzi	ça suffit
the bill	el-hisaab	l'addition
bread	khoubz	pain
meat	lahm	viande
fish	samak/huut	poisson
fruit	fawákih	fruit
vegetables	khódra	légumes
soup	shorba	potage
water	maa	de l'eau
milk	haléeb	du lait
butter	zibda	beurre
egg	baid	oeuf
tea	shay	thé
coffee	kahwa	café
wine	sharáb	vin
red/white/rosé	ahmar/abiad/ bortouqali	rouge/blanc/rosé
beer	birra	bière
salt	milh	sel
pepper	felfel	poivre
sugar	súkar	sucre
breakfast	futóor	petit déjeuner
lunch	áda	déjeuner
dinner	asha	dîner

For a glossary of architectural terms, see page 143.

Crime

As in most Muslim countries, crime rates are relatively low, but pickpockets and theft are on the increase. Always keep your money and bag tightly closed when walking in crowded places such as the *medina* and *souqs*, or on public transport. Theft in the hotel is more likely to be from your fellow holidaymakers than from the hotel staff, but in any case you should always keep your valuables locked away.

Avoid the '*faux guides*', many of whom are con men. They will offer their services as a guide, only to show you a backstreet carpet shop or craft workshop with an uncomfortably heavy sales pitch, where they work on a commission. A typical approach is made as you step out of a taxi: a cheery greeting of 'Hello, don't you remember me? I'm from (the name of your hotel).' In fact, he asked the driver where he picked you up and is a perfect stranger. In the unlikely event that you are assaulted, contact the police immediately.

Police

The Gendarmerie, concerned with state security, dress in khaki, the ordinary police force, the Sûreté, wear blue-grey uniforms, and Traffic Branch officers have a white cap and cuffs. Tunis has a small corps of policewomen, which it likes to keep

The British Embassy, one of the few left in Tunis' Bab el Bahr area

in the public eye to prove its liberated approach.

To report a crime or accident, contact the Sûreté. They usually speak good French, but little English. The Gendarmerie does the road checks in rural areas and frequently stops drivers as a security measure. Tourists normally don't have problems, but do always carry your driving licence, passport and car papers for such occasions.

Embassies and consulates

● **Canada** 3 rue du Sénégal, Tunis (tel: 01 796 577). Also handles Australian affairs.
● **UK** Consulate: 5 place de la Victoire, Tunis (tel: 01 341 444). Embassy: 141–3 avenue de la Liberté (tel: 01 287 293).
● **US** 144 avenue de la Liberté, Tunis (tel: 01782 566).

Emergency telephone numbers

The national emergency telephone number is 197.
● **Ambulance** 491 313/284 808.
● **Fire** 198.
● **Police** 197.

Lost property

Any documents or possessions lost or stolen should be reported to the police (Sûreté), and a certificate of loss should be obtained for insurance purposes. If your passport is stolen, contact your consulate, and if you have lost your credit cards, notify the appropriate agencies immediately.

Health

The greatest danger, as in many holiday destinations, is too much sun combined with an overdose of alcohol and greasy or contaminated food. Drink only bottled water, although tap water is fine for rinsing the mouth, and avoid drinking too many iced drinks in the heat of the day. Try to make sure the food you eat, especially raw vegetables, has been properly washed, and choose restaurants that are popular so the food is always fresh. In case of stomach upset, drink plenty of mineral water. With a serious bout of diarrhoea use a rehydration solution (available at most pharmacies); if symptoms persist, call a doctor.

Use a high-factor suncream, and a total sunblock for children, as well as hats and sunglasses. As mosquitoes can be a nuisance in the summer, take a good insect repellent with you so that you can enjoy dining outdoors at night in peace. There is no malaria in Tunisia. Bees and wasps are rarely seen, and although there are snakes

Tunisian pharmacies are indicated by the sign of a Hippocratic snake

and scorpions in the desert regions in the south, the chances of encountering them are very slim – that said, never forget to check your shoes in the morning. Also remember to wear good boots when you go on desert safari.

Aids is present in Tunisia, as in all parts of the world, so take the necessary precautions. Contact your hotel reception or embassy, or look in the phone directory for a list of doctors (*docteurs*) or dentists (*chirurgien/dentistes*). Consultations are generally cheap. In Tunis, emergency treatment is provided by the **Aziza Othmana Hospital** place de Gouvernement, La Kasbah (tel: 01 662 292).

Vaccinations Unless you arrive from a declared infected zone, no vaccinations are required by law. Some doctors may advise taking precautions against cholera, typhoid and polio.

Pharmacies Found in every village, pharmacies are recognisable by the Hippocratic snake in green on a white sign. They are well stocked and clean, and staff speak fluent French and can offer basic diagnoses. All-night pharmacies are listed in the French-language newspapers.

The Tunisian police force now employs quite a few women

CONVERSION CHARTS

FROM	TO	MULTIPLY BY
Inches	Centimetres	2.54
Centimetres	Inches	0.3937
Feet	Metres	0.3048
Metres	Feet	3.2810
Yards	Metres	0.9144
Metres	Yards	1.0940
Miles	Kilometres	1.6090
Kilometres	Miles	0.6214
Acres	Hectares	0.4047
Hectares	Acres	2.4710
Gallons	Litres	4.5460
Litres	Gallons	0.2200
Ounces	Grams	28.35
Grams	Ounces	0.0353
Pounds	Grams	453.6
Grams	Pounds	0.0022
Pounds	Kilograms	0.4536
Kilograms	Pounds	2.205
Tons	Tonnes	1.0160
Tonnes	Tons	0.9842

MEN'S SUITS

UK	36	38	40	42	44	46	48
Rest of Europe	46	48	50	52	54	56	58
US	36	38	40	42	44	46	48

DRESS SIZES

UK	8	10	12	14	16	18
France	36	38	40	42	44	46
Italy	38	40	42	44	46	48
Rest of Europe	34	36	38	40	42	44
US	6	8	10	12	14	16

MEN'S SHIRTS

UK	14	14.5	15	15.5	16	16.5	17
Rest of Europe	36	37	38	39/40	41	42	43
US	14	14.5	15	15.5	16	16.5	17

MEN'S SHOES

UK	7	7.5	8.5	9.5	10.5	11
Rest of Europe	41	42	43	44	45	46
US	8	8.5	9.5	10.5	11.5	12

WOMEN'S SHOES

UK	4.5	5	5.5	6	6.5	7
Rest of Europe	38	38	39	39	40	41
US	6	6.5	7	7.5	8	8.5

Camping

The Ministry of Youth and Tourism runs official campsites for scouts and school parties, but there are very few organised public facilities: at Remel Plage near Bizerte, Les Jasmins at Nabeul, Le Moulin Bleu at Hammam Plage (20km from Tunis), L'Ideal Camping at Hammamet and Sonia Camping at Zarzis. Except on tourist beaches, however, it is possible to pitch a tent anywhere scenic and suitable, providing you have asked the landowner's permission and/or the local police. Most petrol stations have taps for drinking water and sell fuel for primus stoves. Camping gas is a problem, however, as it is unavailable in portable bottles in Tunisia and is banned on your flight out.

Visitors with disabilities

Facilities are extremely limited in Tunisia and wheelchair access in particular is rarely found in hotels or at sites. The Tunisian organisation **Association Générale des Insufisants Moteurs de Tunis** (Centre d'Orthopédie, Qasr Said, Manouba) may be able to deal with specific queries from disabled visitors on the spot. Before a trip, the **Holiday Care Service** at 2 Old Bank Chambers, Horley, Surrey (tel: 01293 774535) can provide travellers with fact sheets on facilities available for the disabled in Tunisia.

Opening times

During July and August most offices and banks close for the afternoon. General opening times are quite hard to come by, but most banks are open Mon–Thu 8–11.30, 2–6.30, Fri 8–11, 1.15–3 (Jul–Aug, 7–11.30). Most shops are open summer 8.30–12, 4–7; rest of year 8.30–12, 3–6. Restaurants tend to open 12–2.30 for lunch and 7.30–10 for dinner. Museums and sites are often closed on Mon, and generally open summer 9–12, 3–6.30; rest of year 9–12, 2–5.30.

Places of worship

● **Anglican** St Georges' Church, place Bab Carthage, Tunis (services Sun 10am) or 16 rue de Malte, Sousse (Sun 9.30am).

The cathedral at Carthage is now a cultural centre

● **Protestant (French)** Église Réformée, rue Charles de Gaulle, Tunis (Sun 10am).
● **Catholic (French)** Cathédrale de St Vincent de Paul, avenue Habib Bourguiba, Tunis (Mon–Fri 8.15am, 6pm; Sat 6pm; Sun 9am, 1am).

Toilets
Public toilets do not exist in Tunisia, except in railway stations and at airports, so your best bet is to head to the nearest tourist restaurant or hotel. Toilet paper is not always available so be sure you carry some with you. The plumbing is often dodgy, so put your used paper in the waste bins that are frequently provided beside the toilet.

Photography
Taking photographs is no problem in Tunisia but be aware that women and older people may not be too keen to be photographed. Always ask their permission first. Avoid taking pictures of military installations or you risk losing your film and even your liberty. An additional ticket is often required to take pictures in museums and archaeological sites. Film is widely available everywhere in the country, but bring any specialist or video films you require.

Electricity
The current in Tunisia is 220V. Plugs are the two-round-pin variety, so take an international adaptor.

Etiquette and local customs
● As Tunisia is a Muslim country, dress casually but modestly outside beach resorts, covering legs and arms.
● Do not enter mosques unless it is clear that non-Muslims are welcome, and always dress appropriately.
● In hammams do not strip completely, but leave your pants on.
● If invited to a Tunisian home, only take along alcohol as a gift if you are sure it will be acceptable. Otherwise, take a generous selection of pastries or chocolates. Remove your shoes before walking on the carpet.
● Topless sunbathing is illegal, but is tolerated on private hotel beaches.

Tunisia's postal service is reasonably efficient

Tourist offices abroad
● **Canada** 1253 McGill College Bureau, 655 Montreal, H3B 2Y5 Quebec (tel: 0514 397 1182).
● **France** 32 avenue de l'Opéra, 75002 Paris (tel: 01 47 42 72 67).
● **Germany** Fremdenverkehrsamt, Tunesien Goethe Platz 5, 60313 Frankfurt am Main (tel: 069 297 0640). Also at Fremdenverkehrsamt Tunesien Kurfurstendamm 171, 10707 Berlin (tel: 030 885 0457).
● **UK** 77a Wigmore Street, London W1H 9LJ (tel: 0171 224 5561).
● **US** c/o Embassy of the Republic of Tunisia, Tourist Section, 1515 Massachusetts Avenue NW, Washington DC 20005 (tel: 202/234-6644).

Regional tourist offices in Tunisia
In Tunisia there are Offices Nationales de Tourisme in all large towns, and often also a Syndicat d'Initiative which supplies information on hotels, festivals and museums.
● **Bizerte** 1 rue de Constantinople (tel: 02 432 897; fax: 02 438 600).
● **Jerba** route de Sidi Mahrez, Houmt Souk (tel: 05 650 016; fax: 05 655 181).
● **Monastir** Zone touristique de Skanès (tel: 03 461 205).
● **Nabeul** avenue Taieb Mehri (tel: 02 286 737).
● **Sousse** 1 avenue Habib Bourguiba (tel: 03 225 157).

Police patrol the beaches mainly to protect tourists from touts

● **Tabarka** 32 avenue Habib Bourguiba (tel: 08 670 111). Also at boulevard 7 Novembre (tel: 08 644 491; fax: 08 643 428).
● **Tozeur** avenue Aboulkacem Chebbi (tel: 06 454 088).
● **Tunis** 1 avenue Mohammed V (tel: 01 341 077). Also at 29 rue de Palestine (tel: 01 341 077).

The main resorts offer all the watersports, although at a price

HOTELS AND RESTAURANTS

HOTELS AND RESTAURANTS
ACCOMMODATION

See pages 76–7 for general information on Tunisia's hotels.

The hotels listed below are grouped into three price categories:

● **expensive** (£££): over 100D for a double room with bath, including breakfast and taxes.
● **moderate** (££): 50–100D.
● **budget** (£): less than 50D.

TUNIS

L'Africa Meridien (£££) 50 avenue Habib Bourguiba (tel: 01 347 477; fax: 01 347 432). The smartest and most central luxury hotel, with comfortable rooms overlooking the city and the Lac de Tunis. The café-terrace is an excellent place to watch the world go by and The Pub is a favourite downtown meeting-place in the late afternoon or evening.

Les Ambassadeurs (££) 75 avenue Taieb Mehiri (tel: 01 288 011; fax: 01 780 042). Slightly out of the centre, but with good bus connections, this comfortable hotel has rooms overlooking the Belvédère Park. Quite popular with tour groups.

Auberge de Jeunesse (£) 25 rue Saida Ajoula, Médina (tel/fax: 01 567 850). Very well-kept dormitories in the old residence of a bey. Beautiful 18th-century ceiling in the refectory and old tiling in the Salle Polyvalente. In summer you can stay a maximum three nights – booking in advance is preferable. Also offers bike rental.

Carlton (££) 31 avenue Habib Bourguiba (tel: 01 330 644; fax: 01 338 168). Very central hotel with newly refurbished, tastefully decorated rooms, spotlessly clean bathrooms, direct telephone and air-conditioning. Rooms at the back are quieter and the few with shower only are cheaper. Impeccable service. Our first choice in this category, so book ahead.

La Maison Dorée (£) 6 bis rue de Hollande, entry on 3 rue el-Koufa (tel: 01 240 631; fax: 01 332 401). Located near the railway station, this hotel is something of an institution in Tunis. The grandson of the first French owner tries hard to keep up the standards, so rooms are clean and well kept, with furniture dating from the 1950s. Excellent value in this category. Advance booking is essential.

Majestic (£) 36 avenue de Paris (tel: 01 332 848; fax: 01 336 908). A grand turn-of-the-century building with clean, spacious rooms with bathroom. The staff are attentive and the large terrace on the first floor is a great place to sit in the late afternoon or evening with a beer or an apéritif.

Salammbo (£) 6 rue de Grèce (tel: 01 337 498). Very clean rooms with or without showers, but traffic noise can be a problem.

TUNIS ENVIRONS
Carthage

La Reine Didon (££) rue Mendès-France Carthage Hannibal, beside the museum (tel: 01 733 433; fax: 01 732 599). Clean, quiet rooms with splendid views over the sea and Tunis; perfect for exploring the area of Carthage.

Gammarth

Abu Nawas Gammarth (£££) avenue Taieb Mehiri (tel: 01 741 444; fax: 01 740 400). One of the most luxurious hotels along this coast. All mod cons and a splendid setting. Great pool.

Megara (£££) Gammarth Plage (tel: 01 740 366; fax: 01 740 916). Charming old-fashioned seaside hotel in the old palace of a foreign prince, with a swimming-pool set in a tranquil garden by a little beach. Comfortable rooms have large balconies and are decorated in an unmistakable 1970s style, a reminder of family holidays of old. Recommended.

La Marsa

Plaza Corniche (££) 22 rue du Maroc, near the TGM station (tel: 01 743 489; fax: 01 742 554). Tastefully decorated rooms set in a lush garden with a small swimming-pool. Everything is perfect, though it can be very noisy on disco nights.

Sidi Bou Said

Dar Said (££) at the top of the main street (tel: 01 740 471; fax: 01 256 908). Attractive, atmospheric hotel in an old house with a peaceful courtyard, often recommended as a honeymoon hotel. Closed for renovation at the time of writing, so should be even better on reopening.

Dar Zarrouk (££) opposite the Dar Said (tel: 01 740 215). Great views over the gulf, but also closed for much-needed renovations at the time of writing.

Sidi Bou Farès (£) in the street on the left before the Café des Nattes (tel: 01 740 091). The most basic of Sidi Bou's hotels is also set in a lovely old house with eight rooms around a courtyard filled with geraniums and jasmines. Rooms are clean but very simple, most of them sharing a communal bathroom. Book ahead in summer.

Sidi Bou Saïd (£££) Sidi Dhrif (tel: 01 740 411; fax: 01 745 129). A small, pleasant hotel outside Sidi Bou Said, with swimming-pool, tennis-courts and air-conditioned rooms. The view from the terrace is great, the perfect place for a cool beer or an apéritif.

THE NORTH
Aïn Draham

Beauséjour (£) in the centre (tel: 08 647 005). This colonial-style hotel has lost most of its attraction; the best rooms are now in the annexe.

Les Chênes (££) 7km from Aïn Draham in the hamlet of Chênes (tel: 08 655 211; fax: 08 655 396). In an excellent location surrounded by forest on the hills outside Aïn Draham, this hotel with pool and tennis-courts once had a great reputation. Unfortunately, everything has seen better days, though the hotel is still popular with hunters and offers all-inclusive hunting packages (see also panel on page 86).

Béja
Phénix (£) 37 avenue de France (tel: 08 450 188). Cleaner of the two small hotels in town. Communal bathrooms.

Bizerte
Corniche (££) route de la Corniche, 4km out of town (tel: 02 431 844; fax: 02 431 830). One of the most comfortable hotels in town, with its own beach, swimming-pool and a popular nightclub.
El-Feth (£–££) avenue Bourguiba, in front of the mosque (tel: 02 430 596). Completely modern hotel with little character, but the rooms are spotless and the service is friendly.
Le Petit Mousse (££) route de la Corniche, 6km out of town (tel: 02 432 185; fax: 02 437 595). Charming little hotel with rooms overlooking the beach and sea, which also means the road. Quite noisy but well kept. The restaurant is excellent (see page 201). Recommended, but book far in advance as it is fills up quickly, especially at weekends.

Bulla Regia and Chemtou
The nearest place to stay is in Jendouba, 9km away.
Atlas (£) 55 rue du 1er Juin (tel: 08 630 566). Straightforward, but clean rooms and a pleasant garden bar.
Similthu (££) on the road to Bulla Regia (tel: 08 631 695). New hotel but fairly unexciting, with 25 clean rooms.

Ghar el Melh
Only straw huts on the beach, rented per day for camping.

Raf Raf
Dalia (££) Small hotel near the beach, with very clean rooms and a reliable restaurant.

Tabarka
Abu Nawas Montazah (££) (tel: 08 643 532; fax: 08 643 726). Enormous hotel on the beach with excellent watersports facilities, including an Olympic-size pool. Bad insulation means the rooms are very noisy and every step in the hotel is heard.
Les Aiguilles (££) 18 avenue Habib Bourguiba (tel: 08 643 789; fax: 08 643 604). Comfortable modern hotel with well-kept rooms, attentive service and an excellent restaurant (see page 201).

De France (£) avenue Bourguiba (tel: 08 644 577). Definitely a faded glory, but still has plenty of charm. Probably one of the best cheap hotels in town.
Iberotel Mehari (££–£££) (tel: 08 670 001; fax: 08 643 943). Much quieter hotel on the beach, with a good pool and a pleasant restaurant.
Mimosas (££) signposted on the left as you enter town (tel: 08 643 018; fax: 08 643 276). On a hill overlooking town, and set in a lovely garden. The rooms have views over the town and harbour, and service is friendly and personal. Smallish pool. Heating in winter.

CAP BON AND THE SAHEL
Cap Bon
L'Épervier (££) avenue Habib Bourguiba, El Haouaria (tel: 02 297 017; fax: 02 297 258). The best hotel in town, with clean rooms and a good restaurant.
Hotel des Sources Korbous (tel: 02 294 533). Good rooms, but as most clients come to Korbous for health reasons it's not very cheerful or lively.
Pension Anis (£) avenue Erriadh, next door to the fish market, Kelibia (tel: 02 295 777). A recently opened pension, only five minutes from the beach. Offers comfortable and clean rooms with communal bathrooms, plus friendly service. Restaurant (see page 201).

Hammamet
Alya (£) 30 rue Ali Belahouane (tel: 02 280 218; fax: 02 282 365). Very pleasant little hotel run by a retired colonel and his family, who would move the sea to make you feel at home. In summer a *mechoui* (roast lamb) is served on the lovely roof terrace, accompanied by traditional music. Prices go up considerably in season and advance booking is necessary.
Bellevue (£) boulevard Ibn el-Fourat (tel: 02 281 121; fax: 02 283 156). Central, clean hotel on the beach; most rooms have a *belle vue* of the sea.
Les Citronniers (££) rue de Nevers, *en route* to the hotels (tel: 02 280 622; fax: 02 283 142). Another pleasant hotel, with comfortable rooms and a swimming-pool. In season it will often be full with tour groups.
Le Dar Hayet (£££) route de la Corniche (tel: 02 283 399; fax: 02 280 424). A new five-star hotel in the style of a Hammamet villa, with very tastefully decorated rooms, all with locally produced fittings and furniture. Lovely pool with bougainvillaea and a small Moorish café. The service still needs some attention, but this hotel has character and is a welcome move away from the mega-hotels that blight Tunisia's coast. Recommended, especially the ground-floor rooms with sea view and access to a small garden.

195

HOTELS AND RESTAURANTS

Yasmina (££) route de la Corniche (tel: 02 280 222; fax: 02 280 593). Centrally located with comfortable rooms, a good pool and a pleasant, shady garden. More cachet than most in this price category.

Iles Kerkennah

Most hotels on the islands close in winter, and only a few of those that stay open have heating.

Cercina (£) Sidi Frej (tel: 04 215 885; fax: 04 215 878). Open year round, with hot water and central heating. This is a very good hotel, with rooms and bungalows directly on the beach. The patron is very friendly and helpful, and the restaurant serves excellent Kerkennese fish specialities on its large terrace.

Farhat (££) next door to the Grand Hotel, Sidi Frej (tel: 04 281 236; fax: 04 281 237). Tastefully decorated rooms and a great pool, but the beach is almost non-existent. Mediocre restaurant.

Grand Hotel (££) Sidi Frej (tel: 04 281 266; fax: 04 281 485). With 100 rooms with sea view and a lovely pool, this hotel works mainly with British tour agents. All sports facilities and an enjoyable restaurant on the beach.

El-Jazira (£) Er Remla (tel: 04 281 058). Very well-kept rooms with clean communal bathrooms and a restaurant.

El Jem

Club el-Ksar (££) 5km from the site on the road to Sousse. This hotel was not completed at the time of writing, but is due to have three pools and 35 rooms with all mod cons.

Relais Julius (£) near the railway station (tel: 03 690 204). Spacious, simple rooms around a central courtyard. Good value.

Mahdia

Abou Nawas Cap Mahdia (£££) *zone touristique*, Hiboun (tel: 03 680 300; fax: 03 680 405). Large, stylish beach hotel offering watersports facilities and horse riding. Overlooks a wonderful white-sand beach. Mini-club for kids.

Corniche (£) on the Corniche (tel: 03 694 201; fax: 03 694 190). This small and simple hotel offers worn, clean rooms, some with a balcony overlooking the beach. The main terrace is the local hang-out for Mahdia's young men, so the front rooms can be noisy. Service can seem a little brusque.

Rand (£) 20 avenue Taieb M'Hiri (tel: 03 680 525). Small and homely hotel in a central location. Very friendly staff.

Monastir

Most of the hotels cater to the package market, and are expensive and rather uninspiring.

Club Abou Nawas (£££) La Dkhila (tel: 03 466 940; fax: 03 466 948). Whitewashed low-rise hotel in a magnificent garden with an excellent swimming-pool and golf course. Wide range of sports on offer as well as a massage and sauna room, and a mini-club for children.

Kahla (£) avenue du 7 Novembre (tel: 03 464 570; fax: 03 467 881). New hotel with whitewashed rooms with spick and span bathrooms, or apartments for five people. Very welcoming.

Yasmine (£) route de la Falaise, Essouani (tel: 03 462 511). Very pleasant and, for Monastir, unusually small hotel with clean rooms, an excellent restaurant popular with locals and the beach across the road. The staff are very welcoming and don't mind if you sleep on the roof.

Nabeul

Château-Mignon (£) 48 avenue Hosni Abdelwahed (tel: 02 224 365; fax: 02 223 566). Small family-run pension with eight comfortable and clean rooms with bath and balcony.

Club Aquarius (££–£££) on the road towards Cap Bon, 2km from the centre (tel: 02 285 777; fax: 02 285 682). Part of the Club Med group, this hotel offers the sense of being away from it all. Hidden amidst orange groves on a superb beach, offering a wide range of sports facilities and a mini-club for children, it is an ideal place for families with smaller kids.

Les Jasmins (££) avenue Habib Thameur (tel: 02 280 222). Older hotel with cosy rooms and an enjoyable garden.

Les Oliviers (£) rue de Havane (tel: 02 286 865). Clean rooms with bathroom in a small house. Closed in winter. Book ahead.

Port el Kantaoui

There are no cheap options here. All hotels cater for the package market and rarely take in individual travellers.

Diar el Andalous (£££) signposted in town (tel: 03 246 200; fax: 03 246 348). Huge resort, one of the most luxurious in the country, with indoor and outdoor pools and all sports facilities.

Sfax

El Andalous (££) boulevard des Martyrs (tel: 04 299 100; fax: 04 299 425). Well-located, recently built hotel with all mod cons. Ask for one of the quieter rooms at the back.

Ennaser (£) 100 rue des Notaires, near Bab Djebli (tel: 04 299 919; fax: 04 212 901). Simple, recently renovated hotel with some rooms overlooking the ramparts of the *medina*.

Hôtel des Oliviers (££) avenue Habib Thameur (tel: 04 225 188; fax: 04 223 623). This old palace with a splendid façade and lovely pool is not always very well kept and things seem to be falling apart, but it is recommended for nostalgic souls none the less.

Skanès

The majority of hotels in Skanès (near Monastir) only deal with package tours, which means that walk-in rates are high. If you want to stay, it will be necessary to book from abroad.

Sousse

Most beach hotels in Sousse cater to the package market, although some may have vacancies out of season. Don't come looking for faded grandeur: the two hotels with flavour, the Claridges and the Hadrumette, are now very noisy and are not particularly clean.

Chems el Hana (£££) *zone touristique* (tel: 03 226 900; fax: 03 226 076). Elegant big hotel with all the sports facilities and also offering wheelchair access.

Justinia (££) avenue Hedi Chaker (tel: 03 226 381; fax: 03 225 993). Fairly big hotel on the sea front with small, comfortable rooms but no pool.

Medina (£) near the Great Mosque in the *medina* (tel: 03 221 722; fax: 03 221 794). Pleasant hotel in the heart of the *medina* with spotless rooms and good views from the roof terrace. There is even a bar despite its proximity to the mosque. Book in advance in summer.

Les Palmiers (£–££) rue des Palmiers (tel: 03 270 756; fax: 03 270 755). Pleasant rooms, some with sea views and air-conditioning. Good value.

THE INTERIOR
Dougga

Avoid staying overnight in Dougga. Stay either in Le Kef (see page 198) or in the small basic **Hotel Thugga** in Teboursouk (£–££) (tel: 08 465 713).

Douz

Méhari (££) at the end of the Route Touristique near the Ofra dune (tel: 05 495 145; fax: 05 495 589). First of the larger hotels to appear out of the desert and spoil the landscape. Air-conditioned rooms and two pools, one of which is thermal. Avoid the food.

Résidence du 20 Mars (£) next to the bus stop, behind the square (tel: 05 470 269). Well-kept pension run by three brothers from Mali who are passionate about the music from their country. Rooms are basic, clean and lead onto a small but peaceful patio.

Sahara (££) Route Touristique (tel: 05 470 864; fax: 05 495 566). Modern whitewashed hotel with comfortable and tastefully decorated rooms, plus indoor and outdoor pools.

Saharien (£) Route Touristique (tel: 05 495 337; fax: 05 495 339). Cheaper option, with tidy bungalows set in the palmery. Swimming-pool. Can get crowded with tour groups.

Gafsa

Maamoun (££) avenue Taieb Mehiri (tel: 06 222 432; fax: 06 226 440). The most up-market hotel in town, with modern rooms devoid of any character whatsoever, but with air-conditioning. The food is often appalling. Swimming-pool.

Moussa (£) on the road to Tozeur (tel: 06 223 333). Simple but perfectly clean rooms with communal showers and toilets. Can be rather noisy.

La République (£) avenue Ali Belhouane (tel: 06 221 807). Best of the cheap hotels, with newish, clean rooms.

Kairouan

Amina (££) 3km from the centre on the road to Tunis (tel: 07 226 555; fax: 07 225 411). Excellent modern hotel with 62 well-equipped air-conditioned rooms and a swimming-pool. Often booked by tour groups.

Continental (££) near the Aghlabid pools (tel: 07 221 135; fax: 07 229 900). Large hotel with spacious rooms that have balconies overlooking a swimming-pool.

Sabra (£) rue Ali Belhouane, opposite the Bab ech Chouhada (Martyrs' Gate) (tel: 07 225 095). Clean rooms with communal showers (a basin is provided in the room), overlooking the ramparts. From the roof terrace there are magnificent views over the *medina*. Rooms at the back are quieter and there is a good hammam next door. Excellent value.

Le Splendid (££) avenue du 9 Avril 1939 (tel: 07 227 522; fax: 07 220 829). Very central hotel offering excellent value for money. Rooms are spacious and clean, and some have TV. The bar serves alcohol, but as it is popular with local drinkers it can be a bit noisy.

Tunisia (££) avenue de la République (tel: 07 221 855). Comfortable rooms with bathroom or shower and fans, as well as central heating in winter. The rooms at the back are quieter but miss out on a balcony. Impeccable service.

Kebili

Ben Said (£) avenue Bourguiba (tel: 05 491 573). Basic but clean rooms with basin and hot water, communal showers and toilets. The hotel is next to the mosque so don't worry if you've forgotten your alarm clock.

Borj des Autruches (££) signposted from the road to Douz (tel: 05 491 117; fax: 05 491 306). This old military fort was once turned into an ostrich farm, but that didn't work out. Recently it was renovated and converted into a hotel with about 100 comfortable rooms and several pools, including a Moorish bath and a thermal pool. There is a bar on a delightful terrace overlooking the *chott* and oasis. A relaxing place to spend a few days, but book in advance.

197

HOTELS AND RESTAURANTS

Oasis Dar Kebili (££) *zone touristique* (tel: 05 491 436; fax: 05 491 295). Four-star hotel with well-equipped rooms set in a large and beautiful palmery. Little zoo with desert animals.

Le Kef
El Medina (£) 18 rue Farhat Hached (tel: 08 220 214). Fairly new and clean hotel with free cold showers.
Résidence Vénus (£–££) rue Oued Smida (tel: 08 224 695). New hotel with 20 clean rooms, hot showers and central heating. A welcome new addition to Le Kef's rather lacklustre accommodation.
Sicca Veneria (££) place de l'Indépendance (tel: 08 221 561). The most comfortable and clean hotel in town, but ugly and soulless. The bar livens up at night when locals descend on the place for more than just a few drinks.
La Source (£) place de la Source (tel: 08 221 397). Small hotel with rooms around a patio, not always clean and next door to the muezzin's loudspeaker, which calls for prayer just before dawn. The family room is traditionally decorated with stucco and tiles.

Makthar
Mactaris (££) near the triumphal arch (tel: 08 876 014). The only place around; not really welcoming, but the rooms are just about adequate.

Metlaoui
Ennecim (£) on the road to Tozeur (tel/fax: 06 241 920). Faded rooms with bathrooms that have hot water. Edible food. There is no alternative.

Nefta
Caravansérail (££) at the edge of the palmery (tel: 06 430 355; fax: 06 430 344). Beautiful stone building with comfortable rooms overlooking the palmery.
Marhala (£–££) next door to the older **Marhala du Touring Club** (£), on the out-skirts of town on the road to Algeria (tel: 06 457 027; fax: 06 430 511). Brand new hotel with tastefully decorated rooms in traditional style. Lovely pool and garden. Good value.
Les Nomades (£) at the entrance to town from the road to Tozeur (tel: 06 457 052). Traditional rooms with palm-wood ceil-ings set in pleasant surroundings. Shame about the pool (not always clean). Hot in summer as there are no fans or air-conditioning.

Sbeïtla
Suffetula (££) next door to the ruins on the road to Kasserine (tel: 07 465 582; fax: 07 465 582). The best hotel in Sbeïtla. Ideal for seeing the ruins, which are at their best at dawn or at sunset when all the tour buses have left. The rooms are

comfortable and air-conditioned, although the service does not always come up to scratch.

Tamerza
Des Cascades (£–££) turn right in centre of town towards oasis (tel: 06 453 732). A tourist village with badly kept bungalows built of palm wood. The views are stunning, though.
Tamerza Palace (££) (tel: 06 245 214; fax: 06 799 810). Some people find this four-star hotel a good enough reason to visit Tamerza. Clinging to a rock and painted deep ochre in a style influenced by Algeria, it fits in well with the landscape. Beautiful rooms and a fantastic pool. Book in advance in summer.

Tozeur
Grand Oasis (££) avenue Bourguiba (tel: 06 450 522). Attractive hotel overlooking the palmery, plus a tempting swimming-pool. Often booked by tour groups.
El-Hafsi (££) *zone touristique* (tel: 06 450 966). Pleasant, newly built hotel near the Belvédère. Swimming-pool. Already being extended.
El-Jerid (£) avenue Aboul Kacem Chebbi (tel: 06 450 488). Faded hotel, but the rooms are clean and there is a pool and a garden.
Palm Beach Palace (£££) *zone touristique* (tel: 06 453 111; fax: 06 453 911). Five-star accommodation and the most luxurious hotel so far of the many up-market new ones here. Several pools.
Palmyre (££–£££) *zone touristique* (tel: 06 452 020; fax: 06 453 470). One of the few new hotels to make an effort in using traditional architecture and building materials. The rooms are stylishly decorated and have good bathrooms. Inviting pool overlooking the desert.
Résidence Warda (£) avenue Aboul Kacem Chebbi (tel: 06 452 597). Basic but well-kept rooms and very friendly staff. Excellent views from the roof terrace. Recommended.

JERBA AND THE SOUTH
Foum Tataouine
Hamza (£) avenue Hedi Chaker (tel: 05 863 506). Recent hotel, basic but clean.
Sangho (££) signposted on the road to Chenini (tel: 05 860 124; fax: 05 862 177). Ochre hotel with tastefully decorated rooms, plus a pool and good restaurant.

Gabès
Chems (££) off avenue Habib Thameur (tel: 05 270 547; fax: 05 274 485). Large beach hotel with tastefully decorated and spacious rooms, all with balcony. Set in a garden with swimming-pool. Some rooms overlook the sea. The restaurant should be avoided.

Nejib (££) corner of avenues Habib Bourguiba and Farhat Hached (tel: 05 271 686). Comfortable air-conditioned rooms, although noisy as it lies between two main streets. Often used by tour groups.
Regina (£) 138 avenue Bourguiba (tel: 05 272 095). Clean rooms with antique plumbing and wobbly beds, set around a pleasant interior courtyard (less pleasant when a wedding party is being held).

Ile de Jerba
Dar Faiza (££) 6 rue de la République, Houmt Souk (tel: 05 650 083; fax: 05 651 763). In a quiet residential quarter overlooking the Borj el Kebir and the sea, this lovely hotel has clean, simple rooms set in a tranquil garden with a small swimming-pool (Jerba's first), tennis-court, olive trees and bougainvillaea. The villa and garden belonged to a French aristocrat until 1959. Breakfast is served inside or under the trees, and there is a bar and Italian restaurant. Recommended.
Hasdrubal (£££) *zone touristique* (tel: 05 657 650; fax: 05 657 730). Best of the five-star hotels on the beach, offering luxurious, well-equipped rooms with balconies overlooking the garden, swimming-pool and sea. Indoor and outdoor pools, gym, private beach, watersports facilities and several restaurants. Excellent service.
Hotel du Lotos (£) 18 rue de la République, Houmt Souk (tel: 05 650 026; fax: 05 651 763). Overlooking the port, this pleasant hotel (with the same owner as the Dar Faiza) has a terrace overlooking the sea. The blue and white rooms are clean and comfortable.
Marhala du Touring Club (£) rue Moncef Bey, Houmt Souk (tel: 05 650 146). Basic but clean rooms in an old caravanserai, set around a courtyard covered in bougainvillaea. The restaurant-bar in the courtyard can be noisy in the evening. One of Jerba's most characterful hotels.
Sables d'Or (£) 30 rue Muhammad Ferjani, Houmt Souk (tel: 05 650 423). Beautiful old house with 12 basic but lovely rooms with showers ranged around a small central courtyard.

Matmata
Marhala du Touring Club (£) turn right off the road to Toujane (tel: 05 230 015). The nicest of Matmata's three troglodyte hotels. Very basic rooms without door locks and with communal bathrooms. Good restaurant. Often fully booked.
Matmata (££) turn right off the road to Toujane (tel: 05 230 066). Not underground, but more comfortable rooms with bathrooms, and an unpleasant green swimming-pool. Not particularly clean.
Les Troglodytes (££) on the road to Tamerza (tel: 05 230 062; fax: 05 230 173). Modern hotel which, despite the name, is above ground. Pleasant rooms and a pool.

Metameur
Hotel el-Ghorfa (£) Ksar Metameur (call the local post office on tel: 05 640 294). Delightful, basic hotel in the best-preserved part of the *ksar*, lovingly run by the Berber Drifi Hachem. He also organises great trips in the area by camel, donkey or bike to more isolated *ksour* that are rarely visited by tourists.

Zarzis
Most hotels in Zarzis cater for package tours and are vast.
L'Olivier (£) near the bus station (tel: 05 680 637). Best of the cheap hotels, with basic and clean rooms.
Sangho Club (££) 10km from Zarzis on the road to Jerba (tel: 05 680 124). Attractive holiday club with watersports facilities and swimming-pools. Accommodation is in small bungalows built in traditional southern Tunisian style.

RESTAURANTS

See pages 72–4 for more information on traditional Tunisian food and drink.

The restaurants listed below have been grouped into three price categories (all per person for three courses, without wine):
● **expensive** (£££) above 30D.
● **moderate** (££) 15–30D.
● **budget** (£) up to 15D.

TUNIS
Le Bagdad (££) 29 avenue Habib Bourguiba (tel: 01 259 068). Behind an intricately decorated façade is an equally elaborate and plush interior in gold, blue and white. Traditional Tunisian dishes are served up by friendly waiters.
Chez Nous (££) 5 rue de Marseille (tel: 01 243 043). Another of those old-fashioned restaurants with friendly waiters and a décor that has remained unchanged for decades. Pictures of the stars who have eaten here include Edith Piaf, Tino Rossi and even Muhammad Ali. The food is excellent, with a large choice of dishes on the menu.
Club Sandwich (£) 120 rue de Yougoslavie (tel: 01 249 842). Take-away sandwich bar with probably the best sandwiches in town: delicious hot bread stuffed with tuna, potatoes, Tunisian salad, lettuce, olives – and *harissa* on top for those who like it hot. Excellent value!
Cosmos (££) 7 rue Ibn Khaldoun (tel: 01 241 610). Closed on Sun. One of our favourite restaurants in Tunis, really old-fashioned with white tablecloths and a marine-style décor of white stars on a blue ceiling. The waiters are the same year after year, and so is the ageing clientèle, many of whom eat here daily.

HOTELS AND RESTAURANTS

Straightforward but fresh and well-prepared salads, grilled fish and meat. Good-value *plat du jour*.

Dar el-Jeld (£££) 5 rue Dar el-Jeld, Médina (tel: 01 260 916). Exceptionally beautiful traditional house tucked away in the *medina*, now a restaurant. One of the few places outside the home to taste the rich variety of genuine Tunisian cuisine, accompanied here by oriental music. However carried away you get, leave a little space for the desserts as they are delectable. Book well in advance. Closed Sundays and August.

Mahdaoui (£) rue Jemaa ez Zitouna, Médina. Outdoor eatery in the *souq* next to Jemaa ez Zitouna, with fresh and well-prepared dishes such as fish, couscous and *tagines*. Popular with Tunisians and tourists alike. No alcohol and lunch only. Closed Sundays.

M'Rabet (£) Souq et Trouk, Médina (tel: 01 261 729/ 263 681). Downstairs is a pleasant and cool Moorish café, one of the few '*marabout* cafés' left, a tradition dating back to the 16th century. A great location to recover from the heat with a mint tea and a water-pipe. Courting couples discuss their future in the quiet garden, while upstairs is a touristy Tunisian restaurant (££) with a view over Jemaa ez Zitouna and a folkloric show in the evening.

L'Orient (££) 7 rue Ali Bach-Hambra. Brasserie-type restaurant with good Franco-Tunisienne cuisine, fast service and cosy décor.

Le Paradiso (££) 16 avenue des États Unis d'Amérique, Belvédère (tel: 01 786 863). Excellent pastas, salads and European dishes served in a bright décor. This restaurant near the Belvédère is rarely frequented by tourists but is very popular with diplomats and expats. Also serves a good-value *plat du jour* at lunchtime. Recommended.

TUNIS ENVIRONS
Carthage
Le Neptune (££) 2 rue Ibn Chaabat, next door to the Quartier Magon (tel: 01 731 456/731 328). One of Carthage's hidden treasures, this cool, tucked-away restaurant overlooks the Mediterranean and serves grilled fish, seafood and bouillabaisse as well as meat and salads. The menu is excellent value. Wonderful terrace in summer. Recommended. No credit cards.

Gammarth
Les Dunes (££) 130 avenue Taieb Mehri (tel: 01 743 379). Several terraces facing the sea or a cosy room with a log fire in winter. Serves French classics such as onion soup, snails and fondue bourguignonne. Good value and an excellent wine list. Closed Wednesdays.

Les Ombrelles (££) avenue Taieb Mehri, past the Hotel Megara (tel: 01 742 964). The terrace overlooks the sea and the menu proposes a long list of interesting salads and entrées as well as a fresh catch of fish and seafood. Book in advance in season as it is popular with local residents.

La Goulette
Le Café Vert (£) 68 avenue F Roosevelt (tel: 01 736 756). The most popular fish restaurant in town, famous for its *complet poisson*. Simply delicious.

Le Vert Galant (£–££) avenue F Roosevelt. Fish specialities and friendly service.

La Marsa
Ayyam Zaman (Au Vieux Temps) (£££) 1 rue Aboul Kacem ech-Chebbi, to the right of the TGM station (tel: 01 774 322). Only open for dinner. This restaurant is an institution and feels like it should be somewhere in the Provence in France. The French traditional cuisine is excellent and the wine list is a delight. Book in advance.

Café Saf-Saf (£) place Saf-Saf. Very popular family café/restaurant with two terraces served by several stalls selling *briks* and excellent *cassecroute* and *fricassées*. The camel in the middle pumping up water from an old well is there to be photographed. Only open in summer.

Le Golfe (££–£££) 5 rue Lahbi Zarrouk, signposted on the way to Gammarth (tel: 01 748 219). In a lovely villa full of flowers giving directly onto the beach. The house speciality is fresh fish and seafood, all simply but very well prepared, but the meat dishes are equally delightful. Very popular with wealthy Tunisians, so book in advance. Closed Mondays.

Sidi Bou Said
Ayyam Zaman (Au Vieux Temps) (£££) in the street leading past Dar Zarrouk (tel: 01 744 733). Behind a blue door hides a wonderful, typical Sidi Bou Said house with an enchanting terrace, decorated with antiques and tastefully chosen junk from flea markets. From the same owner as the traditional restaurant in La Marsa, serving authentic French food with a few Tunisian specialities, and every day a delightful suggestion from the chef. Book in advance.

La Bagatelle (££) rue Bourguiba, just beyond the place du 7 Novembre. A casual place where local residents meet. No alcohol.

Café des Nattes (£) top of the main street in the village. Tea upstairs in this beautiful Moorish café is a must for anyone who visits Sidi Bou Said. Take your time and linger, smoke a water-pipe and daydream about all the writers and painters who have hung out here, from Flaubert researching his novel *Salammbo*, to Paul Klee and Simone de Beauvoir.

Café Sidi Chabaane (£) at the end of the main street to the right – follow the crowds! Magnificent café with sweeping views over the gulf and a small choice of drinks: mint tea, mint tea with pine nuts (more expensive), good coffee and cold drinks. The place to smoke a *chicha* (water-pipe), made with sweet Egyptian tobacco, sip a tea with a little bouquet of jasmine behind your ear and watch the sun go down or the moon go up – if you're not careful you'll still be here when the new day comes!

Au Petite Suède (£) 12 avenue 7 Novembre (tel: 01 741 843). Two Swedish women married to Tunisian pilots opened this tea-room. Straight out of a Swedish suburb or an IKEA catalogue, but the home-made cakes and pastries are really delicious. Popular meeting-place for young Tunisois.

Le Pirate (££–£££) in the yacht harbour below the village of Sidi Bou Said (tel: 01 270 484). Excellent food, with fresh fish and seafood specialities served in pleasant surroundings, outdoors in the season. Mostly frequented by Tunisians as it lies off the tourist route. Recommended.

THE NORTH
Aïn Draham
Beauséjour hotel (££) in the centre. A cheap but uninteresting set menu, as well as the slightly better à la carte.

Bizerte
Le Bonheur (£) 31 rue Thaabli (tel: 02 431 047). Large restaurant with a good selection of fish and seafood as well as couscous. Several good-value menus and an extensive wine list. Closed during Ramadan.

L'Eden (££–£££) route de la Corniche (tel: 02 439 023). Stunning terrace covered with flowers where fresh fish and seafood specialities are served. Well known to locals, so book in advance.

Le Petit Mousse (££) route de la Corniche, 6km out of centre (tel: 02 432 185). Very pleasant restaurant, the best place in town, with a 1960s décor, picture windows looking out over the sea, and jazz music. Large menu with excellent French dishes. The **pizzeria** (£) in the garden is only open in the evening and serves very good salads, grills and, of course, pizzas. Recommended.

Tabarka
Les Aiguilles (£) 18 avenue Habib Bourguiba (tel: 08 643 789). Tunisian specialities and fresh seafood served either on a pleasant terrace or in a lovely room inside.

La Perle du Nord (£) 53 avenue Habib Bourguiba. Simple seafood dishes served on a great terrace.

CAP BON AND THE SAHEL
Cap Bon
Anis (£) in Pension Anis, avenue Erriadh, Kelibia (tel: 02 295 777). Franco-Tunisian specialities and good fish.

Café Sidi el-Bahri (£) by the port, Kelibia. The perfect place to watch the sun go down and fishing boats set out for the night. Tea, coffee, *chichas* (water-pipes) and soft drinks, but no alcohol.

El-Mansourah (££) from Kelibia's port follow signposts to Hotel Mansour, then take the track to the right (4km from Kelibia's centre). Restaurant built on the rocks overlooking a small beach and the blue sea. As if this wasn't enough, it also serves tasty, reasonably priced food. Try the Muscat sec de Kelibia, a local dry wine.

Hammamet
Achour (££) rue Ali Belahouane (tel: 02 280 140). By far the best restaurant in town for fish and seafood as well as for *agneau à la gargoulette* (roast lamb). Tables are set under the trees in a pleasant garden, with a band playing during summer weekends. Friendly service. Recommended.

201

Le Barberousse (££) Next door to the fortress, *medina* (tel: 02 280 037). This outdoor restaurant on top of the ramparts offers great views over the bay and the rooftops of the *medina*. Good, simple food at reasonable prices.

La Brise (£) 2 avenue de la République (tel: 02 278 910). Very cheap tiled restaurant serving a tasty couscous and other Tunisian favourites such as *brik* and *ojja*.

Café des Muriers (£) at the foot of the fort by the waterside. Excellent place to while away the hours over mint tea and a *chicha* (water-pipe). Very popular.

Café Tutti Frutti (£) avenue de la République, almost next door to La Brise (see above). Meeting-place for young Hammametis, with a big terrace where a variety of fresh juices are served as well as Tunisian and other sweet pastries.

Casa d'Oro (££) 60 avenue Habib Bourguiba (tel: 02 260 099). Slightly out of the centre, with kitsch Italian décor and a quirky pianist. Serves very good fresh pastas and pizzas. Recommended.

Iles Kerkennah
Café Sindebad (£) before the Régal (see below). Lovely fishermen's café.

Le Régal (£) near the harbour El Ataya. Small café-restaurant with really well-prepared seafood and fish. Good value, but no alcohol.

Sefnou (£) Er Remla. Kerkennah specialities served on a great terrace.

La Sirène (Chez Tahar) (££) near the bank in Er Remla (tel: 04 281 118). Excellent fish and seafood served on a pleasant shaded terrace overlooking the sea. Pasta with seafood is delicious but has to be ordered in advance. Alcohol is served.

HOTELS AND RESTAURANTS

El Jem

Bel Espoir de Salem Kachté (£–££) 5km out on the road to Sfax. Excellent fresh fish, as it should be: the owner's brother works at the Ministery of Fishing in Sfax.

Le Bonheur (£–££) next door to the Relais Julius (see page 196) on the road to Sfax (tel: 03 690 306). New restaurant with well-prepared Tunisian specialities.

Mahdia

Le Lido (££–£££) avenue Farhat Hached (tel: 03 681 339). Facing one of Tunisia's largest fishing ports, it comes as no surprise that this is an excellent place to eat fish and seafood. The menu also includes Tunisian salads and meat, and the place is extremely popular with locals (mainly men), especially on Friday nights. It may be wise to book a table in advance.

El-Moezz, Chez Kacem (£) between the main gate and the market. Small restaurant popular with Tunisians coming to eat the freshly cooked *plat du jour*.

Le Quai (££) next door to Le Lido (see above), avenue Farhat Hached. Good grilled fish and stews, but not as good as those at the Lido. Better for lunch.

Monastir

El-Baraka (£) Souq el Karam, behind the Bourguiba Mosque (tel: 03 463 679). Delicious Tunisian cuisine, simple and cheap, served on a peaceful terrace.

Le Pirate (££) in the industrial zone near the fishing harbour (tel: 03 468 126). Closed on Mon and no alcohol. Despite the unpleasant area the food is excellent with, of course, mainly fish on the menu. *Couscous au mérou* (fish couscous) is recommended.

La Plage (£) place du 3 Août (tel: 03 461 124). Generous portions of fresh fish, plus a view of the sea.

Nabeul

Café Errachida (£) avenue Habib Thameur. Charming café for a mint tea and a water-pipe, or for a sticky pastry.

Le Bon Kif (££–£££) avenue Marbella (tel: 02 222 783). The best, and most expensive, restaurant in town, with the best fish and seafood in the region. Stylish décor.

L'Olivier (££) avenue Hedi Chaker (tel: 02 286 613). Excellent menu with French and Tunisian dishes, although perhaps a little expensive for what it is.

Sfax

Le Bagdad (££) 63 avenue Farhat Hached (tel: 04 223 856). Recommended by Sfaxians. We really enjoyed this place, with its excellent food and very pleasant service. Book in advance as it is often full. Closed on Fri.

Le Barraka (£) 4.5km from the centre on the road to Sidi Mansour. Only open during the summer. Although it serves only simple dishes, Le Barraka is a wonderful wooden structure on stilts, surrounded by colourful fishing boats.

Le Corail (£££) 39 avenue Habib Maazoun (tel: 04 210 317). Stylish and elegant restaurant with a very good menu. Delightful salads and lots of fish.

Le Diwan (£) near Bab Diwan. Atmospheric café built into the ramparts, serving mint tea and coffee.

Sousse

Le Bonheur (££) place Farhat Hached. Frequented mostly by sunburned Europeans, this restaurant deserves its good reputation, serving Tunisian and European dishes on a pleasant terrace.

Le Golfe (££–£££) in the Abou Nawas Hotel on boulevard Habib Bourguiba (tel: 03 229 905). Expensive for what it is, as the food is rather ordinary, but the terrace overlooking the sea is great.

Les Jasmins (£) 22 avenue Habib Bourguiba (tel: 03 225 884). Next door to the Cinema Palace. This is a good place for Tunisian dishes; the couscous in particular is recommended. Have a look at the menu and ask what the specialities of the day are as they are often very good. Closed Mon.

Sherif (£) avenue Habib Bourguiba, next to Les Jasmins (see above). According to some, Sherif serves the best ice-creams in Tunisia – we wouldn't disagree!

Sidi Bou (£) 11 boulevard de la Corniche (tel: 03 210 145). Good couscous and mixed grills served by the friendly owner. Eat inside or on the noisy little terrace.

THE INTERIOR

Douz

Café du Théâtre (£) near the tourist office. A pleasant and very popular Moorish café with a courtyard, kept by young people to finance their theatrical productions.

La Rosa (£) avenue du 7 Novembre (tel: 05 495 465). Good, simple food, served in a Berber tent in summer.

Gafsa

Semiramis (£) rue Ahmed Snoussi (tel: 06 221 009). The best food in town, with steamed lamb as the house speciality.

Kairouan

Fairouz (£–££) near avenue Bourguiba in the heart of the *medina*. A cut above the rest, and located right in the heart of the city. Good local cuisine.

El-Karawan (£) rue Soukaine el-Houssein (tel: 06 222 556). Tunisian dishes at moderate prices. No alcohol.

Pâtisserie Segni (£) avenue Bourguiba. The best place to taste the local speciality, *makroud*, a pastry stuffed with dates.

Sabra (£) avenue Farhat Hached. Authenic Tunisian food in a pleasant décor. Try the grills cooked over charcoal.

Le Kef

L'Auberge (£) avenue Bourguiba. Cheap Tunisian dishes

Chez Venus (£) avenue Bourguiba. The best food in town is served here in an enjoyable atmosphere.

Sicca Veneria (£–££) place de l'Indépendance (tel: 05 221 561). Attached to the lively bar, and serving good local food. Friendly service.

Nefta

Café de la Corbeille (£) See page 152.

Ferdaous (£–££) in the palmery. Simple local cuisine. Also has a bar.

La Source (£) avenue Bourguiba at the entrance to town coming from Tozeur. Well-prepared Tunisian specialities and friendly staff, but no alcohol.

Tozeur

To try such Tozeur specialities as *m'tabga* (a folded pizza) or *seffa* (a kind of couscous served with dried fish and lamb), you need to place your order a few hours in advance.

Les Andalous (££) route de Degache (tel: 06 454 196). The best place to try the specialities of Tozeur; call in advance to make your order. In case you didn't book ahead, the other food is of an equally high standard.

Le Petit Prince (££) avenue Bourguiba. Delightful food in pleasant surroundings, although the prices are quite steep.

Restaurant of Club Med Hotel, Ras el-Aïn (££) opposite the palmery (tel: 06 452 445). Excellent and very good-value buffet with plenty of salads, local specialities and grills served in superb surroundings. Open in season for both lunch and dinner.

Le Soleil (£) avenue Abou el-Kacem Chebbi (tel: 06 554 220). Tunisian and European cuisine served in perfectly clean surroundings. Try the couscous, which is particularly tasty.

Le Sud (£) avenue Farhat Hached (tel: 06 450 826). A cheaper place, serving the specialities of Sfax.

JERBA AND THE SOUTH

Foum Tataouine

Try the *cornes de gazelle* (a pastry horn stuffed with almond paste), the speciality of Tatouine, from one of the patisseries on avenue Farhat Hached.

Restaurant of La Gazelle (£) avenue Hedi Chaker. Cheap and well-prepared Tunisian food.

Gabès

Café La Chicha (£) rue Ibn el-Jazzar. Vast terrace in green and white overlooking a small garden. Ideal for a drink or an ice-cream. No alcohol.

Chez Amori (£) 82 avenue Habib Bourguiba. Very cheap and tasty Tunisian specialities served with a smile. No alcohol.

El-Mazar (££) 39 avenue Farhet Hached (tel: 05 272 065). Eat inside among the rustic décor or on the panoramic roof terrace. The French and Tunisian dishes are slightly more accomplished than at l'Oasis (see below).

L'Oasis (£–££) 15 avenue Farhat Hached (tel: 05 270 098). Old-fashioned Franco-Tunisian cuisine served since 1949 by waiters who've seen it all before. Friendly service and simple but pleasant décor.

Ile de Jerba

Baccar (££) place Hedi Chaker, Houmt Souk (tel: 05 650 708). Pleasant décor and well-prepared food, especially the fish.

Central (£) 128 avenue Bourguiba, 100m from the bus station, Houmt Souk. Very popular and clean eatery with good-value Tunisian stews and grills.

La Fontaine (£) avenue du 2 Mars, Houmt Souk. Meeting-place for the local bourgeoisie. Wide choice of home-made ice-creams.

Princesse de Haroun (££–£££) at the entrance to the harbour, Houmt Souk. Vast restaurant overlooking the sea and the harbour, with a stylish interior room and a spacious terrace in the summer. This is Jerba's premier restaurant – and one of the best in Tunisia – with excellent fish specialities and a delicious rice dish with seafood. Very attentive service, plus live oriental music in the evening. Often visited by tour groups, but as it is big there is room enough for everyone. Book ahead for a table with a view.

Restaurant du Sud (££) place Hedi Chaker, Houmt Souk (tel: 05 650 479). One of the best restaurants in the old town, with Tunisian specialities like couscous with fish and a spicy Jerban-style steamed fish. Pleasant terrace outside in the season. The locals hang out here.

Restaurant Tunisien (£) in the market near the fish auction, Houmt Souk. This popular eatery serves only vegetables and meat, while the one opposite has only fish. Both serve cheap but clean Tunisian dishes, and are very popular with locals. Lunch only.

Le Sportif (£) 147 avenue Habib Bourguiba, Houmt Souk. Very cheap but good Tunisian food served inside the little restaurant or outside on the terrace. Equally popular with locals.

Matmata

The best food is served in the hotels (see page 199).

Ouled Aziz, Chez Abdoul (£) in the centre. Delicious Tunisian dishes.

Zarzis

Relais des Palmiers (££–£££) *zone touristique*. Enjoy well-prepared fish and seafood on a palm-shaded terrace.

Index

Principal references are shown in **bold**.

204

INDEX

INDEX

INDEX

Picture credits

The Automobile Association would like to thank the following libraries and photographers for their assistance in the preparation of this book.

AKG LONDON PICTURE LIBRARY 24b; IMAGES COLOUR LIBRARY Front cover; MARY EVANS PICTURE LIBRARY 14a, 30a, 32a, 38b, 40b, 40c, 42b, 61a, 61b, 64a, 64b, 64c, 120c, 140a, 140b; MAGNUM PHOTOS 44b, 44c, 45b, 45c; NATURE PHOTOGRAPHERS LTD 92b (P R Sterry), 92c (S C Bisserot), 93a (P Craig-Cooper), 93b (D Hutton), 93c (R S Daniells); ROGER VIOLLET 68b, 69a, 69b.

The remaining photographs are from the Association's own library (**AA Photo Library**) and were taken by Steve Day, including the back cover and spine pictures.

Acknowledgements

The authors would like to thank the following for their invaluable advice and help during the research of this book: Chawki Alaoui of the Tunisian Information Bureau, London, Ann Noon and staff at the Tunisian National Tourist Office, Tunisair, Results PR, Gareth Wynn and Hertz Tunisia.

Contributors

Copy editor: Susi Bailey
Verifier: Mike Swindell
Indexer: Marie Lorimer